Mountains and Molehills

MICHAEL FOX

Mountains and Molehills

Essays – 2003 to 2007

To my dear friends Elizabeth and Philip
I inscribe this book with the deepest
affection.

Michael Fox

18 October 2007

Weill Publishers, Jerusalem

ISBN 978-965-7405-00-0

Weill Publishers
P.O.Box 7705
Jerusalem 91076

Designed by Yuval Tal, Jerusalem
Printed in Israel, 2007

For Sheila – Who else?

Contents

HEAVILY HISTORICAL

PARTIALLY POLITICAL

SLIGHTLY SACRED

Foreword

Michael Fox is a distinguished lawyer who, quite late in his career, has found a second vocation. I say "vocation," because the pieces he has been contributing to the *Haaretz* newspaper in recent years are something more than casual journalism. They are essays in the old sense – humane, reflective, free-wheeling, idiosyncratic. Like all the best examples of the genre, they repay re-reading, and they fully deserve to be gathered together in book-form.

No one can fail to be struck by their variety. In Fox's pages, Winnie the Pooh jostles Noam Chomsky, Arthur Koestler competes for attention with Tin Pan Alley, P.G. Wodehouse takes his place beside the Messiah. There are reflections on the board game Monopoly and the Da Vinci Code, on Harold Pinter's Nobel Prize and on the use and abuse of four-letter words. And the bill of fare is even more varied than the contents page suggests, since few of the essays stick single-mindedly to their formal subjects. They are almost always enriched by jokes and anecdotes, by stimulating parallels and entertaining digressions.

Few other accounts of Mel Gibson's film about the Crucifixion, for instance, can have begun with reminiscences of Lenny Bruce and ended with musings about Aramaic. And how many other writers would have enlivened a discussion on proportional representation by working out how the bizarre British pop singer Screaming Lord Sutch and his Raving Monster Loony party would have fared if he had run as a candidate for the Knesset rather than for the House of Commons?

Fox's touch is so light that it is easy to overlook how much solid reading and hard thought have gone into his work. The essays are the fruit of experience rather than research, and the quotations which adorn them spring up as naturally as they might in a good conversation. He has plainly got them at his fingertips; he could hardly have achieved the relaxed style which makes his writing so engaging if he hadn't.

Much of what he writes is autobiographical – often openly so (who could forget the pen-portrait of his cantankerous Russian *Bubbe*, for instance?), but indirectly too. A recurrent impulse behind the essays is the urge to recapture the everyday culture of the world he grew up in – its customs and pastimes, its assumptions and attitudes. He is a skilled social historian, while for a contemporary like myself – and we have been friends for over fifty years – there is the added bonus of nostalgia. But it is a temperate nostalgia, which is never allowed to blind us to the less rosy of yesterday's realities.

The familiar essay is the least systematic and the least hectoring of literary forms, and like the good essayist he is, Fox makes his points without preaching. There are many valuable lessons to be learned from the collection – moral, political, cultural – but in the nature of the case they defy simple summary. One of Fox's heroes, George Orwell, called his weekly column in the magazine *Tribune*, "I Write as I Please," and Michael Fox himself might well have adopted that as his motto. He writes as he pleases, and he offers his readers a great deal of pleasure in the process.

John Gross

London, July, 2007

**P**reface

I have included in this book some fifty essays that have appeared over the past four years as a monthly column in the English language edition of the *Haaretz* newspaper. The column is entitled "Musings." I cannot say that I am enamoured of this rubric but I am now stuck with it and I suppose that it is a fair, if bland, description of the rambling nature of the pieces I produce.

How, at the age of sixty-nine, I was picked from obscurity to become a writer of sorts is a story I feel compelled to relate. In March 2003, my wife Sheila and I were having dinner with Jacqueline and David Landau. David, later the Chief Editor of *Haaretz*, was at the time the editor of the English-language edition of the paper. Perhaps searching for a topic of conversation, David asked me, out of the blue, if I was interested in writing a column for *Haaretz*. To this day I do not know what made him think that I had the minimum skills needed to write anything, let alone a column, in a national newspaper. Nor have I dared ask him if he had acted out of impulse or had previously given the matter thought. He knew that I had read a few books but he had certainly never read anything of mine because I had never written anything.

Still, for me, the idea was seductive. The proposal could not have come at a better time. I had some years before undergone major surgery and I was reducing my work load as a corporate lawyer. I was no longer likely to open the batting for England at Lord's but to be a writer would satisfy another boyhood ambition, indeed one that I had never wholly abandoned.

But though I liked the idea, I had great doubts as to whether I could write anything at a level that would pass muster. Sheila, whose judgment has seldom let me down, was strongly in favour of my accepting the offer. So, vehemently, was my long-time secretary, Aliza. Neither of them, I felt, was impartial. They had a confidence in my abilities that I did not feel myself. It was only, on a subsequent visit to London, when I consulted my friend John Gross, of whose critical faculties I have been in awe since he was fifteen, that I decided to give it a try.

To help me on my way, David Landau suggested the subject of my first piece, an article on the forthcoming Hebrew translation of Winnie-the-Pooh by Avirama Golan. Since then I have written an article every month as well as the occasional book review. I do not exaggerate when I say that writing the column has changed my life. To find that, in what is euphemistically called the third age, I could write articles that people would actually read was a heady experience. At a time when I would otherwise have been pottering around the golf course, I have discovered a new career; admittedly not lucrative but hugely rewarding. Not that it has been easy. I find the actual process of writing agonizing and I expect I always shall; even four years on, I have regular fits of despair as I flounder with each new article, sure that this latest one will not work out. But after the agony comes the ecstasy: to read in print something you have written, to receive kind letters and emails from readers who have taken the trouble to write and to meet real readers in person. I have never known a feeling like it.

I cannot name all those to whom I owe thanks. I have already mentioned David Landau. My debt to him and to Jackie, one of my most uncritical fans, is a great one.

That I have fans is a source of great satisfaction to me. I would have found it harder to continue were it not for the friends, family and strangers who, without fail as each new article comes out, take the trouble to write or telephone me.

Joanna Yehiel, a first-class editor, took the trouble, despite her additional responsibilities as editor of the "Week's End" supplement, to steer this fledgling writer through the uncharted seas of authorship. My editors at *Haaretz* will, I know, forgive me for restoring British spelling to this book. It is merely a preference, I realise, but I feel it is more in tune with the subject-matter of my articles.

John Gross is one of Britain's foremost literary critics. He knows good writing yet he has read everything I have written and has gone beyond the bounds of friendship in encouraging me to continue, and in writing an over-generous introduction to the book.

My friend Asher Weill has put at my disposal the wealth of his experience in taking on the task of editing and publishing this book. I am grateful to him for all his help and advice.

Aliza Ozdoba has been my secretary and our close family friend for almost thirty years. Indeed she is part of our family. She is not only unfailingly helpful but takes as much delight in my new career as do Sheila and I.

And finally, my thanks to Sheila. That she should unstintingly encourage me, as she has, is I suppose implied in our marriage contract. In the good life we have led together I would never have expected anything else. But where she has surprised me is in her editorial skills. In the time I have been writing the column I have never once submitted a typescript to *Haaretz* without having Sheila read it first. Her comments are always constructive and to the point and she has always had some helpful observation to make. More than once I have changed an article completely because Sheila thought that I was charging off in the wrong direction.

At the age of seventy-three to publish one's first book is rare. It is an exciting venture for me and I hope my readers will derive as much pleasure from reading the book as I have had in publishing it.

Michael Fox
Herzliya, July 2007

Mountains and Molehills

NOTABLY NOSTALGIC

*R*oots

The number 100 has a special resonance for us. Arbitrary it may be, but when we watch, on a scoreboard or an odometer, two nines languidly sink below the horizon to be replaced by two rising zeroes headed by a brand-new "1," the satisfaction we feel is quite out of proportion to the trivial increment the alteration represents. Thus, we tend to love centenaries. I have only myself to blame that a couple of centenaries of particular significance to me have recently passed by unremarked.

In 1899, my still unmarried maternal grandfather emigrated from the small Lithuanian town of Wirballen near Kovno to settle in the ship-building town of Sunderland in the northeast of England. The little I know of the history of my grandfather, Zaide Joseph Pearlman, I have picked up from an illuminating monograph written about him by my second cousin David Pearlman. The proximate cause of Zaide's emigration was a combination of economic hardship and a reluctance to serve for 20 years in the army of the tzar. Zaide stood the army for about two years, becoming, thanks to his ritual prowess with the ram's horn, a sergeant-bugler. We have a photo of him in his sergeant's uniform looking more a Slav infantryman than the pious patriarch he later became.

My father's father followed a similar track. His year of immigration was 1904. He, too, was a musician in the tzar's army; he played an unspecified wind instrument in the officers' mess. A regret of mine – though one that does not keep me awake at nights – is that, scion that I am of two tootling Zaides, I could have been another Benny Goodman had my parents had the foresight to buy me a clarinet. What I did inherit from both grandfathers was a conspicuous absence of talent for soldiering. Through years of undistinguished service in the reserves of the Israel Defense Forces – including weeks of indescribable tedium on the wrong side of the Suez Canal in the wake of the Yom Kippur War – I retained, throughout, my pristine rank of private.

But to return to Zaide Fox. On February 8, 1904, the Japanese attacked the

Russian naval base of Port Arthur in Manchuria, thus precipitating the Russo-Japanese War of 1904-1905. While half-a-million Russian soldiers (of whom a quarter were ultimately killed or wounded) travelled east to participate in the war, Zaide, with a promptitude for which I shall always be grateful, hotfooted it in the opposite direction. He sailed from Hamburg to the port of London, settling in London's East End. He left behind, in his home town of Berdichev, his wife (my Bubbe) and two small children, one of whom was my four-year-old father. They joined him a year later.

Zaide's name, on arrival, was Abraham Ochs. The immigration officer heard "Ox" and it was as Abraham Ox that my grandfather acquired a modest immortality. His unusual name appeared on the sign above his shop in the Commercial Road and is mentioned as a curiosity in histories of the East End. To the hundreds of Ochses, past and present, who read this and are anxious to claim relationship with me, let me say at the outset that they will first have to prove to me that they are Levites. Although nothing notable seems to have happened to our branch of the Ochses between 70 C.E. and yesterday, we are of the Tribe of Levi and were consequently, while the Temple was standing, sweet singers of Israel.

My pedigree thus stretches back millennia, admittedly with a few trifling gaps, and I will champion that heritage against the challenge of such Ochs upstarts as the founders of the *New York Times*. But we soon gave up on the name. His teacher told my father that he could not go to an English school with the name of Sammy Ox. At the age of six, Dad precociously exchanged the name of Ox, to which he does not seem to have been unduly attached, for the English surname of Fox.

I did not know my Zaide, but I think I should have liked him. For one thing he seems to have been fascinated with the stage, a trait that has reappeared in several of his descendants. He was poor but used to save up for an outing to the Yiddish theatre. On his return home he would, taking all the parts, act out, to the rapt audience of his four children, a near-verbatim version of the play he had seen. I am told that he was a very sweet-natured man. I believe he must have been. All his children had that quality, one that they certainly did not inherit from my grandmother, who – though I know that ancestor worship is an integral part of the Jewish psyche – could not, by any stretch of the imagination, have been accused of excessive amiability.

I had a Russian Bubbe and a Lithuanian Bobbe. My Bobbe, my maternal grandmother, though Yiddish was her mother tongue, wrote, read and spoke English fluently, with a slight Yiddish but heavier Sunderland accent. Bubbe, on the other hand, though she lived in England for close to 70 years, never learned a word of English, partly because she was stone deaf for the last half of her life, but partly, I maintain, because she was plain disobliging. In the conventional, almost stuffy, household in which I grew up, Bubbe was an exotic figure. Despite her extreme piety – she fasted every Monday and Thursday, a rarely observed practice of Jewish ascetics – she later became an icon for my radical feminist nieces, who revered her, in my opinion, for her downright orneriness.

Odd she certainly was. I am sure that she had never read Freud, but she possessed a classic persecution complex. An early riser, she was the first to get to the morning newspaper. Her total ignorance of English did not inhibit her from censoring our reading. She excised from the paper every picture of herself (she always spotted several) and every article that she fancied put her in an unfavourable light so that by the time we managed to get to it, the paper would be in shreds. When television came, she would spend hours in front of the set, haranguing the announcer who, to her fury, would consistently ignore her.

Bubbe had a thing about burglars, something she shared with James Thurber's aunts. One aunt of Thurber's, you may recall, was a timid soul who would leave her jewellery piled outside her door every night with a note to the burglars begging them not to blow chloroform through her door because this was all she had. Bubbe was more combative, resembling more the Thurber aunt who would make a pile outside her room of all the shoes in the house and put the burglars to flight by throwing the shoes along the corridor at intervals during the night. Bubbe favoured a two-strike strategy: She seldom moved in the house without a glass of water in one hand and a pot of pepper in the other. The method must have been effective because the house was never burgled until Bubbe left. Indeed, I cannot imagine any thief foolhardy enough to tangle with Bubbe.

I have lived in the interesting times of the apocryphal Chinese curse, but, thanks to the decisions made a century ago by my now long-dead grandparents, I have led a relatively untroubled life. It could have been otherwise. In that beautiful summer of 1941 – at the same time and on the same planet as I, a seven-year-old English schoolboy was messing about, as small boys do, in the Buckinghamshire countryside – in what might as well have been some nightmarish parallel universe, the seven-year-old children of those who had stayed behind, perhaps distant cousins of mine, were having their heads dashed against rocks to save the cost of ammunition. And I can tell you the dates. On September 11, 1941, the children of Wirballen were killed in the arms of their mothers by their Lithuanian neighbours. And on October 5, 1941, the Germans slaughtered the last of Berdichev's 40,000 Jews.

There is nothing wrong in coming from Berdichev. For a medium-sized, predominantly Jewish town, it had interesting literary associations. It was, of course, the home of the most lovable of all the Hasidic masters, Levi Isaac of Berdichev, but it was also the birthplace of Joseph Conrad and of Vassily Grossman, who wrote "Life and Fate" – to my mind, one of the great novels of the 20th century.

I am sorry that I cannot read Tolstoy or Pushkin in the original, but still I am glad that my grandparents made me a Londoner. Thanks to their prescience, I avoided the grisly fate of my Russian relatives and grew up playing cricket, reading Jane Austen and drinking my beer warm. For that, I owe a great debt to my Bubbe, my Bobbe and my two Zaides. Those centenaries are a cause for private jubilation.

16 February, 2006

Annus Mirabilis

I turned thirteen in 1947. In the world at large it was a year of peaks and troughs, mainly troughs. Britain, too, was having it tough. The British Chancellor of the Exchequer, Hugh Dalton, called 1947 an "annus horrendus." Britain may have been on the winning side of the recently ended war, but it did not feel like it. In many respects, what was later described as the "Age of Austerity" was harder to bear than the war itself. Food rations were below the wartime average and even bread was now, for the first time, rationed. Britain's economy was in dire straits. If you went to a restaurant or stayed at a hotel, you had to produce your ration book. There were no foreign holidays. The amount of food you could serve at a function and the number of guests you could invite was limited by law.

My bar-mitzvah party was a spartan tea in a chilly synagogue hall and, although I cannot remember what we ate, I recall that it was awful. What everyone who was around at the time remembers is the weather. England suffered its harshest winter in living memory. It was cold indoors, too. This was the winter of the notorious fuel crisis. Power stations closed for lack of coal. You were forbidden to heat your house during daylight hours and there were lengthy power cuts every day.

Yet, if – to paraphrase Dickens – it was the worst of times, it was also the best of times and, as if to compensate for the horrible winter of that seesaw year, the summer was glorious. I live now in a country where, for more than half of the year, you can be sure that the sun will shine. To those who have known nothing else, it is not easy to explain how, in a country condemned to almost permanently grey skies, a sunny day can lift the spirits and how a season of such days can remain in the memory half a century later.

P.G. Wodehouse was a fantasist because for him, every English summer is a fine one. In dozens of Wodehouse novels you will find passages like the opening of "Summer Lightning": "Blandings Castle slept in the sunshine. Dancing little ripples of heat-mist played across its smooth lawns and stone-flagged terraces. The air was full of the lulling drone of insects".

The summer of 1947 was that kind of summer. We would cycle for picnics by the river. We would boat on the lake at Regents Park ("Come in number five, your time is up") and there were those long, lazy evenings reading in the garden when all you could hear was the clatter of lawnmowers and, yes, the lulling drone of insects.

But above all, a fine English summer means cricket and, more than anything else, that is what I remember: playing cricket, watching cricket, dreaming cricket. Indeed 1947 was a year for cricket. In that cloudless summer, cricket records were broken by the score. I was fortunate enough to live not far from the home of cricket, Lord's Cricket Ground. My mother would make me sandwiches and my cousins and I would go for the day to watch a game at Lord's. If the game was an international match, known in cricket's peculiar parlance as a "Test Match," we would sit contentedly on the grass in front of the stands from 11:30 in the morning to 6:30 in the evening, a thin rope being all that separated us from our idols on the field. If the sun harmed us, we did not know it. Perhaps the violet rays, like the Orthodox, were not as ultra as they are today.

It was from my place on the grass at Lord's that I was almost within touching distance of Australia's Don Bradman on his last tour of England in 1948. He was not only the greatest cricketer of all time; he was among the greatest-ever players of any game. Bradman's lifetime test match batting average was 99.94. That may mean nothing to the non-cricketer until he is told that the next highest in the annals of cricket was 60.97. That is how this run-making machine dominated the sport.

Still, I had already had my brush with cricketing greatness a couple of years earlier. As a reward for something or other – I think that it was for getting into my new school – my father took me to buy a cricket bat. He collected me from school and we walked to a small shop in Fleet Street where the nice elderly gentleman who owned the shop showed me bats. The elderly gentleman was none other than Jack Hobbs, the finest of all English batsmen, still a legend then though long retired. My father, who had seen him bat in his heyday, was no less thrilled than I was. To the envy of my friends, Jack Hobbs signed my new bat. Had I been given a replica of the Ten Commandments signed by Moses, I could not have treasured it more.

I did not merely watch cricket. I played it, not just in 1947 but on and off until 1968, when I came to live in an effectively cricketless country, Israel. To the best of my knowledge, if you were not born in Bombay, you are not permitted to play cricket in this country. In England, however, they were always looking for people to make up an eleven and they would even take Litvaks at a pinch. In fact, I do not think that I ever met the membership requirements of any team for which I played. But, unlike Groucho Marx, I was always ready to join a club that would not have me as a member.

I played, for instance, with a club of Bohemian writers, journalists and painters who drank red wine between overs. I then played for a side that bore the name of a dodgy clothing company. Its chief financial officer had been persuaded by a young cricket-loving accountant in our circle to invest in equipping a cricket team on the dubious premise that it would have tax advantages. This side drank beer. Finally, I played a few seasons for the "Blue Angel." This team, composed of the raffish habitués of a Mayfair nightclub of that name, drank quantities of almost anything. The club did not have its own ground – nightingales might sing in Berkeley Square, but you cannot play cricket there – so we would play any village team in southern England that would have us. Village cricket is England. You play at the centre of the village, on a green surrounded by oaks and elms, bordered at one end by a Norman church and, at the other, by a pub. For all I know, the church was also open for business after the game, but the pub won hands down.

All this was later than 1947 but it was in 1947 that I achieved my cricketing apotheosis. It was neither a batting nor a bowling performance that I recall so vividly nearly 60 years later. It was a catch I took in a school game and it was – why conceal the fact under the cloak of false modesty? – the finest catch in the history of cricket. Some of the protagonists in that immortal game are no longer alive and I fear that others will have forgotten it – such being the solipsistic nature of memory – but I shall bear with me until my dying day the memory of that achievement of the long, sunny summer of 1947.

One of the reasons that cricket may seem like a priesthood to outsiders is the arcane argot of the game. The positions on the cricket field bear weird names like gully, point, cover and slip. So don't giggle when I tell you that on that day I fielded at silly mid-off. It is a position a couple of feet in front of the batsman and I would not field at that position today for all the oil in Saudi Arabia. Had King David been the captain of a cricket XI, silly mid-off is where he would have placed Uriah the Hittite. But I was younger then and when the ball popped up from the bat, I twisted my body diving at my own feet to snatch the ball a moment before it touched the ground. I ended up on my back with the ball held triumphantly aloft in my right hand.

"Old men forget," said Henry V to the poor deluded troops who were about to risk their lives for him at the Battle of Agincourt, "yet all shall be forgot, but he'll remember, with advantages, what feats he did that day." Well I remember that catch – with advantages. In a longish life, I have had, I suppose, the occasional triumph but nothing will ever rival that moment of glory in the beautiful summer of 1947.

14 June, 2006

_O_ _h! What a Lovely War_

In another three days I shall be seventy. It is a time for retrospection. I have led a happily uneventful life in an era that has been far from uneventful, indeed a time of upheaval and cataclysmic change. The 1940s, the decade between my sixth and fifteenth birthdays, saw the bestialities of Auschwitz and the establishment of the Jewish state. Truly, in the unforgettable words of Charles Dickens's "A Tale of Two Cities," it was the best of times and the worst of times.

Stingo, the narrator of William Styron's "Sophie's Choice," speculates on what he calls the "time relation" when applied to the Holocaust. The day that his heroine Sophie entered Auschwitz, Stingo recalled that he was doing something utterly banal in Raleigh, North Carolina. Of course, this strange characteristic of time – that, at any given moment in the history of the world while most people are following their quotidian pursuits, somewhere some unspeakable act of cruelty is taking place – is not confined to the Holocaust, but it is difficult to think of a better example of it. Styron quotes George Steiner who writes that, at the same hour as a particularly bestial murder was being committed in Treblinka, "the overwhelming plurality of human beings …were sleeping or eating or going to a film or making love or worrying about the dentist… The two orders of simultaneous experience are so different, so irreconcilable to any common norm of human values, their coexistence is so hideous a paradox… that I puzzle over time".

While I and my cousins were fishing for tiddlers in a country pond, my friend Guy – a boy of my age – was hiding in Paris together with his mother; his father was by then a French prisoner of war in the hands of the Germans. They were lucky; thanks to good French friends who risked their lives daily to protect them, they survived the war and Guy went on to a distinguished career in France and Israel. He remained close to his rescuers and had the satisfaction of seeing each one of them declared Righteous Gentiles by Yad Vashem. But

Guy frequently thinks of his cousin – his childhood playmate in pre-war Paris – who was deported to and perished in Auschwitz. His was the more typical fate of a European child in those times. I was infinitely luckier than Guy. Thanks to the Royal Air Force and to that narrow sliver of water that separates Britain from the Continent of Europe, I not only escaped the common European fate of a Jewish child, but – with a slight blush of shame – I remember the Second World War as a time of delight.

Shortly after the outbreak of war, my family moved from London to a town in rural Buckinghamshire. This was a common experience, as London families fanned out to dormitory towns in the Home Counties to escape the Blitz. Towns in Surrey, Kent, Buckinghamshire, Hertfordshire and Berkshire saw an influx of Londoners, many of whom stayed on after the war. Among them were Jewish families who set up provisional communities with makeshift synagogues in halls and disused churches in country towns that had barely seen a Jew before.

My friend John Gross has beautifully recaptured that time in his memoir "A Double Thread." He was evacuated to Egham, a Surrey town on the Thames, a river that played a memorable part in my own life.

Growing up in the country was liberating. Adults were either absent or preoccupied and the roads were virtually empty of motor traffic; petrol was only available for essential purposes and most families had got rid of their cars. High Wycombe, where we lived, is a country town in the Thames Valley, nestling in the Chiltern Hills. It has little claim to fame though the balcony of its celebrated inn, the Red Lion, was the scene of a famous election address by the town's most celebrated resident, Benjamin Disraeli. With his unrivalled sense of history, Winston Churchill addressed a large crowd from the same balcony when running for election in 1945. Not that it did him any good. An ungrateful nation threw out Disraeli's greatest Tory descendant and elected the opposition Labour Party.

Although High Wycombe is a sizeable town, we lived outside it at the top of Marlow Hill, one of the hills that encircle the town. The small and temporary wartime Jewish community held services in a Methodist church in the town, about three miles from our home. Walking there on a Shabbat was easy enough but returning up the extremely steep hill was tougher.

What brightened the steep walk up Marlow Hill was that the left side of the hill was bordered by the magnificently extensive grounds of Wycombe Abbey, one of England's poshest girls' schools. The girls had been evacuated to a part of the country deemed safer than High Wycombe and their places were taken by the US Eighth Air Force which was quartered there in strength. They must have been puzzled at being quartered in a girls' school at all and totally bewildered by the bulletin board in a dormitory with the legend "'if in trouble ring for a mistress".

They certainly made their presence felt in our town. Radio comedians claimed that there were only three things wrong with the GIs: "They're overpaid, oversexed and over here." Well maybe they did cause some resentment but, for a small boy, their friendliness was overwhelming. At a time when sweets were an untold luxury, we would follow the soldiers in the streets with the cry "Got any gum, chum?" I don't believe we ever met a refusal. I trace my own lifelong liking for Americans to the kindness of those homesick young men.

A number of the GIs were, of course, Jewish and the local families vied with each other to invite them home. We had a half dozen regular Shabbat guests. I remember most of them, and all with affection. Lou Sells from Chicago took me once to the cinema, a rare treat. The Rex was the only cinema that our town boasted. We saw "The Destroyer" starring, I believe, Edward G. Robinson.

I trace my addiction to the printed word to those times, though I have little recollection of what I read. I know that I read "The Swiss Family Robinson" a dozen times but it is the "Just William" books by Richmal Crompton that I remember best. I know that I was about seven when I started reading them because I recall feeling resentful that the protagonist should be as old as eleven. I am afraid that that tousled, anarchic small boy became a role model for my own coterie.

I was fortunate enough to have ready-made companions. I have an affectionate relationship with my two sisters but, one being significantly older than I and the other considerably younger, they could not be friends for me in my childhood. But I was blessed with several cousins of about my age including two who lived five doors away. We also had four cousins in the northern city of Leeds with whom we spent the holidays.

Every summer our Leeds cousins came to us for August. We roamed the countryside, picking hazelnuts, elderberries, wild strawberries and blackberries in profusion from the hedgerows. We fashioned our own bows and arrows, played cricket and rounders (the English version of baseball), found caterpillars and butterflies for our "zoo" and, I am now ashamed to say, collected birds' eggs. We also set up a museum with the odd foreign coin, and our prized pieces of bomb shrapnel, and the black stuff the German planes threw out to confuse our radar. And the river beckoned. We would go swimming and boating on the Thames at Marlow ten minutes away.

In December each year it was our turn to go to Leeds, an unlovely city, which had the great advantage, from our parents' point of view, of having been totally overlooked by the Luftwaffe. Our cousins lived in Harehills, today an extreme example of inner city blight but then a leafy suburb. We were a walk away from Gledhow Valley Woods where we raced twigs in a stream, a game I now know as Poohsticks. If there was snow, there was tobogganing in Roundhay Park. But the greatest delight of all was the pantomime, a peculiarly British Christmas institution involving music and slapstick comedy. Leeds was rich in theatres (it doesn't do so well for football teams) and there were usually three pantomimes running simultaneously and we got to see them all. Traditionally the pantomime features a "'Dame," a comedian dressed up as an unappealingly vulgar elderly woman and the "Principal Boy"' another cross-dressing role – this time an attractive young ingénue disguised – unsuccessfully – as a boy, usually a prince.

Of course the war was ever present and we could not avoid being aware of it. We were by peacetime standards deprived though we scarcely knew it. Bananas were a rapidly fading memory; chocolate was strictly rationed: I think we received about a bar a month. We had to make do with our pre-war toys. There were occasional air raids and we witnessed the odd dogfight but our town was largely spared. One year – it was probably 1941 or 1942 – we were visiting my grandparents in Sunderland, a shipbuilding town in the far north of England. While I was there, Sunderland suffered its heaviest air raid. We cowered in the shelters all night. In the morning I was taken into the centre of the town to see the damage. Landmarks that had been familiar to me were razed to the ground, even the great department store Binns was gutted. The excitement that a newly ruined landscape holds for a small boy is well conveyed in John Boorman's film "Hope and Glory." In his story of a nine-year old boy in wartime London I found many echoes of my own wartime experience, down to the idyllic summer days of boating on the river.

In January, 1945, my life changed and I started my new school in London staying during the week with my grandmother who, by then, had moved down from Sunderland to London. Hitler had not yet quite shot his bolt and I had some of my most fearful moments of the war as we ducked under our desks at the sound of an exploding V2 rocket.

In a few months it was all over, but oh it was a lovely war!

5 March, 2004

*I*n Praise of Tin Pan Alley

"If there is still any doubt that Lennon and McCartney are the greatest song writers since Schubert, then next Friday – with the publication of the new Beatles double LP – -should surely see the last vestiges of cultural snobbery and bourgeois prejudice swept away in a deluge of joyful music making, which only the ignorant will not hear and only the deaf will not acknowledge".

This pronouncement by Tony Palmer created the stir it was designed to create when it announced the imminent arrival of a new Beatles record in 1968. Palmer, the pop music critic of the London *Observer*, intended his preposterous generalization to shock. It smacks of the Beatles' own self-assessment – immodest but not inaccurate – that they were more famous than Jesus Christ.

I can leave it to the heavyweights to spring to the defence of the dozens of classical composers of lieder and operas who wrote songs of great beauty in the one and a half centuries that intervened between the death of Schubert and the rise of the Fab Four. Carmen and Traviata hardly lack "joyful music making." Perhaps we should be grateful that Palmer conceded us Schubert.

But, classical music aside, what I find impossible to forgive is that Palmer, a historian of the popular song, should so sweepingly have ignored the titans of Tin Pan Alley. Certainly Lennon and McCartney wrote some fine melodies but there is an unbridgeable gulf between them and the creative geniuses who formed the Golden Age of the American Song. That age lasted roughly from the 1920s until 1954, the year that Bill Haley and his Comets recorded "Rock Around the Clock".

The outstanding composers of the Golden Age were George Gershwin, Jerome Kern, Irving Berlin, Cole Porter, Richard Rodgers and Harold Arlen. Of course there were others – notably Hoagy Carmichael who wrote the evergreen "Star Dust" – but it was these six who wrote, with astonishing consistency, the melodies that made the era famous.

Gershwin apart, the composers of Tin Pan Alley did not seek to belong to the world of classical music. They were conscious of their limitations. But why complain? They gave us gorgeous, soaring, lilting melodies: tunes to sing in the shower, tunes to whistle in the street. If you are an addict like me you will, merely by reading the titles of the songs that I mention here, find that those songs invade your mind and like a "warning voice that comes in the night" – in the words of Cole Porter's "I've Got You Under My Skin" – "repeat and repeat" in your ears. In his absorbing book "The Poets of Tin Pan Alley," Philip Furia finds it surprising that 85 percent of the songs of early Tin Pan Alley were about love. Certainly if he expected them to be about stamp-collecting he would have been deeply disappointed. They gloriously, wittily and unashamedly celebrate romantic love.

In Tin Pan Alley the music reigned supreme. Even the best of the lyricists – outstandingly Ira Gershwin, Oscar Hammerstein, the incomparable Lorenz Hart and, of course, Irving Berlin and Cole Porter who wrote both their own music and lyrics – knew that the words must be subservient to the melody. Many composers worked with several lyricists. Each of the three best known Harold Arlen songs, "Stormy Weather," "Over the Rainbow" and "That Old Black Magic" was written by a different lyricist. Jerome Kern worked with many librettists including – somewhat surprisingly – P. G. Wodehouse, who wrote some of the songs of "Show Boat".

That their lyrics were frequently ephemeral did not worry the Tin Pan Alley poets. Take Cole Porter's "You're the Top." It piles up a witty list of metaphors ("you're a Berlin ballad … you're a Waldorf salad,") to express the perfection of the loved one. Many will have little meaning to a contemporary ear. What is "the nose on the great Durante" and what is so special about cellophane, newly invented when Porter first wrote the song? Take also Richard Rodgers' "Manhattan" in which Lorenz Hart, perhaps the most gifted of all the Tin Pan Alley lyricists, alludes to a now long-forgotten Broadway hit show:

Our future babies
We'll take to 'Abie's
Irish Rose'
We hope they'll live to see it close.

In a later version it is "South Pacific is a terrific show they say…" and my Ella Fitzgerald recording updates it to "My Fair Lady." I expect the latest redaction of that immortal song refers to "The Producers" but none will match Hart's deft rhyming scheme.

The changes wrought by time to these lyrics can also reflect changes in sensitivities. Our prurient age has consigned "Thank Heaven for Little Girls," "My Heart Belongs to Daddy" and "Little One" to near oblivion. An even more arresting example is the history of the words of "Ol' Man River" from Jerome Kern's "Show Boat." Oscar Hammerstein's original 1927 lyric has "Niggers all work on de Mississippi..." By 1928 the first words had become "Coloured folks..." In 1936 it metamorphosed to "Darkies all..." and in 1946 "Here we all..." The 1994 Broadway revival caps it with the pallid "Brothers all..."

By and large they were a remarkably homogeneous bunch. The archetypal Tin Pan Alley songwriter, whether composer or lyricist, was a Jew from New York. It is tempting but dangerous to build a theory on this undeniable fact. The melodies possess no strikingly Jewish flavour but the lyrics, particularly of Hart, have a wit and sophistication that we often associate with Jewish New York.

Cole Porter was conscious of standing out as the token goy. The scion of a wealthy Wasp family, he sought to succeed in this alien environment. He confided to Richard Rodgers that he had found the formula for writing hits. "Simplicity itself" he told Rodgers "I'll write Jewish tunes." And he did too. Rodgers found it "one of the ironies of the musical theatre," that Porter – particularly with his frequent use of the minor key – should be the most "Jewish" of the song-writers of the Golden Age.

Irving Berlin, however, had no interest in writing Jewish tunes. Musically illiterate all his life – he had an assistant who transcribed his melodies – he tried to distance himself from his origins, though he could not escape them. Philip Furia instances "the Yiddish penchant for answering a question with another question" which Berlin employs by answering the question "how deep is the ocean?" with "how high is the sky?"

Of them all Berlin knew best how to satisfy his public as is evident from the success of "White Christmas," often called a "secular hymn." Francois Villon, the mediaeval French poet who pined for *les neiges d'antan* – the snows of yesteryear – could hardly have foreseen the moneymaking possibilities in those snows. Berlin, a musical alchemist, did; he turned snow into dough. Like Villon, and like Orson Welles, who made Citizen Kane's toboggan "'Rosebud'" the symbol of his desperate yearning for the innocence of his childhood, Berlin recognized the potency of snow in the collective subconscious

A book by Jody Rosen in 2002 has been devoted to the history of "White Christmas." Arguably the most popular song of all time it is a phenomenon that merits a book. Aside from the record-breaking version by Bing Crosby (which sold 31 million copies), it has been recorded hundreds of times and has sold at least 125 million copies (some estimates reach as high as 400 million). There are versions in Hungarian, Japanese, Swahili (!) and – the imagination boggles – Yiddish. The Bing Crosby version was the best-selling single of all time until 1998. In that year Elton John wrote "Candle in the Wind" for the funeral of Princess Diana. We can only regret that Irving Berlin was not around then to sanctify that apotheosis of kitsch.

In his novel "Operation Shylock," Philip Roth pays mock homage to the success of "White Christmas" and another Berlin hit, "Easter Parade" by depicting them as Berlin's Jewish revenge on Christianity – turning Easter into a fashion show and Christmas into a holiday about snow.

The only song that approaches "White Christmas" in canonical status was written by two New York sophisticates – Harold Arlen and Yip Harburg – for a film about the adventures of a country girl from Kansas. For many, "Over the Rainbow" is the greatest of them all. Philip Furia growls that its popularity "was yet another signal that a flood of sentimentality… was about to engulf New York urbanity, from top hat to tails." Maybe; but it is, by any standard, a beautiful ballad.

Each of the great Tin Pan Alley composers was prolific. It is near impossible to select a representative song for, say, the consistently brilliant Rodgers or the long-lived Irving Berlin: but putting my money where my mouth is, I conclude by naming six songs, one by each of the six, that can knock the socks off anything by Lennon and McCartney.

So, *douze points* to Gershwin's "Summertime," Kern's "All the Things You Are," Porter's "Night and Day," Berlin's "Always," Rodgers' "My Heart Stood Still" and Arlen's "Over the Rainbow".

Match those if you can, Tony Palmer.

22 August, 2003

A Most Ingenious Paradox

In my youth there was scarcely a suburb of London that did not boast its own live theatre. These theatres specialized in "variety" – shows in which singers, comedians, dancers, jugglers, acrobats and magicians would, in turn, vie for the attention of an often critical audience. Variety is sadly dead now and the theaters have become bingo halls or supermarkets. To paraphrase Villon: Where are the shows of yesteryear? But, while I lament the decline and fall of the Hackney Empire, it is the Golders Green Hippodrome that, for me, evokes golden memories.

I recently rescued a large laundry basket from our basement. I found it buried deep among the detritus formed there by my wife's life-long inability to throw anything away. The basket contained hundreds of old theatre programmes, prominent among them some from the Hippodrome, testifying to half-a-century of enthusiastic theatre-going. Despite its name, the Hippodrome did not stage chariot races but, for half a crown (there were eight of them in a pound), the price of a seat in the balcony, you could see almost anything else. We saw ballet, magicians, stage hypnotists and telepathy acts. Straight plays often visited the Hippodrome as pre-West End tryouts; the programmes remind me that it was there that I saw Peggy Ashcroft as Hedda Gabler and that great comedy actress Kay Kendall as Elvira in Noel Coward's "Blithe Spirit".

But what, for me, made the Hippodrome special was the annual visit of the D'Oyly Carte Opera Company with its repertoire of the light operas of Gilbert and Sullivan. I recall, as of yesterday, my first exposure to a Gilbert and Sullivan opera at the Hippodrome. It was a performance of "The Gondoliers." From the opening chorus "List and learn, ye dainty roses, roses white and roses red," I was enraptured. My adolescent enthusiasm for G & S has gone into remission in recent years, but when a friend, claiming that I had introduced him to the Savoy Operas, suggested I write about that immortal – though quarrelsome – pair, I found myself overcome by nostalgia.

The operas of Gilbert and Sullivan have imprinted an indelible impression on the popular culture of the English-speaking world. William S. Gilbert (1836-1911) wrote the words and Sir Arthur Sullivan (1842-1900) wrote the music. The comic operas they wrote together in the late 19th century were performed at London's Savoy Theatre and, from the start, enjoyed huge success. They have never lost that popularity. The story of their sometimes stormy collaboration has been recounted in numerous books and films. The excellent Mike Leigh movie "Topsy-Turvy" about the making of their best-known opera, "The Mikado," is only the most recent.

It is not easy to explain the enduring appeal of Gilbert and Sullivan. It is surely not because of Sullivan's music. He wrote two songs, "Onward Christian Soldiers" and "The Lost Chord," which are still performed. But, otherwise, his reputation outside the operas he wrote with Gilbert did not long survive his death. The Savoy Operas chiefly owe their success to Gilbert's clever lyrics and lunatic plots. The names of Gilbert and Sullivan are linked for eternity like bacon and eggs (tfu-tfu-tfu!), Abbot and Costello (ditto) and Romeo and Juliet. Although almost invariably the composer is given sole credit for an opera (you never hear of the operas of Mozart and da Ponte,) Gilbert's was always the first name and not for alphabetical reasons; he was the dominant partner. Almost uniquely in the annals of musical drama, the words came first. Gilbert provided the lyrics to which Sullivan had to fit the music.

Not that Gilbert was incapable of writing words to existing tunes. My father, an ardent Gilbert and Sullivan fan, told me a story about Gilbert that I regret not following up. Before he got together with Sullivan, so the story goes, Gilbert attended a service at the Bevis Marks Spanish and Portuguese Synagogue in London and was so struck by the haunting tune of the Adon Olam hymn that he wrote a poem about a Jewish cabdriver to the melody. In trying to trace it recently, I came upon one of Gilbert's Bab Ballads, entitled "The Bishop and the Busman." It is about a Jewish bus driver and I expect it is what Dad was referring to. A sample stanza goes: "It was also a Jew, / who drove a Putney bus / for flesh of swine however fine / he did not care a cuss".

I wish I had not made this discovery because it has caused me to modify my hitherto unqualified reverence for Gilbert. He was a fantasist who had his Lord Chancellor marry a fairy, so I suppose that I can allow him the equally outlandish instance of a Jewish bus driver from Putney. But even if he was having an off day, how could the man who wrote "The Mikado" produce a verse that sounds as if it was written for your nephew's bar-mitzvah by one of his less talented friends? And lastly, try as I might, I could not fit this dreadful piece of doggerel to any known melody for Adon Olam. Unless some kind reader can help me out on another Gilbert poem that would fit my father's story, I must reluctantly conclude that he got it wrong.

Generally, Gilbert was a versifier of a high order. The great Tin Pan Alley lyricists looked up to him as a master. But, witty and deft as his verses undoubtedly are, their topicality often makes them hard for a modern audience to understand. Texts of the operas nowadays appear with annotations because many of the references can convey nothing except to specialists in the period. And sensibilities change. True, you can easily excise from "I've Got a Little List" the words "the nigger serenader, and the others of his race." But you can hardly throw out from "The Mikado" that most plaintive (and, to my mind, most mawkish) of ballads, "Titwillow." It raises a snigger today – and no wonder! If you check Google for the words of Titwillow, you will not be able to avoid seeing the "sponsored links." The first three are: "BoobSex with Amateurs," "Watch Big Breast Movies" and "Sexy Adult Models." Surely not quite what Gilbert had intended.

The English-speaking world has been remarkably successful in exporting its culture, so I find it mildly surprising that the Savoy Operas, so loved wherever English is spoken, have failed totally to gain a foothold in other cultures. I have tried out the names of Gilbert and Sullivan on educated French and Israeli friends and have been met with a blank stare. If you are a "Roosian, a French or Turk or Proosian," you are not only unlikely to have fallen under the spell of G & S; you have probably never heard of them. I have been unable to find any reference in the literature to any performance of a Gilbert and Sullivan opera in any foreign opera house. Yet I do not think that G & S is inherently untranslatable. Broadway musicals have been translated into many languages, including Hebrew. Even the most culturally insular of English writers, P.G. Wodehouse, can now be read in Hebrew. There is a new, reasonably adequate, translation into Hebrew of "Right Ho, Jeeves," entitled *Tov Veyafe, Jeeves*.

The one reference to a translation of Gilbert and Sullivan I have seen is to a performance in New York this year of "The Pirates of Penzance" in Yiddish. If you got a perverse kick out of reading "Winnie Ille Pooh" in Latin, *Di Yam gazlonim* might be to your taste. I'll go for the original English. The much-parodied lyrics of the Gilbert and Sullivan operas have proved to be fertile ground for faux-Yiddish comedians. I still have an LP autographed by two former clients of mine who toured Britain in the 1960s with an act called Goldberg and Solomon, in which they performed such rib-ticklers as the "Tailors of Poznance," "Trial by Jewry" and "Three Little Maids from Shul".

Good things have been happening to Gilbert and Sullivan in recent years. For long the only operas of theirs that you could see were those of the touring companies owned and controlled by the D'Oyly Carte family, whose jealously guarded copyright prevented the staging of any competing productions. This stranglehold made for stale and unimaginative performances. With the expiration of the copyright in 1961, the 50th anniversary of Gilbert's death, bright new productions popped up all over the world. Although I have ceased to be an addict, I go to see such new performances whenever I can.

If anyone from the excellent Light Opera Group of the Negev is reading this, I urge them to go back to their first love and once again produce a Gilbert and Sullivan opera. Yes, the music is pedestrian, the plots creaky and the lyrics outdated. But the paradox is that together they provide a wonderful theatrical experience. A paradox, a paradox, a most ingenious paradox! Ha! Ha! Ha! Ha! Ho! Ho! Ho! Ho!

25 November, 2005

LARGELY LITERARY

*O**rwell and I***

Before the easy options of television and computers were available, reading was the only avenue of entertainment for a solitary child. Like a starving mouse that gnaws at wood I would read everything in my home that came to hand. It led to a certain imbalance in my early reading. Our home possessed attractively bound sets of classics, which you could buy by the yard, at absurdly low prices, through the sales promotions of national newspapers. I thus found myself reading novels by Benjamin Disraeli and Anatole France. Like Everest, they were there.

Of a slightly different category were the bright orange books bound in cloth. These were the publications of the Left Book Club collected by my older sister, then a groupie of Professor Harold Laski at the London School of Economics. In its heyday in the thirties the Left Book Club, a popular anti-fascist but fellow-travelling publishing venture, printed the work of several promising authors. It was, for instance, through reading an anthology entitled "In Letters of Red" that I first came across the poems of W. H. Auden and Louis MacNeice. And it was through a Left Book Club publication on our shelves that I first encountered George Orwell. The book was "The Road to Wigan Pier." This grim description of the author's experiences living among mining families in the north of England was unlikely to appeal to an eleven-year old but I found it surprisingly readable. I was not to know that I was reading the work of a writer who would in later years be considered one of the century's finest writers of English prose.

So much has been written about Orwell that I feel that I owe the reader an apology for adding yet another article about him. The recent centenary of Orwell's birth saw an abundance of books and articles on Orwell, including a thoughtful piece in the pages of *Haaretz* by Dr. Eli Shaltiel. I have no fresh insights to offer nor can I compete with the Orwell professionals. But I want to talk of what Orwell has meant to me.

It was much later, in my last years at school, that I again encountered Orwell. It must have been only shortly after "Nineteen Eighty-Four" first came out – in 1949 shortly before Orwell's death – although I have no recollection of reading any review. The late forties and early fifties were the opening years of the Cold War – a term, incidentally, that Orwell coined. Much of liberal opinion tended to take the same tolerant view of communism that it takes today of international terrorism. An adolescent pink, I too went through a stage of anti-Americanism; indeed there was a lot to be critical about in the years of Senator McCarthy and the execution of the Rosenbergs. In the papers I read – the *Manchester Guardian* and the *New Statesman* – this tended to express itself in a softness, which I shared, towards the Soviet Union.

And then I started reading Koestler and Orwell. My eyes were first opened by Koestler's novel "Darkness at Noon" and by his powerfully uncompromising anti-communist essays in "The Yogi and the Commissar." I was thus softened up for reading Orwell's two great anti-totalitarian novels "Animal Farm" and "Nineteen Eighty-Four" and then Orwell's essays on politics. My continued reading of Orwell over the years has done much to shape my own views of the world.

"George Orwell" was the pen name of Eric Blair (1903-1950). Over 50 years after his death his stature is so unassailable that rival political ideologies claim him for their own. He is hard to pin down because he possessed an independence and integrity that compelled him to view every question afresh.

Orwell's fame today is chiefly derived from the two anti-totalitarian novels that he wrote towards the end of his sadly short life. "Animal Farm" is a brief fable (less than 100 pages long) that tells of animals that forcibly take over a farm from its harsh owners and, after initial successes, are slowly corrupted by their own power. It closely mirrors the events of the Russian Revolution and the triumph of Stalinism. In Orwell's terrifying vision of the future, "Nineteen Eighty-Four," thought itself is controlled, the past is constantly rewritten and there is a permanent state of war. Central to the novel is a theme to which Orwell reverts time after time in his writings – the perversion of language for political ends. Even if you have not read these novels you know the expressions that have become common currency in our culture. Who does not know that Big Brother is watching you, that all animals are equal but that some animals are more equal than others, or has not heard of doublethink, newspeak, the thought police and the two-minute hate?

To appreciate Orwell to the full it is necessary to go beyond his novels and to read his essays and journalism. The four volumes of his essays, journalism and letters edited by his widow Sonia Orwell and Ian Angus contain the real Orwell.

You cannot open any of these books without finding something of interest. Orwell's principal preoccupation was politics but his essays also show a wider variety of interests. He writes penetrating literary criticism; there are essays on Kipling, Dickens, Yeats and Tolstoy that never violate his self-imposed canons of commonsense. He has a love of popular culture and writes refreshing essays on boys' comics, saucy postcards and English cooking.

Orwell's writings are characterized by two closely connected qualities – a patent honesty and a limpid, colloquial prose style. These are the virtues that have made him widely read even after much of his subject matter has become obsolete. Few today are interested in the Spanish Republican War – that bloody precursor to a greater Armageddon – but his classic piece of reportage on that war, "Homage to Catalonia," remains as fresh as ever.

As is evident from his novels, it is the perversion of language that, for him, is the principal feature of a totalitarian state of mind. Many have tried unsuccessfully to imitate his deceptively simple style. He even tells you how to do it. In his essay "Politics and the English Language" he lays down rules for writing that are so dauntingly austere that they are likely to inhibit you from ever putting pen to paper.

Lionel Trilling's old-fashioned epithet for Orwell – that he was a "virtuous" man – perhaps captures him best. But it will not do to be too adulatory. To quote Auden on Yeats "he was silly like us." He never rid himself of the prejudices of his upbringing as a member of the British ruling class. He distrusted foreigners, natives, homosexuals, intellectuals and members of the working class. He makes the occasional casually insensitive remark about Jews. A remark that has always stood out in my mind is an entry from Orwell's diary for October 1940 in which he says that he wants to verify the rumour that Jews greatly predominate among the people sheltering from the Blitz in the London Underground. It appears that they should have remained above-ground so as to give the Luftwaffe a sporting chance.

But Orwell knew he had these prejudices and succeeded in transcending them. Nothing is more revealing than an essay that he wrote in 1945 entitled "Notes on Nationalism." If you are jealous of America or dislike Jews, he says, you cannot get rid of those feelings by thinking about them "but you can at least recognize that you have them, and prevent them from contaminating your mental processes." He returned to this theme a number of times most particularly in his discerning essay "Anti-Semitism in Britain".

Inevitably, people have speculated on what Orwell would have thought had he been alive today. I do not find such reflections futile. To consider what Orwell's opinions on a contemporary issue would have been is to apply to such an issue Orwell's own gold standard of decency and commonsense.

So let me hazard some guesses.

In the best of the recent books on Orwell, Christopher Hitchens' perceptive "Orwell's Victory," Hitchens points out that, almost alone of the intellectual class of the time, Orwell was not fatally compromised by accommodation with any of those "man-made structures of inhumanity," which form the three great subjects of the 20th century: imperialism, fascism and Stalinism. Had he lived, St. George would surely have taken his sword to that fourth 20th century dragon, Islamic terrorism. I pass on whether he would have supported the war on Iraq but he would have despised those on the left who, in seeking to understand the motives of terrorists, condone them. He would certainly have had a field day with the recent pronouncement of the Archbishop of Canterbury urging America to recognize that terrorists can "have serious moral goals".

That jealous defender of language would have poured scorn on post-modernism, cultural relativism and all other manifestations of political correctness that confuse incoherence with profundity. The man who called Sartre a bag of wind would surely have derided Derrida and the excesses of radical feminism and Afrocentrism.

What about Israel? Orwell was unsympathetic to the Zionist cause and there is nothing in the subsequent history of the State of Israel that might have led him to change his mind. But he knew a double standard when he saw it. He would surely have wondered what made Israel uniquely evil in the eyes of the heirs of those woolly European intellectuals for whom he had such contempt in his life and why they should refrain from criticizing infinitely more oppressive regimes, merely because they were not Western.

The poet William Wordsworth, in his radical days, called on that great 17th century apostle of liberty John Milton to redress the wrongs that Wordsworth saw as prevalent in the England of the start of the 19th century. He wrote: "Milton! thou shouldst be living at this hour: England hath need of thee".

Orwell, the world hath need of thee.

17 October, 2003

H anging on a Comma

What must make the lives of film studio chiefs, theatrical impresarios and book publishers enthralling – as well as nerve-wracking – is the sheer impossibility of predicting the reaction of the public to their offerings. Legends abound of the ones that got away. Look at all those sucker publishers who turned down Harry Potter. At times rejection is a badge of honour. The Salon, the official art exhibition of the French Academy, refused admission to so many painters of quality that Napoleon III ordered that a new exhibition, called the "Salon des Refusées," be held for the artists who had been turned down. The list of artists who in 1863 proudly exhibited their work at this home for rejects reads like a roll call of the greatest of 19th century French painters – including Manet, Boudin, Fantin-Latour, Pissarro and Cézanne.

Sometimes you are more surprised at what is published than at what is rejected, though a bold gamble may occasionally come off. Lying unread on hundreds of thousands of coffee tables, for instance, is a tedious but hugely successful account of cosmology: Stephen Hawking's "A Brief [it just seems long!] History of Time." Cosmology aside, if you were asked to pick a subject for a surefire worst-seller you might initially suggest a history of butterfly-collecting in the Balkans or the folkloristic aspects of Patagonian bellringing. Pretty soon, however, you would plump for a book on punctuation.

But as every literate person on both sides of the Greenwich Meridian now knows, the latest British publishing sensation is on that sleep-inducing subject. It is called "Eats, Shoots and Leaves: The Zero Tolerance Approach to Punctuation" by Lynne Truss, and as Michael Handelsaltz wrote in *Haaretz*, is selling in hundreds of thousands. As well as being successful it is both witty and instructive. Handelsaltz was too modest to mention that he is credited in the book's acknowledgments. He provided to the author the unsurprising information that, though Hebrew is written from right to left, the question mark in Hebrew faces the same way as it does in English.

Life without punctuation is tough and I speak with rare authority. I am a lawyer who occasionally reads classical Hebrew. As such, I have manned the ramparts of those last twin outposts of the punctuation-challenged, the legal and the Hebrew. When I started my legal career half a century ago, we were taught that we must draft a legal document so that it could be read without punctuation. To be compelled to punctuate was a confession of failure.

Lawyers no longer draft without punctuation although you can see why they are wary of it. A fortune, sometimes a life, can depend on one of these tiny dots or squiggles. Lynn Truss tells how Sir Roger Casement, the Irish patriot accused of treason against Britain in the First World War, was allegedly hanged on a comma. His counsel argued that the absence of a comma in the Treason Act of 1351 led to an ambiguity that should exonerate the accused. The judges walked over to the Public Records Office to examine the original of the statute, written in Norman French. They detected a faint virgule (the comma's predecessor) and Casement was duly sent to the gallows.

The Hebrew language too is uncomfortable with punctuation. The Torah scroll is unpunctuated; reading it is a specialized skill. But since the work of the Masoretes over a thousand years ago, the Hebrew text of the Bible is not only pointed to compensate for the absence of vowels, each word carries a cantillation mark. The cantillation mark indicates how the word is chanted but is furthermore a form of punctuation, serving to assist in the interpretation of many a difficult text. As for the Talmud, the standard texts are to this day unpunctuated.

It would be easy to devote an article to the hilarious examples of bad punctuation that Truss gives in her entertaining book like the "greengrocer's apostrophe" as in 'potato's' and 'tomato's.' I will content myself with the racist graffito "Nigger's out" under which a wit had scrawled "But he'll be back soon." My politically correct spell-checker refused to allow me to type that "n" word though in other respects it is admirably broadminded; I tried it with a choice selection of four-letter words which it passed without demur

Evelyn Waugh, as elegant a writer as graced the 20th century, was a confident punctuator, but many a good writer was not. In a letter to Nancy Mitford, Waugh told her that, like theology, punctuation was not her subject. Almost half a century ago I wrote a juvenile pastiche of Waugh's style for a literary competition. I am only grateful that the master himself was unlikely to have seen it as it was published in the *New Statesman and Nation*, a journal I assume he despised – or would have done had he acknowledged its existence. I took a passage from "Brideshead Revisited" as my model for the parody. What I remember is that I was impressed by, and studiously imitated, his liberal use of the comma and perhaps it was that that won me the prize of, as I recall, a five-guinea book token.

The success of Truss's book, and of a string of other recent books on the English language, gives me reason to hope that there is a revived interest in good writing in this age of the sound bite, the text message and the blog. In his 1980 review of the "Letters of Evelyn Waugh," Clive James wrote that "unless the telephone is uninvented," the book he was reviewing might be the last great collection of letters by a great writer. Waugh, the archetypal old fogy, hated the telephone and the typewriter; he wrote his quirky, misanthropic, prejudiced but always entertaining letters and postcards in a crabbed, barely legible, longhand.

Heaven knows what he would have thought of the computer but the advent of electronic mail has surely made it apparent that Clive James's obsequies for the art of correspondence were premature. The written word has again become the favoured method of communication between people separated by any distance. Not every writer has the Luddite instincts of Evelyn Waugh and there are good writers today who are finding that their lives have been made easier through the benefits of modern technology. I am convinced that literature will one day be enriched by the correspondence of real writers who use a computer but take pains with what they write.

But there is an awful lot of muck polluting cyberspace. According to a recent article in Time magazine, there are about 500 billion documents on the Internet. That number of monkeys on that number of keyboards could surely produce a Hamlet in no time to speak of. Linguists speculate on the language that is emerging from emails and blogs as a new medium of expression, part writing part speech. All I know is that I would find the junk that crams my inbox every day a little less repulsive were it not so appallingly spelled and punctuated. When my own posthumous collection of emails is published I hope that the person raking over my literary remains will choose not to print the letters from venal civil servants in Nigeria generously proposing to share with me their stash of $40 million or the messages from kindhearted ladies touchingly offering to remedy my most intimate shortcomings. They might well, however, be tempted to print the semi-literate rant I recently received from a correspondent in Montreal who called me, to my delight, a self-hating Jewish *Haaretz* writer. At last I've arrived.

Spelling and punctuation apart, so much of what we find ourselves reading today is pretentious or incoherent. I have tried without success to trace a remark that I have heard attributed to Bertrand Russell: that if you don't understand something you read, the chances are that it is nonsense. I shudder to think of what George Orwell, who believed that bad writing was what distinguishes a totalitarian state of mind, would have said of the distortions of the English language that you see today emanating from the religious right, the European left, the wackier side of feminism or the English departments of American universities.

In his essay "Politics and the English Language," Orwell voices one of his deepest concerns. He writes: "Modern English, especially written English, is full of bad habits which spread by imitation and which can be avoided if one is willing to take the necessary trouble. If one gets rid of these habits one can think more clearly, and to think clearly is a necessary first step toward political regeneration: so that the fight against bad English is not frivolous and is not the exclusive concern of professional writers".

Hunched over our laptops, we write more than ever before. Orwell, Waugh and Lynne Truss would agree on one thing: that punctuation, spelling and clarity of expression matter. We should take it to heart.

6 February, 2004

_W_innie-the-Pooh

I trace the frailty of my adult ego to a bruising childhood encounter with Christopher Robin. My early years were spent in a suburb of London which in the thirties, though hardly _Judenrein_, was far more English than it is today. Christopher Robin, the real-life son of A. A. Milne, was himself in those days barely out of his teens. His father's stories and poems featuring him and his winsome friends of the Forest had already taken the world by storm. Our leafy corner of Christopher Robin's city was not excluded from this cultural hurricane and my mother was blown along with it.

I ought, perhaps, to blame E. H. Shepard whose enchanting illustrations had imprinted Christopher Robin's image upon the minds of umpteen million readers of the books. My mother yearned for her lamb to resemble her literary idol. Mercifully I do not remember if I was ever put into a smock as the two-year-old Christopher Robin is depicted, but I do recall, with a mortification that has lasted to this day, that at the age of four, I was made to wear the outfit – grey flannel coat buttoned up to the top and a grey felt hat – that the little blighter wore when he went down to Buckingham Palace with Alice.

Ours was not a particularly rough neighbourhood but it was not Eaton Square either and as I walked to the synagogue enduring the ill-bred, but totally excusable, sniggers of the local urchins, I knew what I would be in for when I got to shul. I was greeted with catcalls. The pack was led by a seven-year-old whom I have never forgiven and now lives in Haifa in respectable retirement – oblivious of the scars he wrought on my psyche.

But Christopher Robin has stayed with me. Even now, as I walk along a street, I find myself avoiding the lines between the paving stones. True the bears are unlikely to get me if I tread on a line but childhood habits die hard. Between 1924 and 1928, A.A. Milne published four books for children, the two books of verse "When We Were Very Young" and "Now We Are Six" and two books of stories "Winnie-the-Pooh" and "The House at Pooh Corner".

The books were all illustrated by Shepard, who is as indispensable to the Pooh books as Tenniel is to Lewis Carroll. All four books were sensationally successful and have remained so; but though he lived until 1956, Milne only wrote one other children's book. At the time he wrote the books, he was already a well-known dramatist and humorous writer for *Punch*. The children's books were for and about Christopher Robin, Milne's only child who had been born in 1920.

The two Pooh books take the form of stories, told by the author to Christopher Robin, of the adventures in the Forest (a thinly disguised version of Ashdown Forest, where the Milnes had their home) of his nursery toys, Winnie-the-Pooh (a Bear of Very Little Brain) with Piglet, Eeyore, Owl, Kanga, Roo, Rabbit and Tigger.

Already at his death, A.A. Milne's children's books had become a planet-wide phenomenon. They had sold over seven million copies, a number that has multiplied several-fold in the succeeding years. The books have been translated into 25 foreign languages and in 1960 a Latin version, "Winnie Ille Pu" sold 100,000 copies in its first printing, becoming one of those inexplicable best-sellers – like Stephen Hawking's "A Brief History of Time" – that everyone buys but nobody reads. By the time that the sequel "Domus Anguli Puensis" appeared, the novelty had worn off. Apparently not even Latinos were reading Latin.

Winnie-the-Pooh has become a major cultural point of reference. If you have the stomach for it you can now read "The Tao of Pooh," "The Wisdom of Pooh," "Pooh's Workout Book," "Pooh and the Psychologists," "Pooh and the Millennium," "The Te of Piglet," "Pooh and the Ancient Mysteries" and four books in the series "Pooh on Management." The hundreds of Web sites devoted to the immortal bear dispel any further doubts of Pooh's lasting appeal. Indeed Winnie-the-Pooh has received the ultimate accolade. To the horror of Milne and Shepard purists, he has received the full Disney treatment.

In Israel, Winnie-the-Pooh achieved cult status in a much loved Hebrew translation by Vera Israelit. Avirama Golan, who writes for *Haaretz* on social affairs, is now completing a fresh translation of the book. She is a celebrated figure in Israeli literary circles. For the past four years, Golan has hosted a television programme devoted to new books. Her great love is children's literature and she teaches children's literature translation at Tel Aviv University. Among the books she has translated is "Peter Pan," to her the greatest of all children's books.

It is not in a spirit of rivalry that Golan has embarked on a new translation of "Winnie-the-Pooh" for she yields to none in her admiration for the work of Vera Israelit. But the Hebrew language has moved on and the half-century old translation, brilliant as it is, does not speak to a new generation of young readers. Indeed it is hard to believe that its mandarin style – what Israelis disparagingly refer to as *ivrit shel Shabbat* ("Sabbath Hebrew") – can ever have appealed to the intelligent first-graders for whom Milne intended the books. Avirama Golan, on the other hand, writes the way the children of today speak.

To translate a work like "Winnie-the-Pooh" is to walk a tightrope. On the one hand, its references must be understood by young Hebrew readers; on the other hand it must communicate a feeling for the culture in which the book is steeped. For Pooh is a quintessentially English bear. Not only is he English; he is a bear of the upper middle class, living in a wood with his privileged friends. What, asks Avirama, is an Israeli child to make of Owl – a pedant with intellectual pretensions – residing at The Chestnuts? Homes in Israel do not have names, only numbers. Golan's *tsameret armonim* nicely conveys Owl's pomposity.

Golan does not find the Pooh phenomenon hard to explain. For her, these books are great literature having a subtext subtly communicating the thoughts and values that are the essence of the finest children's classics. She instances Milne's treatment of the still modish issue of identity. In "Pooh Goes Visiting," in a passage that is sure to stir feelings of recognition in any child, Rabbit challenges Pooh's certainty that he is indeed Pooh Bear:

> *He took his head out of the hole, and had another think, and then he put*
> *it back, and said:*
> *"Well, could you very kindly tell me where Rabbit is?"*
> *"He has gone to see his friend Pooh Bear, who is a great friend of his."*
> *"But this is Me!" said Bear, very much surprised.*
> *"What sort of Me?"*
> *"Pooh Bear."*
> *"Are you sure?" said Rabbit, still more surprised.*
> *"Quite, quite sure," said Pooh.*
> *"Oh, well, then, come in".*

The Pooh books share with other English children's classics – "Peter Pan," "The Wind in the Willows," "Alice in Wonderland," the Narnia books and now the Harry Potter series – the same comfortable, privileged background: rural, upper class and predominantly male. Much the same can be said of the Fellowship of the Rings cycle; the Shire is a Tory Heaven – the name of a long-forgotten novel by Marghanita Laski – exuding Tolkien's deeply conservative values.

Avirama Golan, whose worldview is unabashedly liberal and feminist, acknowledges this and regards it as part of their appeal. For Israelis growing up in the fifties and sixties, the Pooh books had the attraction of an alien world. Avirama refers to an essay of Amos Oz on the theme of the Forest and the strange fascination this had for his generation, a generation that did not travel and that garnered all its ideas of the outside world from literature.

It is questionable if the Pooh books can bear the weight that their admirers have put on them. Certainly "Winnie-the-Pooh" is children's literature of the highest order. The books read beautifully, are truly funny, and show an uncanny understanding of how a small child thinks. But the stories are for reading aloud to children of about five years old, and Milne never intended otherwise.

Milne, who took himself very seriously, never wanted his literary reputation to hinge on books written for children. He had written a number of light comedies, which are no longer performed, and a couple of novels that have sunk without trace. Milne was particularly upset by the ridicule heaped on him by Dorothy Parker who, in the New Yorker, treated these stories as having pretensions to which they never aspired. In his autobiography, published ten years later, Milne wrote: "The books were written for children. When, for instance, Dorothy Parker, as 'Constant Reader' in the New Yorker, delights the sophisticated by announcing that on page five of 'The House at Pooh Corner,' 'Tonstant Weader fwowed up" (sic, if I may), she leaves the book oddly enough, much where it was".

It was unfair – for one thing the Pooh books do not use that kind of baby talk – and it rankled. But, whether he liked it or not, the Pooh books became his literary epitaph and the work by which he had hoped to be judged proved to be ephemeral.

At the conclusion of "The House at Pooh Corner," Milne sends Christopher Robin to school and, with an almost audible sigh of relief, bids farewell to Winnie-the-Pooh:

> *So they went off together. But wherever they go, and whatever happens to them on the way, in that enchanted place on the top of the Forest a little boy and his Bear will always be playing.*

Milne sought, like Prospero, to drown his book deeper than did ever plummet sound. But Winnie-the-Pooh, the Bear of Very Little Brain, remained to haunt him – to our lasting gratitude.

30 May, 2003

The Voice of Cassandra

"On the eve of the defeat of Communism one of its boldest enemies had been reduced to the level of a half-forgotten crank who was reviled as a philanderer and wife-beater when he was recalled at all." Thus David Cesarani on Arthur Koestler, in the introduction to his life of Koestler, "Arthur Koestler: the Homeless Mind." Koestler deserves a better epitaph than that. The epitaph he wanted is the sentence that closes his two wonderful volumes of memoirs. His books had been burned by both the Nazis and the Communists. "To be burned twice in one's lifetime, is, after all," writes Koestler, "a rare distinction".

Arthur Koestler (1905-1983) was the archetype of the rootless cosmopolitan Jew. Born in Budapest, he studied in Vienna, emigrated to Palestine, moved to Berlin, lived in Paris, reported on the Civil War in Spain and finally settled in Britain. He is chiefly remembered today for his masterpiece "Darkness at Noon" (1940,) a brilliant denunciation of the Soviet system written when the intelligentsia was still in the thrall of Moscow. He had formidable linguistic talents. Though Hungarian was his mother tongue, he wrote his early work in German and then switched to English, a language he wrote so flawlessly that he has been compared to those other foreign masters of English, Conrad and Nabokov.

Cesarani does not like Koestler as a person – he sensationally refers to him as a serial rapist and a habitual drunkard – but he does full justice to Koestler as a writer. To understand Koestler, thinks Cesarani, you must look at his Jewish roots.

Koestler is disliked in Israel, yet no other major Jewish writer of the 20th century has so affirmed his Jewish identity as to devote years of his life to the Zionist cause and live in the Land of Israel. Israel is full of streets and squares named after now forgotten Zionist apparatchiks. Of the thousands that pass through Tel Aviv's Bograshov Street each day, not one in a thousand could tell you who Bograshov was. Yet the author of "Darkness at Noon" who lived on that street and whose novel "Thieves in the Night" (1946), arguably did more than any other to influence international opinion in favour of a Jewish state, remains uncommemorated. Here I declare a personal interest. On my first visit to Israel in 1953, I stayed in what had been Koestler's apartment on Bograshov Street as the guest of my old Hebrew teacher who lived there after Koestler left.

Koestler's infatuation with Zionism is documented in "Arrow in the Blue," the first volume of his memoirs. Straight out of university in Vienna he became secretary to the charismatic Vladimir Jabotinsky, one of those few "guardians of the holy grail," in Koestler's words, who never disappointed him and to whom Koestler remained devoted until his death. Koestler never abandoned his identification with the opinions of Jabotinsky even though he termed him "the spiritual father of the Palestine terrorists." In "Thieves in the Night" he expressed those opinions. The novel alienated him from many of his close friends including Teddy Kollek, to whom he had dedicated the book. It was seen as advocating that the end justifies the means, a doctrine that Koestler had famously rejected when applied to communism. Not for the last time, Koestler had to do some fancy footwork to reconcile directly opposing views.

"Arrow in the Blue" is well worth reading, if only for its colourful descriptions of the yishuv in the days of the British Mandate. Koestler did not find life easy in Palestine. He did not fit in to the kibbutz where he was first sent and he almost starved in Tel Aviv. But he learned Hebrew and claimed to have invented the Hebrew crossword puzzle.

Another intriguing piece of Koestleriana relates to the origin of the name of the central character of his most famous novel. When Koestler thought up the name Rubashov for the old-guard Bolshevik of "Darkness at Noon," he could not remember where he had heard the name before. Only years later was he reminded that, when he had lived in Palestine, the editor of the leading newspaper *Davar* was called Rubashov. Rubashov became a man of even greater consequence in 1963 when he was elected the third president of the State of Israel under his Hebraized name of Zalman Shazar.

Upon the establishment of the state, Koestler publicly renounced Judaism and Zionism. In "Promise and Fulfilment" (1949), he argued that Jews now had a straightforward choice. They could emigrate to the land for which they had been praying for 2000 years or cease to be Jews; he chose the latter. Koestler's views brought him into conflict with the redoubtable Isaiah Berlin who was, by nature, averse to stark choices. He pointedly asked how one goes about ceasing to be a Jew.

Having rejected communism and Zionism, Koestler then said farewell to politics altogether. In 1955 in "The Trail of the Dinosaur," he publicly turned his back on the political writing that had earned him his international reputation. "Cassandra's voice has grown hoarse," he wrote, "and is due for a vocational change." Instead he trained the powerful searchlight of his intellect on a bewildering variety of nonpolitical subjects. He became one of the most effective advocates for the abolition of capital punishment; he wrote persuasively on cosmology; he adopted contrarian and increasingly nutty positions on Darwinism, behaviourism, euthanasia, coincidence, telepathy, humour and the nature of creativity.

But he could not leave the Jews alone.

In 1976, nearly thirty years after his trumpeted renunciation of Judaism, he published "The Thirteenth Tribe," his book about the Khazars. For almost four centuries, the Khazars, a nomadic people that had migrated from central Asia, held sway over a huge area of southeastern Europe. The Khazar empire became a major European power comparable, according to the great historian J. B. Bury, with the empire of Charlemagne. What has intrigued historians and archaeologists of this little-known empire is that at some time during the eighth century of the Common Era, the Khazars converted to Judaism, an event that captured the imagination of contemporary Jews such as the great poet Yehuda Halevi, who made the Khazars the subject of his monumental philosophical work "The Kuzari".

In the "The Thirteenth Tribe," Koestler argues that the Khazars, having disappeared as a separately identifiable people during the tenth century, re-emerged as the Ashkenazi Jews of central and eastern Europe. The book was savaged by virtually every reputable historian. The standard view, for which there is copious evidence, was that the Ashkenazis had migrated eastwards from France and Germany centuries later than the time of the disappearance of the Khazars. How else to explain Yiddish, a language principally derived from German or the absence of any trace of the Khazar culture or language among the Jews?

But to cross swords with scholars had never daunted Koestler. He was a polymath of such intellectual power and such hubris that he took on, on their own turf, physicists, biologists, historians and psychologists. Yet the old Jewish adage applied as much to Koestler as to any other brave soul who quixotically chooses to tangle with experts: By me he was a historian, but by a historian he was no historian.

Koestler had an agenda for his preposterous theory. If he could thereby prove that he was descended from nomads of the steppes rather than from that awkward desert people who were always causing so much trouble, perhaps he could finally get rid of that outsize Jewish chip on his shoulder. Arab propagandists – notably Abu Mazen whose doctoral dissertation relies on Koestler's book – seized on Koestler's thesis as conclusive proof that the Jews had no historic entitlement to the Land of Israel. Koestler had not intended that, though he had anticipated it. In an appendix to the book he argues that the Jews had acquired the right to the country by international law. Once again, Koestler wanted to have his cake and eat it too.

So Koestler is persona non grata in Israel and he has, of course, been airbrushed from the history of the Revisionist Zionism that he served. We tend to shun our dissenters. Spinoza waited 300 years for a street in Jerusalem. We are unlikely in our lifetimes to see a Chomsky Street or a Leibovitz Avenue; and, sadly, we shall never see a Koestler Boulevard. Our High Priests of Zionist correctness will see to that.

But before we cast Koestler into that corner of the outer darkness that we reserve for our perceived renegades, let us take a look at an article he published in *The New York Times* magazine in January 1944, entitled "On Disbelieving Atrocities." He writes of the impossibility of convincing the civilized world of "the greatest mass-killing in recorded history" that "goes on daily, hourly, as regularly as the ticking of your watch." He admits to being a "maniac," a Cassandra who is "screaming" of the killing of the total Jewish population of Europe.

Drunken rapist perhaps, renegade maybe, but it is as one of the great screamers that we should remember Arthur Koestler.

28 May, 2004

*J*oy in the Morning

If you have read George Eliot's novel "Daniel Deronda," you will have encountered the musical genius Herr Klesmer, "a felicitous combination of the German, the Sclave [Slav], and the Semite." He is a sympathetic character, but he is a foreigner and the ever-so-English George Eliot cannot resist poking gentle fun at him. "One may understand jokes without liking them," he says. "I have had opera books sent me full of jokes; it was just because I understood them that I did not like them.... But, in fact... I am very sensible to wit and humour." Through Herr Klesmer, George Eliot is voicing an axiom: To claim that you possess a sense of humour is to admit you haven't got one, and to write of humour in the abstract is to court an accusation of humourlessness.

So don't ask me why I laugh at P. G. Wodehouse. I just do and do so immoderately. If you have never read Wodehouse, it is hard to describe his appeal. No one writes like him; he is *sui generis*. His stories portray a lost realm of innocence, an imaginary world of dotty earls, dim young men about town, fearsome aunts, dyspeptic tycoons, erudite valets, portly butlers and bungling burglars. His plots are masterpieces of farcical complexity. Every line of dialogue is a comic gem. He claimed that there were two ways of writing novels. One was the way of going deeply into life; the other was his way – "making a sort of musical comedy without music".

It would be a mistake to dismiss Wodehouse as an entertainer of ephemeral importance. Sean O'Casey called him "English literature's performing flea," but serious writers and critics have treated him seriously. He has been called "the greatest living writer of prose" and "the funniest writer ever to have put words on paper." Praise of this order is fatuous – Wodehouse is, after all, a trivial writer – but it is incontestable that he is supremely funny and, by any measure, a skilful stylist.

I have just finished reading "Wodehouse," a biography by Robert McCrum, the literary editor of *The Observer*. I approached it with some caution. I read a fair number of biographies and frequently – as in the case of lives of statesmen – a biography is a good way of getting a handle on a certain period. I think, for example, of Ian Kershaw's magnificent biography of Hitler. In the case of literary biographies, though, you often wonder what a detailed description of an author's life would add to your appreciation of his work.

Still, I am a lifelong Wodehouse fan and I thought it might be interesting to know more about him. Wodehouse was a dull, stuffy, pipe-smoking Englishman whose absorbing interest was his work. He had no conversation and, in company, showed no sign of having a sense of humour. He was astonishingly prolific, a veritable writing machine. His first novel was published in 1902 and his last book, which he was working on when he died, was published in 1975. In that working lifetime of more than seventy years, he wrote at least 96 novels, wrote and collaborated on 16 plays and wrote for 28 musicals together with such titans of Tin Pan Alley as Jerome Kern, George Gershwin and Cole Porter.

In his largely boring life, one interesting thing happened. In 1940, P.G.Wodehouse and his wife were living in France and were overrun by the invading German forces. He was sent to a series of German internment camps, ending up in Tost in Upper Silesia. This internment prompted him to write later: "If this is Upper Silesia, what must Lower Silesia be like?" In 1941, the Germans, realizing the propaganda value of having a famous British writer in their clutches, took him out of the internment camp and feted him at the luxurious Adlon Hotel in Berlin, in return for which he made five broadcasts of "a non-political nature." In Britain all hell broke loose and not surprisingly; his native country was fighting a desperate war against Germany and here was Wodehouse being funny on German radio. There were calls to have him tried for treason, and libraries withdrew his books from circulation.

In 1945, George Orwell, contrary as ever, published an essay entitled "In Defence of P.G. Wodehouse." Orwell contended that Wodehouse had been, at most, guilty of stupidity; he was a political innocent as was evident from his books. Yet he should not get away so lightly; the broadcasts were indeed innocuous in content, but he was more than simply stupid. Even Wodehouse's dimwitted character Bertie Wooster would have known better. Apolitical though he was, Wodehouse was aware that Germany was at war with England and that, already in 1941, the Germans had done some particularly foul things. The truth is that Wodehouse was unwilling to sacrifice his personal comfort for any principle. A moral eunuch, he opted for the easy life.

If you are a devoted Wodehouse reader, this episode must cause concern. We frequently read the work of serious writers whose views are abhorrent to us, but if we read an author solely for entertainment – as we do in the case of Wodehouse – it should matter to us if he is racist or fascist or anti-Semitic. Had I believed Wodehouse to be a fascist sympathizer or an anti-Semite, I would not have been able to read him with enjoyment. So it is pleasant to report that though Wodehouse may have been a fool and a poltroon he was no kind of hater and I concur with his biographer's conclusion that Wodehouse – who had happily spent the 1920s in New York in the almost exclusively Jewish world of musical comedy – was no anti-Semite.

Nor was he a fascist. If you are going to read only one Wodehouse book, try his 1937 novel "The Code of the Woosters." With its devastating caricature of would-be dictator Roderick Spode, it is Wodehouse's one attempt at political satire. The fearsome Spode, a "big chap with a small moustache and the sort of eye that can open an oyster at sixty paces," is a thinly-veiled portrait of British fascist leader Sir Oswald Mosley. He leads a party whose adherents wear black shorts ("footer bags," in Wooster slang). Bertie is told that they are to be distinguished from the Blackshirts – Mosley's outfit – because by the time Spode formed his association, there were no shirts left. Spode bullies Bertie but, assured by the infallible Jeeves, Bertie's ever-resourceful and awesomely erudite "gentleman's gentleman," that he will be able to make the terrible Spode wilt by uttering the word "Eulalie," Bertie goes into an anti-Spode tirade, using a vocabulary that is uniquely, unforgettably and untranslatably Wodehouse: "The trouble with you, Spode, is that just because you have succeeded in inducing a handful of half-wits to disfigure the London scene by going about in black shorts, you think you are someone. You hear them shouting 'Heil Spode!' and you imagine it is the Voice of the People. That is where you make your bloomer. What the Voice of the People is saying is: 'Look at that frightful ass Spode swanking about in footer bags! Did you ever in your puff see such a perfect perisher?'"

The dictator gets his comeuppance because Jeeves has discovered that Spode secretly designs ladies' underclothing and is the owner of an emporium on Bond Street known as Eulalie Soeurs. Says Bertie: "Good Lord, Jeeves! No wonder he didn't want a thing like that to come out".

> "No, sir. It would unquestionably jeopardize his authority over his
>   followers/"
> "You can't be a successful dictator and design women's underclothing".
> "No, sir."
> "One or the other. Not both."
> "Precisely, sir."

The man who wrote that was no fascist. This is in the class of Chaplin's "The Great Dictator."

And one last cheer for Wodehouse. When I was seriously ill some years ago and told that my days were numbered, I kept going by re-reading Wodehouse. One novel tells of how Bertie Wooster finds himself in one horrifying predicament after another during a stay in deepest rural Steeple Bumpleigh. The book's title, "Joy in the Morning," is taken from Psalm 30. In this moving psalm, which is recited daily by observant Jews, the psalmist thanks God for his recovery from a severe illness. As they shake the dust of Steeple Bumpleigh off their feet, Bertie, whose greatest scholastic achievement, as every Wodehousian knows, was a prize he won at his preparatory school for Scripture knowledge, happily quotes to Jeeves: "Weeping may tarry for the night, but joy cometh in the morning".

Psalm 30 is a psalm that has a special meaning for me, and "Joy in the Morning" is one of my favourite books. For that joy in the morning that he brought me at a low time in my life, I shall remain eternally grateful to P.G. Wodehouse.

18 February, 2005

*P*inter's Prize

A small country craves recognition for the achievements of its citizens. The pride that Israelis feel at their nation's unhappily rare successes in international sport may, to outsiders, appear to be out of all proportion to their global significance. Yes, Gal Fridman's gold medal at last year's Olympics occasioned celebration, but in the cold light of the morning after, we were forced to admit that, in terms of international sporting importance, windsurfing is down there with beach volleyball and synchronized swimming. Much the same goes for the basketball successes of Maccabi Tel Aviv. Do we not perhaps exaggerate the importance of the triumphs of a team, composed largely of lofty African Americans, in a competition whose star players would never hold a place in the humblest NBA team?

But Nobel Prizes are another story, and when we get them we have something to brag about. Last year two Israeli scientists shared the prize for chemistry; this year half of the prize for economics was awarded to an Israeli mathematician. Breathes there the Israeli with a soul so dead that did not warm at seeing, on the front page of *Haaretz*, the photograph of a patriarchal Robert J. Aumann, surrounded by his beaming children and grandchildren, each male from the age of three upward clad in the obligatory Nobel uniform of white tie and tails, topped with the not-so-obligatory skullcap?

Alfred Nobel, who died in 1896, left his considerable fortune to fund the annual award of five prizes (the sixth, for economics, was added in 1969) to "the persons who have most benefited humanity" in the areas of literature, physics, chemistry, world peace and medicine or physiology. You might not think of Nobel himself as a benefit to humanity; he invented dynamite. The prizes are today worth around $1.3 million apiece, but it is not merely for their monetary value that they matter. A Nobel is the pinnacle of scientific achievement; there is nothing to match it.

The awards to scientists seldom generate controversy. Few laymen have strong views on the respective merits of chemists, but everyone thinks he knows something about peace. While the other prizes tend to be awarded for lifetime achievement, the Nobel Peace Prize can be given for a perceived contribution to peace that is often too recent to prevent its appearing absurd in the light of later history. Awards for so-called peace-making in Vietnam, Northern Ireland and, of course, the Middle East proved to be premature. In the eyes of many, the peace prize was eternally tarnished with the award of a share of the 1994 honour to Yasser Arafat. It is probably a good thing that dead people are not eligible for the prize; otherwise the committee might have made a posthumous award to Genghis Khan.

It is not only the peace prize that enrages people. The literature prize too is almost guaranteed to kick up a storm. The criteria applied by the selection committee, composed of Swedish academics, have changed over time. They have occasionally got it right – in more than 100 selections, there has to be some gold among the dross – but they have also made some unforgivable omissions. If you wrote a history of 20th century literature based on Nobel winners alone, you would have to omit Joyce, Kafka, Proust, Auden, Virginia Woolf, Cavafy, Mandelstam, Akhmatova, Borges, Brecht, D.H. Lawrence, Nabokov and Orwell, not to mention 19th century names that were considered but rejected during the early years of the prize, like Mark Twain, Tolstoy, Ibsen, Strindberg, Chekhov, Conrad and Henry James. As for writers who won the prize, I have the list before me and the names of far too many of them – writing in such mainstream languages as Occitan, Icelandic, Serbo-Croat and Yiddish – would qualify for inscription on the Tomb of the Unknown Author.

Politics, the curse of the peace prize, has far too frequently also played a part in the award of the Nobel Prize for Literature. That Pasternak and Solzhenitsyn were out of favour in the Soviet Union weighed as much with the committee selecting them for the prize as did their undoubted literary qualities. Now that Soviet Russia is not around, it is the nose of the United States that the Nobel committee loves to tweak. In 1997 the prize was awarded to the Italian dramatist Dario Fo, who called 9/11 "the legitimate daughter of the culture of violence," and last year it was awarded to Austrian writer Elfriede Jellinek, whose main claim to fame is that, like Fo, she is an unrepentant communist.

The award of the prize for 2005 to the British playwright Harold Pinter was true to form. I concede that he is not the worst writer ever to have won the prize – in that he faces stiff competition – but it is hard to believe that what motivated the committee was not Pinter's passionate and well-publicized opposition to the war in Iraq and his almost pathological hatred of America, rather than his literary achievement. Pinter hates everything American with a loathing that passeth all understanding. The United States, he says, is "the most feared, most powerful and most detested nation the world has ever known." The 9/11 atrocity, for him, was "an act of retaliation against constant and systematic manifestations of state terrorism on the part of the United States over many years in all parts of the world." Of course anti-Americanism is the common currency of the European left, but Pinter's tirades are so visceral that one can only compare them with the more extreme manifestations of anti-Semitism.

In recent years Pinter has turned to poetry. He proudly publishes the results on his web site. These poems are embarrassingly bad; few are free of obscenities and most express anti-American sentiments of an adolescent crudity. It is hard not to avoid the conclusion that the mind behind this doggerel is a shallow one. Still I will allow myself to quote one Pinter poem in its entirety: "I saw Len Hutton in his prime / Another time / Another time." I would like to put in a good word for this poem. Devoid though it may be of literary merit, it is short; it is free of profanity and it exhibits one of Pinter's redeeming virtues: his love of cricket. Hutton, once a famous cricketer, was one of Pinter's idols – and one of mine. I can forgive Pinter much for having preferred the solid stylist Len Hutton to the flashy swashbuckler, Denis Compton.

But it is as a dramatist that Pinter should surely be judged. Not all critics would agree with the view of Pinter represented by Michael Kustow, who as Pinter's close associate is surely *parti pris*, in a recent article in *Haaretz*. To write as adulatory an article as did Kustow, you have to be not only an admirer of Pinter's writing, but also wholly in sympathy with his political stance. To a great extent, the reception by the critics of Pinter's prize accorded with their political views – but not entirely. And there were those wholly unsympathetic to his rampant anti-Americanism, who nevertheless gave him credit for bringing a new voice to the English theatre.

The critics from the right who depicted Pinter as some kind of charlatan can surely not have seen his earlier plays "The Caretaker," "The Birthday Party" and "The Homecoming." Employing the everyday speech of his commonplace characters, he creates a unique atmosphere of dread. His talent lies in his unerring ear for the spoken word. He was once an actor and he has an instinctive understanding of that mysterious bond created between an actor and his audience. For good reason he shares with Kafka the distinction of having had an adjective – *Pinteresque* – coined to describe his idiosyncratic style. That he is no phony is also apparent from the craftsmanship of the scripts he wrote for such classic films as "The French Lieutenant's Woman," "The Servant" and "The Go-Between".

Pinter is best known for what he does not say. The typical Pinter stage direction is pause or silence. What people admire in Pinter is the hole, not the bagel. I am reminded of John Cage's "4'33" – a musical composition that, according to Grove's Dictionary of Music, "has no sound added to that of the environment in which it is performed." In other words, the work is performed in complete silence for four minutes and 33 seconds. Like the garden shed that won this year's prestigious Turner Award for Art, the arts are more and more resembling the new clothes of Hans Christian Andersen's emperor.

Still, Pinter's pauses work and his best plays are unquestionably powerful pieces of theatre. But the Nobel Prize is supposed to be for literature and, for me, literature is something that you read. I can't read Pinter. His plays only come alive on the stage. If asked whether Pinter deserves the prize, my response would be a quotation taken at random from almost any page of his plays: Silence.

23 December, 2005

*B*enefit of Clergy

One day in the late 1300s, the father of English poetry, Geoffrey Chaucer, was fined two shillings for striking a Franciscan friar on Fleet Street. Some 600 years later, in a swanky Manhattan restaurant, Bob Dylan's mother, Mrs. Zimmerman, was heard complaining that, although her famous son gave her naches, he was not eating enough. What these diverse stories have in common is that they are anecdotes about writers and, as such, are among the many that appear in "The New Oxford Book of Literary Anecdotes".

Anecdotes are not necessarily funny, though many in this book are, but most of them are revealing about the authors whose foibles make the book so entertaining. What strikes the casual reader is the extraordinarily antisocial character of so many of the poets, dramatists and novelists that people the book. Chaucer merely hit his friar, but the 20th century American writer, William Burroughs, went one better: in a grisly, and presumably drunken effort to emulate William Tell, he placed a glass on his wife's head, intending to shoot it off with his revolver. His aim, tragically, was off and he shot her through the temple.

Homicide apart, the book provides a host of other stories about writers on behalf of whom you would have been ill-advised to offer yourself as a character witness. You might have been honoured to host F. Scott Fitzgerald, but I doubt if you would invite him again if he amused himself, as he does in one of the anecdotes, by throwing your valuable Venetian wineglasses over the garden wall. And aren't you glad that you were not one of the children of Evelyn Waugh? When the first consignment of bananas arrived in Britain after World War II – there were no bananas throughout the duration of the war – the government decreed that every child in the country should get one banana. The famous novelist called his three children to watch him while he guzzled all three of their bananas, to which he added their rations of sugar and cream.

And how about Dylan Thomas? On one occasion, at a dinner given by Edith

Sitwell, Thomas and his then wife spent the evening fighting and hitting each other. The evening ended with Mrs. Thomas thrusting her elbow into the ice cream and then ordering the famously staid T.S. Eliot to lick it off. If you were sufficiently dedicated to literature to have Thomas as a houseguest, his polishing off your liquor cabinet and trying to bed your wife would be the least of your worries. He was also unabashedly larcenous. John Gross includes a story where a hostess caught Thomas trying to slink off with an object that can only have been of use to him at a pawnshop – her electric sewing machine. Yet, although you would not have wanted your daughter to marry him, this was the man who wrote "Do not go gentle into that good night." So, should we care if an artist whose work we admire turns out to be a drunkard, thief, murderer or rapist?

George Bernard Shaw's play "The Doctor's Dilemma" asks the question in dramatic form. The play is Shaw's assault on the medical profession, but it also puts forward an interesting test case in ethics. Rather improbably, the distinguished physician of the title has a chance to play God. He has two dying patients and is only able to save the life of one of them. One is a dull doctor who devotes his life to the poor. The other is a totally amoral but brilliant painter. Shaw, perverse as ever, kills the artist and, in doing so, asks provocative questions about the artist's relationship to society.

George Orwell raises the same question in his essay on the autobiography of Salvador Dali, which he describes as "a book that stinks." In the field of aberration, Dali was an infant prodigy. He proudly tells his readers of how, at five, he threw another boy off a suspension bridge and, at the same age, caught a wounded bat and ate it live together with the ants with which it was encrusted. As he grew up, he really got going and confesses to, or rather boasts of, an array of perversions of which sadism, necrophilia and coprophilia are among the mildest. Orwell allows that Dali is a brilliant draughtsman – he will not go so far as to call him a painter or an artist – and asserts that there are two approaches to a man like Dali. There are those who, because he is so detestable, will not admit that he has talent and there are those who, because of that same talent, refuse to find any fault with him. One ought, writes Orwell, to be able to hold in one's head simultaneously the two facts: that Dali was both a good draughtsman and a disgusting human being.

Orwell is not, I think, saying that our knowledge of an artist's character should affect our judgment of his works, still less that his work should be suppressed because he is a bad hat. What he is saying is that genius gives no special right and that a sociopath who paints or writes well remains a sociopath.

This is so self-evident that I am surprised that it should ever be called into question. But what if it is not the artist's character that offends, but his opinions? What if he is a bigot or, as has been so often the case, an anti-Semite? Call it the Wagner test. Richard Wagner was a world-class anti-Semite and a loathsome individual to boot, but the reasons that his works have been barred from the opera stages and concert halls of the State of Israel have less to do with what he was and more to do with what he symbolizes. The ban is indefensible. There is no justification for withholding from the Israeli public the music of a composer whose work is part of the standard repertory of Western orchestras. Those who seek to perpetuate this boycott are not indulging in any spirit of self-sacrifice; they would not go to a Wagner opera or concert even if they could. They merely believe that they are taking revenge against a long-dead anti-Semite.

We take other anti-Semitic artists in our stride in cases where – like Wagner, as I understand it – they keep their anti-Semitism out of their work. We take pleasure in a Degas dancer; we read "The Brothers Karamazov" despite the virulently anti-Semitic views of the artists who created them.

More than that: Where the work itself is plainly anti-Semitic, Jews do not object if it has acquired the patina of age. Jews are villains in Chaucer's "Prioress' Tale," Marlowe's "Jew of Malta" and Bach's "St. John Passion," but these works of art are protected by virtue of their classical status. Sometimes we positively revel in anti-Semitic portrayals. How else to explain the popularity in Israel of "The Merchant of Venice"? Even more extraordinarily, Jews not only tolerate the villainous Jewish Fagin of "Oliver Twist," but turn the book into a popular musical and translate it into Hebrew. But what do you say to the following?

> *My house is a decayed house,*
> *And the jew squats on the windowsill, the owner,*
> *Spawned in some estaminet of Antwerp,*
> *Blistered in Brussels, patched and peeled in London.*

You do not have to fully comprehend these lines, taken from "Gerontion," a poem by T.S. Eliot, to sense the contempt that suffuses them. No one who takes even a passing interest in modern literature can ignore Eliot, a central figure of 20th century English poetry. In reading any collection of Eliot's early verse it will not take the casual reader long to find poems hostile to "jews" as he belittlingly described them.

When literary anti- Semitism lost its respectability after the Holocaust, Eliot's only revision to these poems was to give his Jews an upper-case "J." Even though, in a letter to Groucho Marx of all people, he expressed his admiration for the State of Israel, Eliot was unquestionably anti-Semitic. A Jewish literary critic, Anthony Julius, goes further. In "T.S. Eliot, Anti-Semitism, and Literary Form," Julius, who in another life is a leading London lawyer, argues that in these early poems the anti-Semitism was more than incidental: It was integral to the poems. Eliot put anti-Semitism to imaginative use, says Julius, and his poetry is one of anti-Semitism's few literary triumphs.

Some admirers of Eliot will not have it that he was an anti-Semite though the evidence is clear-cut. One should, to paraphrase Orwell, be able to hold in one's head that Eliot was both a great poet and an anti-Semite.

On Dali, Orwell said that his defenders were claiming for him some kind of "benefit of clergy." T.S. Eliot wrote wonderful, cerebral, verse but he was a bigot. We should grant him no benefit of clergy.

8 September, 2006

FRANKLY FRIVOLOUS

O, *My Offence is Rank*

For all but irredeemable nitpickers, the 21st century began when all the numbers changed on our calendars on 1st January 2000. The opposing opinion in this futile debate – one that crops up every century – maintains that a century transition occurs at the start of each '01 year. It has reason on its side but little else.

The reason is that Dionysius Exiguus – the sixth century monk who instituted the now universal system of dating years from the putative date of birth of Jesus of Nazareth – started his count with the year one. Western mathematicians had not yet developed a concept of zero so Dionysius was reduced to starting his count on Jesus' first birthday. But Dionysius got it wrong anyway. Herod the Great in whose lifetime – according to the New Testament – Jesus was born, died in 4 BCE so Jesus must have been at least four years old when Dionysius reckoned he was born. Not that anybody celebrated the millennium in 1996.

I have a minor personal interest in settling this unresolved, indeed irresolvable, question. The exact date of my father's birth is shrouded in mystery. The Julian calendar, which makes Russians celebrate the October Revolution in November, ruled in Berdichev in those days and this already complicates the calculation. Added to that, my grandmother, who I recall as being naturally anarchic, would surely have misinformed the authorities of the date of the birth of her eldest son. Jewish mothers have been protective of their sons in that way since the days of Yocheved the mother of Moses. But, taking all these factors into account, I can still be reasonably certain that Dad was born in 1900. I have no desire to attach to it a significance that it does not merit but having a parent born in the 19th century adds a certain je ne sais quoi to the conversation at a 21st century dinner party.

The big battalions in the form of popular sentiment are overwhelmingly on my side in the century debate. There were no millennium celebrations on 1 January 2001. They all took place in the previous year. Certainly there was no doubt that the 21st century commenced in the year 2000 in the minds of those who indulged in that media-driven compulsion to compile, in milestone years, lists ranking people and achievements in some perceived order of importance.

The end of the century saw a prodigious number of these lists, which come in two principal forms: the pontifical and the popular. A pontifical list is purportedly authoritative. Orthodox, conventional, it is prepared by committees of *bien pensants*. A popular list is based on polls of readers or worse, of Internet surfers. The results of these polls produce aberrations that beggar the imagination, not only because popular taste is so often at odds with that of the mandarins but because special interest groups canvass for the most bizarre of candidates and voters indulge in ballot box stuffing to a degree that would bring a blush to the cheeks of a Likud vote contractor.

Compare, for example, the pontifical and the popular lists of the 100 best novels in English of the 20th century. The Modern Library, which is responsible for the two lists, bravely juxtaposes them on its web site. The "Board's List" is headed by "Ulysses" and "The Great Gatsby." You can cavil at this pontifical list (Henry James first appears at number 26, way below the politically correct choices of Ralph Ellison and Richard Wright. Joseph Conrad is first seen at 67 with "Heart of Darkness") but it is broadly predictable. The "Reader's List" well illustrates the pitfalls of inviting public participation. Delightfully erratic, it has four novels by Ayn Rand and three by L. Ron Hubbard in its first ten. Both these writers have a considerable following among the mentally unhinged.

Ayn Rand, (born Alicia Rosenbaum) is the icon of the libertarian right. L. Ron Hubbard, having concluded that writing science fiction was insufficiently rewarding, invented a new religion, Scientology, which has been raking in the shekels from the gullible ever since. You will also be intrigued to learn that the 100 Best Novels include seven by Charles de Lint (no, neither have I) whose family must have had a busy time during the run-up to the poll.

The screwballs had even more fun with *Time's* "Person of the Century." The magazine's own selection was Albert Einstein, followed by Franklin D. Roosevelt and Mahatma Gandhi. No surprises there. But Time could never have foreseen the results of its invitation to the Internet public to express its considered opinion on this weighty historical question. Those well-meaning souls – perhaps you were among them – who ran an energetic campaign in support of Yitzhak Rabin (Person of the Century? Come on, get serious!), were rewarded for their zeal. They almost got what they wished for. Thanks to their sterling efforts, Rabin was elected runner-up Person of the Century. And there he is – wedged for eternity between the winner Elvis Presley and third place Adolf Hitler. I rest my case, Your Lordship.

Perhaps, to make their list less bland, the voters in the BBC's list of "Great Britons" should have taken advice on multiple voting from the Knesset. The list has some gems but is not nearly as chaotic as one might have hoped to see from a genuinely popular list. True, the relatively obscure Victorian engineer Isambard Kingdom Brunel was ranked second – thanks to the efforts of the students of London's Brunel University. True also that Brunel was followed at number three by Princess Diana. But a list that includes in its top ten Churchill, Darwin, Shakespeare, Newton, Nelson and Cromwell hardly meets the heterodox expectations we have of a popular list. Where was Screaming Lord Sutch? Did nobody vote for Sir Oswald Mosley?

But the list that, for me, took the biscuit was a list that had the temerity to call itself "Songs of the Century." It was prepared by the Recording Industry Association of America and the National Endowment for the Arts – you can't get more pontifical than that, can you? For aficionados of the popular song, the list is an outrage. Irving Berlin's cloying, but commercially successful "White Christmas" apart, you will look in vain in the top 50 for songs by the true masters of 20th century popular music – Gershwin, Kern, Berlin, Rodgers, Cole Porter. Instead, as decreed *ex cathedra* by the august bodies that organized the 365-long list, the sixth greatest song of the 20th century was "Boogie Woogie Bugle Boy" credited superfluously to the Andrews Sisters. As if any but that toothy trio could have perpetrated it. And the infamy continues: number eight is, wait for it, "Take Me Out to the Ball Game".

It may be that I am giving to a subject that is essentially frivolous an importance that it does not deserve but it seems to me that throwing these rankings open to the opinion of a wide public is wholly salutary. Nothing can bring out the total banality of the ranking enterprise than to reduce it to absurdity. I am not advocating relativism. By any civilized standard, Mozart is superior to Salieri, and Tolstoy to John Grisham. Nor do I deny the cultural or educational value of a closed, unranked list of masterpieces like the Great Books programme, which is taught in American universities so as to bring literature to a generation that no longer reads.

What I find offensive is the effort to measure the unmeasurable, that trivializes what is too important to be trivialized. In what sense is Roosevelt superior to Gandhi? Do we need to decide whether Shakespeare should be ranked above Goethe, or van Gogh allotted more points than Raphael? By all means let us have an inventory of great books or paintings. But don't seed them like tennis players.

It is by no means self-evident why we are so fascinated with this urge to place people or their achievements in order of importance. We can accuse a recidivist ranker like *Time* of cynically exploiting its public in order to increase its sales, but I believe that the obsession to rank is deep-rooted within us. Whatever its ancestry, what has made the ranking phenomenon ubiquitous in recent years is professional sport. Money is an incontrovertible yardstick. If Tiger Woods and Serena Williams earn the most, they are the best. It is when we transfer our passion for winners and losers to areas that are not so easily quantifiable that we come unstuck. Had "Songs of the Century" openly advertised itself as an index of commercial success, one could have thought it vulgar but there would be no true cause for complaint. But the list purported to make qualitative judgments and that is unforgivable.

I close with a heresy. It is my firm conviction that anyone who heads his list of best films with "Citizen Kane" or "Battleship Potemkin," has never seen the Marx Brothers in "Duck Soup".

27 June, 2003

****Profanity

It's good to see that Lars Porsena is back with us; a recent issue of the *Economist* reported a renewed search for his tomb. As anyone with a doctorate in ancient history knows, Lars Porsena was an Etruscan king who ruled in central Italy around 500 BCE. Those old enough to remember a time before learning poetry by heart went the way of carbon paper, the slide rule and the sabre-toothed tiger, will recall Macaulay's once-famous poem "Horatius," which features Lars Porsena as one of the guys in black hats. The poem describes the heroism of the Roman Horatius who, with two comrades, stood guard on a bridge over the Tiber to hold off Lars Porsena's Etruscans. The poem opens:

> *Lars Porsena of Clusium*
> *By the Nine Gods he swore*
> *That the great house of Tarquin*
> *Should suffer wrong no more.*
> *By the Nine Gods he swore it ...*

These lines were sufficiently familiar to the reading public in 1927 for the poet, novelist and scholar, Robert Graves, to give the title "Lars Porsena" to his book-length essay on "The Future of Swearing and Improper Language." In 1974, the by then elderly poet wrote a new introduction to the book, asserting that swearing had virtually ended in Britain because the age of sexual permissiveness initiated by the pill had rendered pornography no longer shocking. He didn't get it quite right because swearing is more prevalent today than it ever was, but it is true that bad language has lost its sting. We have become so hardened to reading and hearing four-letter expletives that the coinage of profanity has become irreparably debased.

Even with my sheltered upbringing, I cannot recall a time that I did not know the bad words; children acquire them by osmosis. There was one word that filled us with awe and whose utterance unfailingly reduced us to fits of guilty giggles. The word was "britches" and, for the life of me, I cannot understand today how it achieved its totemic power. For my part, bad language has never lost its facility to shock. I accept it in literature – sometimes it is necessary – and I admit that Tony Soprano would lose his credibility if he substituted "My goodness" for his favourite word, but, like many of my vintage, I feel uncomfortable uttering an obscenity, let alone committing one to paper.

It is a commonplace that when Hebrew speakers feel the need to swear they must resort to Yiddish or Arabic. Yet, as the "Song of Songs" and the sonnets of Immanuel of Rome can testify, a paucity of dirty words has not prevented Hebrew from producing erotic poetry of passionate intensity. For that matter, when, 2,000 years ago, Hebrew was last a spoken language, there were words that were unacceptable in polite company. The Bible itself contains words that, according to the Masoretic tradition, may be written but not uttered. In reading aloud the "cursing" sections of Deuteronomy, euphemistic expressions must be substituted for words in the text – for the sexual act and for an embarrassing medical condition – that are deemed improper.

Over the centuries bad language has had its ups and downs. Chaucer uses four-letter words liberally. Shakespeare is only a trifle more circumspect. London's latest Hamlet, the 23-year old Ben Whishaw, who plays the Prince as a snivelling adolescent, turns a notorious double entendre in the play-within-a-play into a single entendre (and, incidentally, loses the point of a not-very-good joke) by openly pronouncing a notorious four-letter word at which the text only hints.

But *autre temps, autre moeurs*. The Victorians raised the bar again. The word "leg" could not be uttered in polite society. For saying "'Damn me," the Captain of Gilbert and Sullivan's "HMS Pinafore" is demoted to the rank of able seaman. And quite right too, thought Lewis Carroll, who castigated Gilbert for permitting those dread words to be repeated by "a bevy of sweet, innocent-looking girls ... I cannot find the words to convey to the reader the pain I felt in seeing these dear children." Sweet innocent girls and dear children were something of a Carroll speciality – "taught to utter such words to amused ears grown callous to their ghastly meaning." And you think I'm a prude!

In the 20th century things went downhill fast. A revealing case history is that of George Bernard Shaw's "Pygmalion." The phonetics professor Henry Higgins has wagered that he can pass off the Cockney flower girl Eliza Doolittle as a duchess by teaching her to speak properly. But though he can teach her correct pronunciation, he can hardly wean her off bad language because he himself uses it abundantly. When the play was first staged in 1914, the audience was shocked into laughter that lasted a full 75 seconds as Eliza (played by Shaw's friend Mrs. Patrick Campbell who, at the age of 49, was surely an excessively mature Eliza,) exclaimed "Not bloody likely" in her newly-acquired cut-glass accent. When the play was turned into the Broadway musical "My Fair Lady" some 40 years later, the word "bloody" had become hopelessly devalued. In the Ascot scene, Julie Andrews' Eliza was compelled to urge her horse Dover to "Move yer bloomin' arse!" Today, that expression has in turn lost its bite and in recent productions of the musical it scarcely raises a titter.

Once you get to the modern age, obscene language almost becomes the norm, though not without a struggle from the Mrs. Grundys. "Lady Chatterley's Lover," which deploys all the four-letter words, is not my favourite D. H. Lawrence novel, but James Joyce's "Ulysses," which is likewise replete with obscenities, is arguably the greatest novel of the 20th century. Both these books were originally banned and as late as 1948, the London Sunday Times urged the banning of Norman Mailer's "The Naked and the Dead" for using "incredibly foul and beastly language," which turned out to be a word that Mailer had himself bowdlerized to "fug." By 1971, when a poem by Philip Larkin opened "They f*** you up / Your mum and dad ...," the morality police did not even put up a fight.

The "f" word is both potent and protean. In a vivid demonstration of the parts of speech of an English sentence, one of my teachers gave us a complete sentence that he claimed he had heard used by a mechanic in the army: "F***! The f***ing f***er's f***ing well f***ed." Used both as an expletive and in its dictionary sense of the sexual act, the word is one of the most ubiquitous in the English language. Dorothy Parker employed both senses memorably when asked by a friend why he had not seen her for some time: "I've been too f***ing busy; and vice versa," she replied.

Inhibited though I am, I implore my fellow prigs to be tolerant when they hear bad language. For one thing, the speaker might be suffering from "Tourette's Syndrome" – a neurological disorder characterized by tics and spasms but also, in some cases, by the sufferer's uncontrollable use of obscene and scatological language. The condition was thought to be a rare one, but as Oliver Sacks – who gives an interesting and sympathetic case history of a Tourette's sufferer in his best-selling "The Man Who Mistook His Wife for a Hat" – discovered, it is quite common.

Tourette's is said to be particularly widespread among Ashkenazi Jews. Certainly a shared trait of both Jews and Touretters is an eagerness to embrace famous people as their own. Dr. Johnson's habit of touching every post as he walked along Fleet Street has usually been attributed to superstition but, coupled with his constant tics and other compulsive rituals, he has reasonably been claimed to have had Tourette's. To my regret, Dr. Johnson was not an Ashkenazi Jew (nor any other kind, for that matter), and neither was Wolfgang Amadeus Mozart who, according to a theory popularized by a documentary on BBC's Channel 4, suffered from Tourette's. In his brief life, Mozart composed the most beautiful music ever written, but he also had a notoriously foul mouth. We are used to discovering that the artists we admire do not necessarily live admirable lives, but it is nevertheless hard to reconcile the exquisite sounds Mozart produced with his reported profanity.

Did Mozart have Tourette's? Was Napoleon a manic-depressive? Did Rembrandt suffer from rosacea? Was El Greco astigmatic? Speculating on the diseases suffered by historical personalities in the light of later medical knowledge has become a popular sport of science writers in recent years. Freed from the fear of malpractice suits – Moses, though retroactively diagnosed with temporal lobe epilepsy by one bold medical Monday morning quarterback, will not be suing anyone – these posthumous diagnosticians can safely ascribe a venereal disease to the chastest of saints.

Personally, I don't give a f*** if Mozart used every obscene word in the dictionary and then added a few more for good measure. He also wrote "Don Giovanni".

26 November, 2004

Save the Medusa

C.P. Snow was both a novelist and a physicist. Although he did not, perhaps, reach the peak of either profession, he had earned the right to declare – in his celebrated 1959 lecture, "The Two Cultures" – that Western intellectuals were "split into two polar groups," the literary and the scientific. There were scientists, he maintained, who had never heard of Charles Dickens and writers who could not describe the Second Law of Thermodynamics.

While his reproach directed against the literary establishment was undoubtedly well founded, I think he was being unfair to the scientists. For some years I have been a devotee of essays written by eminent scientists, a form of literature that, to my mind, has never been given its due. Some of the finest minds in science have put their hands to writing prose of enduring quality.

In no area of science has literature been so well served as in natural history and none wrote better than the late Stephen Jay Gould. From 1974 to 2001, Gould wrote a monthly essay for *Natural History Magazine* and never failed to entertain with his blend of wit, culture and elegant prose. Whether he was writing on Bach, Byron or baseball, or supplying significant trivia such as that Abraham Lincoln and Charles Darwin were born on the same day, he always had something of interest to say and always said it well.

Above all, he communicated to his readers the inexhaustible wonders of nature. In one essay in which, in his delightfully discursive way, he discussed the Sleeping Beauty legend, Bruno Bettelheim and Adam Smith, he pondered the extraordinary cases in nature where organisms of a presumed lower order adhere to the most sophisticated of biological clocks. Gould instanced a species of bamboo that flowered in China in the year 999 and since then has, without fail, flowered every 120 years.

And then there is the periodical cicada, a kind of locust, which does something quite as spectacular. Every 17 years, in the eastern states of the United States (13 years for a variant species in the southern states), this cicada, which has been whiling its time away underground during the intervening period doing whatever it is that periodical cicadas do in their leisure hours, suddenly emerges into the light of day, like the prisoners in "Fidelio," to feed, reproduce and die. Their appearance is totally predictable and naturalists are on location waiting for a sight of the periodical cicada as eagerly and surely as astronomers wait for an eclipse.

Mathematicians love prime numbers and some evolutionary theorists, including Gould, believe that it is significant that 13 and 17, the intervals for the emergence of the two species of periodical cicadas, are prime numbers. It is possible, they argue, that these species obtain an evolutionary advantage against predators by emerging in prime number cycles. Personally I find it odd. Call me a speciesist but to me it seems improbable that even the most pointy-headed cicada is going to be able to work out that it has to stay in the muck for a number of years that is a positive integer not divisible without a remainder by any positive integer other than itself and one.

The cicada has, by the way, an extensive fan club manifested by a proliferation of web sites with names such as "Cicada Watch" and "Cicada Mania." This last site provides answers to "Frequently Asked Questions" like "Is there such a thing as an albino cicada?" a Question as Frequently Asked, I imagine, as "Do oysters lay tefillin?"

All this is by way of introduction to what I believe to be a novel observation made by two amateur naturalists, a married couple without scientific credentials, whom modesty inhibits me from naming. The biological calendar to which the bamboo and the cicada adhere is based on the solar year but we have come across a creature that, surely uniquely, relies for its synchronicity on the Jewish religious calendar. To distil a fairly complex subject into a few words, the Jewish calendar – which regulates the days on which religious holidays fall – is what is technically known as a luni-solar one. The basic unit of the Jewish calendar is the lunar month, but a periodical adjustment is made so as to keep the Jewish year broadly in harmony with the seasons. Thus, Yom Kippur will not fall each year on any given date of the Gregorian calendar but will always be in the early autumn.

For upwards of 30 years my wife and I have lived in Herzliya (this is how I spell it though there are as many ways to spell the name of my town as there are reputed to be of spelling the name of Shakespeare), a coastal town north of Tel Aviv. Almost every morning we take a walk along what little beach the developers of an environmental disaster known as the Herzliya Marina have left its unfortunate inhabitants. For a brief period each summer, our walk is impeded by the corpses of hundreds of jellyfish.

Rhopilema nomadica, to give the Herzlian jellyfish its correct scientific moniker, is known in Hebrew as a "medusa," which is its generic scientific name. For a brief period each summer, the jellyfish arrive in swarms and land inert on our beaches, in pulsating quivering blobs, resembling most the unappealing dessert that has given it its name. The infestation lasts for nine days. On the tenth day, their corpses having been bagged by workers from the municipality, the jellyfish disappear and, like some insubstantial pageant faded, leave not a rack behind.

Now here's the interesting bit. The nine days during which the jellyfish engage in their orgy of self-destruction do not coincide with any particular period of the Gregorian calendar. In this the jellyfish differs from the cicada. But those days do coincide remarkably with a particular period of the Jewish calendar. The corpses first appear with the new moon for the Jewish month of Av and they disappear after the Fast of the Ninth of Av, the anniversary of the destruction of both the first and second temples. The Jews call these very days that precede the Fast the Nine Days and they have a special religious significance. They are days marked for mourning and are believed to be days of ill omen.

Of course, there is a rational explanation for this ostensibly astonishing synchronicity. The tides that bring in the hapless jellyfish are influenced by the moon. That the jellyfish indulge in their spectacular self-immolation during a particular phase of the moon is thus less surprising than might first appear. Still, they have not chosen any nine days; they have chosen the Nine Days, days on which it is forbidden, under Jewish law, to bathe in the sea.

Rabbis who, often on thinner evidence, ascribe supernatural causes to events that are rationally explicable, should surely be enthusiastic in finding in nature such a striking vindication for one of their prohibitions. For who, however willing to flout the laws of the rabbis, would want to defy the authority of their marine acolytes in the form of shoals of suicidal but still toxic jellyfish? If I were in the preaching business I would compare those jellyfish to the heroes of Masada; they sacrifice themselves for a cause.

Yet I would not expect our religious authorities to take the jellyfish to their bosoms, even figuratively. You might be prepared to sit in the cabinet with a jellyfish but you certainly would not want your daughter to marry one. Nor would you want to eat one even though certain types of jellyfish are a delicacy in Japan. In the words of Leviticus, jellyfish are an abomination. Although the official stance is that there are no gradations under the dietary laws and that food is either kosher or non-kosher, it seems to me that jellyfish in aspic might be regarded as different in kind from inadequately washed lettuce.

And now back to literature for a moment. The jellyfish has made its modest contribution to English literature. Were it not for the humble jellyfish we would not have the novels of one of the finest English writers of the 20th century. In Evelyn Waugh's autobiography "A Little Learning" he describes how, at a desperately low time of his life, he decided to put an end to it all by drowning himself in the sea. He swam far out but, on being attacked by a school of jellyfish, he returned to shore.

Like the equally unloved cockroach and mosquito, the jellyfish appears on no known list of protected species. But while Greenpeace and the Sierra Club campaign for the horseshoe bat, the dormouse and the natterjack toad in the name of biodiversity, let's have one small cheer for that venomous but vital contributor to "Brideshead Revisited." My friends, join me in sporting a button to protect that unsung invertebrate ally of the religiously correct.

Save the Medusa!

27 August, 2004

Codeswallop

"Arrogant fools, have you not noticed that I have been listening tonight as you discussed these poems?" The Goon Show's Bluebottle? Wrong. The author of this deathless piece of dialogue is Dan Brown, whose cloth ear for the rhythms of human speech has done little to hamper the success of his novel "The Da Vinci Code," a book that has broken every conceivable publishing record. This – to put it charitably – undistinguished novel, about a conspiracy to suppress the record of a marriage between Jesus and Mary Magdalene, has created an unprecedented buzz. Celebrated in spin-off books and a host of websites, the book has set off a feeding frenzy of Bible scholars and art historians. A film is being made of it, of course. With its revelations of Jesus' sexuality, the movie will truly have the right to call itself the Passion of the Christ. According to *Time* magazine the Code has spawned an industry that includes Code-themed dinners, Da Vinci Code tours of the Louvre, academic analyses, seminars and scholarly Catholic books refuting the Code. Perhaps Colin Dexter could resurrect his famous inspector with "The Morse Code".

When it comes to escapist literature I claim some modest expertise. In a long and largely misspent life (what corporate lawyer can claim otherwise?), I can assert that I have devoured more than my share of mysteries, spy novels and thrillers. But I prefer my junk to be literate junk – what George Orwell called good bad books.

No one could claim literacy for Dan Brown. He seems to have a thesaurus but no dictionary. The blurb tells us that he has taught English and creative writing at Amherst College and Phillips Exeter Academy. Let us hope that he does not include his own books in the curriculum. He confuses "simple" with "simplistic" and "disinterested" with "uninterested," he misuses the term "laissez faire;" he goes wrong on the words "literally," "chastising," "travesty" and "leery." If, like me, you can happily read a book without once encountering the word "plethora," you will be sorry to hear that he first discovers the word on page 174; for the remainder of this long book we are treated to a plethora of plethoras.

For the benefit of that section of the public that (a) reads this column, (b) has not read the book and (c) chooses to ignore my advice to give the book a miss, I shall give only an outline of the plot. Jacques Saunière, the director of the Louvre Museum, is shot by Silas, a giant self-flagellating albino monk. (Why always albinos? Can't thriller writers pick on midgets or hermaphrodites for a change?) When not occupied in thrashing himself or thinking holy thoughts, Silas moonlights as a hit man for the sinister right-wing Catholic brotherhood, Opus Dei. He shoots Saunière so as to cause him maximum pain ("pain is good, monsieur") but also – more importantly for the story – to give him 15 minutes to drag his bleeding body round the Louvre leaving for the hero and heroine fiendishly difficult clues in the form of anagrams and mathematical riddles. Taking as long to die as Hamlet, Saunière contrives to contort his dying body into the unnatural shape of Leonardo's Vitruvian Man – another clue. If you think this is macabre, Brown's previous novel "Angels and Demons," which also features villainous Catholics, has the assassin remove the eye of his victim so as to operate a retina-activated door to a secret laboratory.

Our hero is Robert Langdon, met already in "Angels and Demons," a Harvard professor of "religious symbology" who has been listed by Boston Magazine "as one of that city's top ten most intriguing people." Either "top" or "most" is superflous but I suspect that, at Amherst College, Dan Brown teaches symbolic tautology.

The female protagonist is Sophie Neveu, a police cryptographer who is the granddaughter of the murdered man and also – sorry, this sounds like that old Danny Kaye routine – a Merovingian princess, but we don't find this out until much later. Her grandfather brought her up but Sophie has refused to have anything to do with him for ten years because she arrived home unexpectedly one day and saw him playing the central role in an orgy. Let's face it; you would also have been upset had you caught your zeide *in flagrante delicto*. Not having taken a course in religious symbology while majoring in cryptology, Sophie was not to know that grandpère was not a dirty old man at all but, as the Grandmaster of the Priory of Sion (one of those secret societies that have helped Brown pay off his mortgage with spare change for an executive jet) was officiating in an ancient fertility rite known as *hieros gamos*. How wrong could she be! She thought he was having fun.

Saunière is the last custodian of the Holy Grail and it is to the location of the Holy Grail that he has left the clues for Robert and Sophie. The other three custodians, all providentially living in Paris, were bumped off by Silas on that same busy evening that Silas caused grandpa to make his terminal tour of the Louvre. Considering that Silas administers to himself a good penitential flogging after each murder, it was a hard day's night – even for an albino monk. The Holy Grail is not, as you believed, a goblet but a secret – guarded for centuries by the Priory – revealing Jesus' union with Mary Magdalene, which marriage produced a child.

The action moves from one location to another while Langdon and Sophie evade Silas and some Clouseau-ish French policemen who are also after them. They are aided by Sir Leigh Teabing who was knighted by the Queen for his "extensive history of the House of York" and who, being a knight and thus a true English aristocrat like Sir Elton John, says things like "I see you travel with a maiden" and "the new medication gives me the tinkles." You may well ask why this knight is different from all other knights.

Some critics, who should know better, have praised Brown for his erudition. I find this astonishing. As scholars have not failed to point out, the book is studded with howlers. He helps himself liberally from one loony cult book after another. You never get the impression that he has done any kind of serious research; often it is apparent that he has little knowledge of his subject matter. Much seems to have been taken from a far more scholarly thriller, Umberto Eco's "Foucault's Pendulum" which also features the Freemasons, the Templars, the Rosicrucians, the Illuminati and speculates upon a union between Jesus and Mary Magdalene.

While we are at it, I can think of at least two other thrillers in the same genre that are worth ten "Da Vinci Codes." One is Lionel Davidson's brilliant "A Long Way to Shiloh" (published in the USA by Harper and Row as "The Menorah Men,") a fictional search for the seven-branched candelabrum from the Temple. The second is a 1962 novel by James Hall Roberts called "The Q Document" about the search for the vanished Aramaic source document of the synoptic Gospels of Mark, Luke and Matthew. I recommend some enterprising publisher to reissue these novels so that the public can learn the nature of a quality thriller.

So how are we to account for the runaway success of this pretentious piece of airport trash – apart from its justifying H. L. Mencken's adage that no one ever went broke underestimating the taste of the American public?

First, I have to acknowledge that the book has a certain vitality. Despite Brown's relentless urge to press information on us, the action unquestionably moves. If one suspends one's disbelief, the book has a kind of breathless attraction that is hard to resist. Furthermore, Brown has succeeded in striking two contemporary cultural mother lodes: conspiracies and the life of Jesus.

Brown has successfully surfed the conspiracy wave. What distinguishes Brown from Umberto Eco and other writers of esoteric thrillers is that Brown seems to believe the nonsense he purveys. He opens each novel with a solemn announcement headed: "FACT" and then goes on to assure us that the cults of which he writes exist. His earlier book, "Angels and Demons" dealt with the Illuminati, a staple of the conspiracy industry. In this book we are given for good measure at least three conspiratorial cults – the Priory of Sion, Opus Dei and the Templars. We are promised that the next Brown novel will deal with the Freemasons. We shall, no doubt, be told that those amiable buffers, who cavort around in funny aprons so as to have an evening away from their wives, are plotting to take over the world.

As for me, I take a serious view of conspiracy theorists. I belong to a people that has too often been their victim. I am not being totally facetious when I say that I expect a future Dan Brown novel to open:

"FACT. The Elders of Zion exist".

25 June, 2004

Weddings, Israeli Style

The Book of Ecclesiastes (*Kohelet*) reveals such a depressing view of the human condition that it is hard to understand how it found a place in the Bible. Indeed, the book's almost total lack of conventional religious sentiment made its admission into the biblical canon a matter of hot dispute among the rabbis. A verse that illustrates the book's profound pessimism and reflects a worldview that is more Calvinist – if you will forgive the anachronism – than Jewish, is Ecclesiastes 7:1: "It is better to go to a house of mourning than to go to the house of feasting." I am light-years from being an authority on wisdom literature, but I will venture an interpretation of the verse. It is my view that King Solomon, the reputed author of Ecclesiastes, had just returned from a Jerusalem wedding.

It is hard to challenge Solomon's status as an authority on weddings. He had had 700 weddings of his own and with 700 sets of in-laws, must have been obliged to go to thousands more. So why did the wisest of all men hate the weddings of the Land of Israel? Let us examine the evidence.

Many of the films I have seen recently featured weddings. There have been monsoon weddings, Georgian late weddings and big fat Greek ones; but no movie could prepare the uninitiated for an Israeli wedding. You, who sympathize with the plight of the average Israeli – subjected, as he is, to bombings, reserve duty, heavy taxes and road rage – do not know the half of it. Israelis also have to endure Israeli weddings.

Secular or religious, in Savyon or in Dimona, the ubiquitous feature of an Israeli wedding is the noise. It is not just that you cannot hear what your neighbour at the table is saying – that could be the only good thing that happens to you all evening – but the din is so painful that if a political prisoner were subjected to it, he would make an emergency call to Amnesty International.

My wife and I have a standard wedding kit consisting of two sets of earplugs and a corkscrew. No explanation is needed for the earplugs but without the latter, you can suffer the fate of Tantalus. There will be a bottle of wine on your table, but you will lack the means to open it. The waiter you ask to open the bottle will go off, purportedly to fetch a corkscrew, and, like Captain Oates, never be seen again.

The earplugs will remain handy during the blessed but sadly brief period that the music is switched off. Remember that the greatest bore in literature, Coleridge's Ancient Mariner, was also a wedding guest. Your neighbour at table will tell you, not of an albatross (which reminds me of my trip to the Galapagos Islands – I can show you the photos when we next meet at a wedding), but of his prostate. The return of the band will not silence him and courtesy will require you to try to follow him by lip-reading.

And be careful if you bring a gift. According to a television programme I saw recently, it is a solecism of the worst order to give the couple any gift other than money. I was amazed to learn that, among young Israelis, the parents do not pay for the wedding. The couple pays on the proven assumption that they will clear a substantial profit on the evening.

A minor compensation is that speeches are rare at Israeli weddings. It has been tried, but Israeli guests will not listen to speeches – even from their host. If you are really unlucky, you might, in place of a speech, get entertainment from the family. This generally takes the form of a song with verses that neither rhyme nor scan, providentially inaudible but inordinately long, sung by children who should be in bed and egged on by parents who should know better.

I have left the ceremony for last. Never be afraid of being late for the ceremony. However late you contrive to be, the ceremony will be later. But eventually, the ceremony will take place. Expect anything! Israeli ceremonies come in all shapes and sizes, but are always unpredictable. I was at one wedding where the officiating rabbi had liberally helped himself to the sacramental wine before the ceremony. He stood more or less upright while the bride, a skimpy bridal dress just covering her nakedness, tripped down the aisle to the deafening sound of the music from "Star Wars." When she arrived under the canopy, the rabbi somehow got through the Hebrew blessings, but was defeated by the tongue-twisting Aramaic of the marriage contract. He should have taken lessons from Mel Gibson.

To be fair – something I find it hard to be when it comes to weddings – the shameless mockery of the marriage service that is so common in this country is not generally found where the participants are from traditional backgrounds. Where the couple is religious, you would not see (as I have seen) the bride accompanied to the canopy by a samba band led by a shapely young woman clad in a bikini, playing the maracas.

You might well ask why, if people have such contempt for custom, they go through the travesty of what is, after all, a religious ritual. To understand why they do, you will need a little background.

In Israel there are two truths that we hold to be self- evident. The first is that Jerusalem is the eternal, indivisible capital of the Jewish people and if I forget that, may my two typing fingers lose their cunning. The second is that Israel is the only democracy in the Middle East.

I have been pondering this last axiom while reading of the issue that has lately dominated public discourse in the United States: gay marriage. It is not a question frequently debated here. Israel is not about to legalize same-sex marriage for the simple reason that it even raises obstacles to opposite-sex marriage. Democratic Israel – light unto the Gentiles, beacon of enlightenment amid a fog of bigotry, island of freedom in a sea of oppression – has laws of personal status that would seem harsh to an ayatollah. I do not discuss here the archaic Jewish laws of divorce or the pitiful situation of the *aguna*, the wife who cannot trace her husband and is therefore unable to remarry. My subject is marriage.

If one of the pair is not recognized as Jewish by Jewish law, as is the case with some half a million of Israel's new citizens from the former Soviet Union, they may not marry under Jewish law. If you are a Cohen – born into the priestly caste – you may not marry a woman who has been divorced. If you are the product of such a union, or if you are the child of an adulterous union, you may not marry at all unless you are lucky enough to find an unfortunate in the same position.

Fair enough, you might say. If you choose to marry according to religious law, you must abide by the rules, the rules in this case being those laid down over the centuries by *halacha*, the time-hallowed corpus of Jewish law. If you cannot have an Orthodox wedding, you can marry according to Conservative or Reform rites; or if you are not religiously inclined, you can always exercise the rights of the citizen of any Western democracy and marry under its civil laws. Well, no; actually, you can't. The only democracy in the Middle East does not permit civil marriage and insists that marriages can only be conducted by an Orthodox rabbi.

When a bill for the legalization of civil marriage was recently introduced in the Knesset, it was roundly defeated. It found little support even among the supposed standard-bearers of civil rights. Government ministers from the Shinui party, elected on an anti-clericalist platform in the last general elections, betrayed their voters by abstaining. Perhaps even worse, most Knesset members from the once-great Labour Party failed to support it.

It remains a matter of astonishment to objective observers that a nation, outwardly Western, with democratic institutions, still compels those of its citizens who wish to marry to do so according to the rites of a religion in which they may not believe. The alternatives are unappealing. One is non-marriage. Couples live monogamously together in stable relationships and produce children without troubling to go through a ceremony they regard as meaningless. Others will leave the country in order to go through a civil marriage, which – strangely – is then recognized by Israeli law. The tourism industry of Cyprus has Israel's marriage laws to thank for much of its income.

But those who wish to regularize their union in Israel in the only way legally possible must go through an Orthodox ceremony. If they treat it with disrespect, can they be blamed?

30 April, 2004

*T*he Games People Play

"**D**id you know you have something in common with Mel Gibson, Sting, Keanu Reeves, Joan Collins and Queen Elizabeth II?" You might think this to be a leading question of the order of, "When did you stop beating your wife?" Certainly, you would never guess the answer. It turns out that we and they all play Scrabble – or so maintains the official Scrabble web site.

I don't know about you, but I have not held a Scrabble tile for a decade, and the thought of joining this ill-assorted quintet is unlikely to tempt me back. Celebrities they undoubtedly are, but like W.S. Gilbert's House of Lords, they make "no pretence to intellectual eminence or scholarship sublime".

For a board game that demands a modicum of literacy, you would surely be more impressed if told that Einstein, Bertrand Russell and Saul Bellow had shared your passion for the game. Anyhow, Mel Gibson probably plays the Aramaic version and if you played the Queen, would you dare challenge her if she misspelled "corgi?"

Why I went off Scrabble was that it turned scientific. When it achieved its original popularity around 1954, it was a pleasing and mildly challenging word game. But then the nerds moved in. Scrabble congresses sprang up all over the place. The game began to acquire a distinct odour of midnight oil. Earnest competitors committed to memory words that could be used in tight corners. The *reductio ad absurdum* was when a 15-year-old boy won the Scrabble championship of Britain using, in succession: reasted, xi, janes, tak, mino, rah, uvea and harn. You need short words for the end game? Despite the protests of my spellchecker, never challenge gi, ch, ea, zea, ae, ne, ee, mo, ny, da, ai, jo, si, ar, ex, st or oe: All of them are legal. Well, I ask you! Is that a game or a university entrance exam?

Chess had gone the same way earlier. To play chess today you have to digest books of openings. It has become a game for obsessive psychopaths.

There are now several Scrabble dictionaries providing definitive answers to challenges. When I played Scrabble with two friends in the 1950s, what I needed was an aischrolatreian dictionary. You knew it already but, just in case you forgot, "aischrolatreia" is the worship of filth, dirt and smut. Our game had one rule; you could not be challenged for erroneous spelling, but the word you chose had to be plausibly obscene. You would be amazed at the latitude that this gave to our fertile undergraduate minds.

If your regular opponent keeps beating you, there are other ways of varying games so as to stave off the monotony. Try, for instance, the enjoyably alcoholic mode of handicapping employed in Graham Greene's "Our Man in Havana." In place of the conventional pieces in a game of draughts (checkers for the Yanks), the novel's characters play with whisky miniatures. Each time a player removed his opponent's piece, he had to drink it. As intoxication overcame the better player, he started making mistakes. Inebriation is a great equalizer.

My own favourite board game is Monopoly. Unlike Scrabble and chess, the game is still relatively untainted by professionalism. There are, of course, Monopoly championships – I expect there are also Ludo trophies, and what could be more natural than a ladder in a Snakes and Ladders league? – but the hard men seem to have left Monopoly to the millions who play it for fun.

Five-hundred million people have played Monopoly in 26 languages. America, where Monopoly originated, situates its game in Atlantic City, though few Americans have been there. The obvious choice was surely New York City; it is probably the dreary nomenclature of its thoroughfares that disqualified Manhattan. Throwing a dice to move your thimble from 7th Avenue to 54th Street has about the same sex appeal as painting the Mona Lisa by numbers.

No wonder the British game is more popular. Who does not know Fleet Street, Oxford Street and Piccadilly? An Australian friend tells me that all the countries of the former Commonwealth – the cricket-playing countries, if you like – have the British game. My friend denies that his Australian version sends you for transportation instead of jail.

Although I have lived most of my life in Israel, my pronounced English cultural chauvinism has prevented me from taking up Hebrew Monopoly. Aside from the gimcrack appearance of the Israeli set, the glamour is missing. Dizengoff Street is surely a poor substitute for Mayfair or the Rue de la Paix.

Monopoly aficionados can point to dozens of versions that the game has generated over the years. There is Disney Monopoly, Lord of the Rings Monopoly, Arsenal Monopoly and many more. Surely the strangest, and certainly the most moving, is the Monopoly now on display in Yad Vashem. It was produced on a printing press in the Theresienstadt ghetto and played there. The streets are actual sites in the ghetto.

The latest edition of Monopoly has created something of a stir in London. Spurred by the ravages of inflation and the changes wrought by gentrification, the manufacturers have created "Monopoly Here and Now." You now collect two million pounds for passing "Go" but, on the other hand, have to pay four million for the equivalent of Mayfair. I learned to play Monopoly long before I had a glimmer of what a mortgage was. I could not pronounce "matures," but if I landed on something called an "annuity" I knew I would collect 100 pounds.

I rarely play Monopoly these days, partly because the modern sets are so tawdry. Although I first played during the 1940s, our set must have been from before the war. The tokens were beautifully crafted pieces, made of nickel; the houses and hotels were of wood, so different from today's shoddy plastic simulacra. If my wife is already worrying about my next birthday present, F.A.O. Schwarz has the perfect solution for her. For the man who has everything they are selling, at the knockdown price of $100,000, the "One-of-a-kind Monopoly." This special edition comes in a locking attaché case made with Napolino leather and lined in suede, and contains: 18-carat-gold tokens, houses and hotels; a rosewood board; street names written in gold leaf; emeralds (what else?) around the Chance icon; sapphires around the Community Chest; and – you are going to like this – rubies in the brake lights of the car on the Free Parking space. There is only one vulgar touch in this otherwise perfect monument to good taste: the money is real, negotiable United States currency. Apart from the moral hazard of tempting players to supplement their holdings by surreptitiously diving into their wallets, the manufacturers could, by substituting fake money for the real money give a discount of $15,140 – the amount of Monopoly money that comes with a standard set.

I am storing up a few priceless Monopoly facts to keep the table enthralled at the next wedding I attend. I shall let you in on a few of the choicest. The longest game ever played lasted 70 days. Can there be anyone who finds that interesting? But your fellow guests will be all agog when you inform them that the record for a game under water was 45 days. I suppose players are allowed to come up for air whenever they land on Free Parking. And what about the longest game in a bathtub – 99 hours? The imagination boggles. My source does not tell me whether the bath contained water, nor what you do when your toes start shrivelling.

Confession time. Why do I no longer play board games? The truth is I am a bad loser. My life-time partner, an avid games player, claims that I kick the board over whenever the game is going badly for me. While I vehemently deny doing that, except from inadvertence, it is true that I hate losing. It is not as if I lack experience. I have spent much of my life losing at games. Take golf. Over a period of some 50 years, I have spent enough on lessons to pay off the national debt of a mid-sized country, but I remain incapable of making contact with the ball, except by accident. I do not know how I acquired this unsporting streak. Certainly not from my father who adopted the ethos of cricket as his own. He would surely have become secretary of the Berdichev Cricket Club, had he not left the town at the age of four. "When you get to the Pearly Gates," he used to tell me, "you will not be asked 'did you win or lose?' but 'did you play the game?'"

I did not know it at the time, but I later learned the perfect riposte. In the words of the American football coach Vince Lombardi, I would have said, "Show me a good loser and I'll show you a loser".

Well said, Vince.

2 September, 2005

Ashkenazi Eggheads

Older British readers will recall the late, great television and radio comic, Tony Hancock. In his unforgettable TV sketch "The Blood Donor," Tony, nobility personified, volunteers to give blood. He has second thoughts when he learns that the amount of blood he is expected to donate is a pint ("... a pint! That's nearly an armful. I'm not going around with an empty arm for anyone"). Tony calls the doctor a "legalized vampire," but changes his mind when he is told that his is a rare blood type. He puffs himself up with pride: "I always knew that we Hancocks were different from the rest of the herd. Well, we can't hog it all".

A Hancockian feeling of mindless superiority is what seems to have animated a number of people of my acquaintance on learning of an article published in a recent edition of the *Economist*. According to the report, an American scientist, Gregory Cochran, has come up with a theory that the reputedly higher intelligence of Ashkenazi Jews (as distinct, I suppose, from Ashkenazi Baptists) has a genetic basis and has developed over the generations by means of natural selection.

I am an Ashkenazi who can trace his Litvak pedigree all the way back to his grandfather, but I find myself unconvinced by any theory of Ashkenazi cerebral superiority, whether by nature, as Dr. Cochran would have it, or by nurture. Our neighbourhood is full of Ashkenazi Jews, but the only evidence I can find for their superior intelligence is their success in concealing it.

But even if there were something to it, why would we Ashkenazim want it to get around? Being cleverer does not make you more loved. I phoned our local Elder of Zion. "The Elders are furious," he told me. "We've succeeded in keeping the fact under our hats for centuries. We had a near escape in the 18th century when Manny Kantorovitz started attracting attention. We had to have his name changed quickly to Immanuel Kant. But usually we are able to operate under deep cover. Now we shall have to work on damage control. We have already started sending out dumb Ashkenazim as a smokescreen; you can spot them by the orange ribbons on their cars".

As instances of Ashkenazi brainpower, the *Economist* heads its article with pictures of Freud, Einstein and Mahler. What these geniuses have in common, aside from being Ashkenazi Jews, is that they were all native German speakers. The incomparable contribution of German Jews to modern civilization has been chronicled most recently by Amos Elon in his outstanding book "The Pity of it All," but another characteristic of Ashkenazim, the Jewish sense of humour – which can be seen at its finest in American fiction of the past half century – is more frequently ascribed to Jews of Eastern European origin. German Jews are thought to lack the shtetl-born self-mockery that characterizes Jewish humour. Indeed the yekkes seem to have, over the centuries, acquired by osmosis that imperviousness to irony that is said to characterize their Teutonic hosts.

Of course, not everyone cares for the humour of the Ashkenazi Jews. The novelist Kingsley Amis hated it. He dismissed Saul Bellow, hated Woody Allen, but preserved his greatest detestation for Philip Roth whom he has described as "one of the unfunniest fellows in the world." Amis' equally famous writer-son Martin, on the other hand, loves Ashkenazi humour. He adulates Bellow and admires Roth, though he understandably found Roth's repulsive novel "Sabbath's Theater" hard going: "You toil on, looking for the clean bits," he writes.

A man with a nice line in self-deprecatory Ashkenazi humour is A.J. Jacobs, whose recent book "The Know-it-All" attests, if not to the high intelligence of Ashkenazi Jews, to a stereotypical Ashkenazi doggedness in the pursuit of knowledge, often confused with intelligence. Jacobs, who starts, if he is to be believed, almost as ignorant as a newborn baby, sets out one day to read the whole of the "Encyclopaedia Britannica." Although he has a day job as an editor of *Esquire* and is subject to all kinds of distractions, he succeeds, in little more than a year, without cheating too much, in reading and, more impressively, digesting all 32 volumes of the Britannica. His motive in doing so is revealed by the secondary title: "One Man's Humble Quest to Become the Smartest Person in the World." By acquiring knowledge of quirky facts, Jacobs hopes to shine at cocktail parties (he fails hilariously) and (with equal lack of success) to score off his maddeningly erudite brother-in-law Eric.

Jacobs is certainly smart and he is not just any old Ashkenazi Jew. He was born into the Ashkenazi purple. He has been told that he is a descendant of Elijah, the Gaon of Vilna, but until he reaches the volume of the Britannica that contains the entry on that towering figure of 18th century Jewish scholarship, he knows nothing of his illustrious ancestor. Jacobs should place greater value on his pedigree. He has inherited at least one enviable trait from the Gaon: his prodigious memory.

Jacobs, in the throes of his efforts at mopping up everything that's worth knowing, and plenty that isn't, marvels that there are actually people who read books for fun. In love with facts and immersed in celebrity culture, he is blind to the pleasures of literature. He apparently sees himself as absolved from having to read "Anna Karenina" because he has read the Britannica's synopsis of the novel.

But now that he is the smartest person in the world, Jacobs might try to become the most literate. If he does, my friendly bookseller, Amazon.com. is there to help him. During a recent virtual browsing expedition I stumbled upon an ad that was hard to resist. Penguin Books is just about to release the complete collection of the 1,082 titles of the Penguin Classics, and Amazon, as philanthropic a bunch of chaps as you will find anywhere, is giving you a once-in-a-lifetime opportunity to save $5,327.75 by buying the collection from them for only $7,989.99.

But don't mortgage your home yet, because you will need to buy a new one to house the 1,082 titles, which if laid end to end (Amazon doesn't tell you why you should choose such an eccentric way of arranging your books) would measure 52 miles. If, Amazon goes on relentlessly, you stacked the books one on top of the other, they would tower 828 feet ("almost as tall as the Empire State Building") and – it must be said – almost as tall as the tale Amazon is spinning here. A biblical literalist in Amazon's marketing department must have been reading the Book of Numbers, where the number of Israelites wandering through the Sinai Desert is inflated by a factor of about a hundred.

But, inflated numbers aside, I think I am going to have to reconsider my business relationship with Amazon. How can I give my custom to people who I am convinced are about to be taken away in an unmarked van? It's not the price of $8,000. That, with difficulty, will purchase a set of silver toothpicks from Tiffany's. But why would Amazon think that anyone would buy a collection of paperback books that stretches for 52 miles?

If, having gone through the Britannica from a-ak to zywiec, A.J. Jacobs were to take my advice and read the Penguin Classics, he would start with Edwin A. Abbott and end with Emile Zola. Now, I will lay you reasonable odds that Jacobs has never heard of Abbott, who merits no entry in the Britannica – or not, at any rate, in my 1976 edition. I, on the other hand, have heard of this obscure Victorian divine who, thanks to the democracy of the alphabet, heads Penguin's list of the great names of world literature. Abbott was, in his time, one of the great headmasters of the slightly posh boys' day school in London that

I attended. His book "Flatland: A Romance in Many Dimensions" is Abbott's fictional attempt to popularize the notion of multidimensional geometry. Don't try and beat me to the movie rights; you read it here first.

As he ascends the Empire State Building, climbing from Abbott to Zola, pausing for breath at Dante, Darwin, Defoe, Descartes, Dickens and Dostoyevsky, Jacobs will meet the great figures of world literature, but he will not encounter a single Ashkenazi. If he were to persevere and go on to the Penguin Modern Classics, he could read Proust, Kafka and Bellow. But the classics, as defined by Penguin, are certified Ashkenazi-free. Not free of Jews, however. Josephus and Spinoza appear, but they spoke neither German nor Yiddish. Nor for that matter did Philo, St. Paul, Maimonides or Disraeli.

Ashkenazi chauvinists should take note. We might try to acquire that rarer Ashkenazi commodity, humility. Let us aspire to mediocrity; it could make us more popular.

8 July, 2005

It Ain't Necessarily So

English is today the unchallenged international language of communication. Just as well. Having English as a first language seems to render its possessors incapable of learning any other. So, it was with a feeling that, for once, history had been kind to me that I learned recently from an erudite American friend that in 1776, English became the official language of the United States and thus the world language of the future, by a margin of only one vote. Its rival was German; the thought of having to wrap my tongue round that barbarous language and use words like – to quote an example given by Mark Twain – *Generalstaatsverordnetenversammlungen*, was hard to contemplate.

But I need not have worried. There never was such a proposal, nor, to cite alternative versions of the story, were Greek, Latin or – believe it or not – Hebrew serious contenders. The story is simply an instance of what in modern parlance is called an urban legend, a widely disseminated piece of folklore with no factual basis.

You can study urban legends at university. Jan Harold Brunvand, a professor at the University of Utah, has devoted his life to urban legends and written several books on the subject. I suppose I should not be surprised. After all, I read last week (another urban legend?) that you can now get a B.A. at the Ben-Gurion University of the Negev in customer communications management, which – translated into the victorious language of 1776 – means learning how to answer the telephone.

I am less impressed than I used to be at learning that there are more than 15 million Internet sites that Google thinks might interest me on the subject of urban legends. I have not tried, but I suspect that as you pass the ten million mark, they begin to be of marginal relevance. Still, out there in cyberspace, there is no lack of people bursting to tell me about urban legends. Most legends cited by the web sites are of mind-numbing triviality. Try telling the assembled guests at dinner that you had heard on the BBC that a lion had mutilated 42 midgets in a Cambodian ring-fight and see if you are invited again. And who cares that there are no alligators in the sewers of New York, or that gerbils were never found in any of the extraordinary and unmentionable places that myth has placed them?

But not all urban legends are frivolous. I think with a blush of how often I have astounded my friends with what I believed were little-known facts that turned out to be neither little known, nor facts. Despite what you may have heard to the contrary from me or from some other big mouth, there are more words for "snow" in English than there are in Eskimo. The Nazis did not manufacture soap from the bodies of their victims, nor did they make lampshades from human skin; they did far worse, but not that. In one of the columns that George Orwell used to write for the left-wing weekly *Tribune*, he gave examples of fallacies that he himself believed to be true at one time. Some of those he quotes survive today and I had believed most of them. Everyone knows that bulls are infuriated at the sight of red. Isn't that why matadors wear red? Well, no! Apparently bulls are colour-blind. And Orwell goes on inexorably. It is not true that a swan can break your arm or leg with a swipe of its wing. And you won't get lockjaw if you get a cut between your thumb and forefinger. As for the belief that you can die if powdered glass is put in your food, don't bother to put crushed glass in your mother-in-law's lemon tea. It won't work even though I have read more than one murder story that hinges on just that belief.

Rumour was rife in World War II and urban legends abounded, but the Hitler stories were in a class of their own. With the publication of several biographies, much of the mystery and all of the myths surrounding the Führer have now been swept away. But some of them had a good run for their money. Those of you still breathing who were around during the war may still think of Hitler as Schickelgruber – Churchill's derisive pet name for his arch foe. Had that really been his name, the war might have been shorter. Germans reputedly have a negligible sense of the ridiculous, but even they would surely have found it hard to say "Heil Schickelgruber" without falling on the floor with laughter like the centurions in "Life of Brian." So I am sorry to report that Adolf was always Hitler, his father Alois having changed their surname from Schickelgruber to Hitler before the future Führer was born.

Then there was the story that Hitler had a Jewish grandfather. This story, widely circulated in the 1920s and 1930s, was revived by Hans Frank, the Nazi governor general of Poland, in the memoirs he dictated just before his execution. According to Frank, Hitler's unmarried grandmother gave birth to Hitler's father while serving as a domestic in the home of a Jewish family called Frankenberger. The alleged natural father was the 19-year-old son of the house, on whose behalf Frankenberger Senior had reputedly paid regular instalments to support the child. But Ian Kershaw, Hitler's latest and, in my mind, best biographer has firmly knocked this story on the head. Not only was there no family by the name of Frankenberger, there were no Jews at all in that part of Austria in the 1830s.

One feature of Hitler of which you have surely heard but never taken seriously is his alleged testicular deficiency. It was the theme of a ribald ditty sung to the tune of "Colonel Bogey." I have no information on poor old Goebbels who, as the rhyme goes, had no balls at all, but there actually is some evidence, admittedly dubious, from the autopsy the Russians carried out on the Führer's burned carcass that Hitler did indeed have only one testicle.

The myth I was sorriest to abandon was the one about good King Christian of Denmark. The legend was around for a long time, but it obtained worldwide circulation with the screening of the popular movie "Exodus." A bad film from a worse novel – perhaps a sequel called "Leviticus" would have been better – it nevertheless had its memorable moments. The author Leon Uris had a fixation with blond, blue-eyed, gun-toting sabras who became his stereotype Israelis. In the film a moving story is told by the young – blonde and blue-eyed, of course – Danish Jewess. The story goes that, when his Jewish subjects were compelled to wear a yellow star, King Christian put one on his own clothes and walked through the streets of Copenhagen wearing it. Only a few years ago, in a letter to *The New York Review of Books*, did I learn that there was no truth in the story at all; indeed the Jews of Denmark were never required to wear the yellow star. So another illusion bites the dust.

The late prime minister, Menachem Begin, had an overwhelming desire, common among many of us, to share interesting facts with his interlocutors. This didactic streak came to the fore at the September 1978 signing ceremony of the Camp David agreements on the lawn of the White House. In his speech, the prime minister complimented President Jimmy Carter on the enormous amount of work he had put in. He added: "As far as my historic experience is concerned, I think that he worked harder than our forefathers did in Egypt, building the pyramids." One hopes he had worked harder because, by the time the Children of Israel arrived in Egypt, the Great Pyramids were already in situ and had indeed been there for 1,000 years or so – the time that separates us from William the Conqueror or Rashi.

Not that the nuggets of information supplied by Begin – assiduous disseminator of urban myths though he was – were always inaccurate. I have only my admittedly shaky memory to rely on, but I recall a televised meeting with President Sadat in which Begin, to break the ice, decided to discuss the weather.

He earnestly explained to the Egyptian president that they were experiencing what Israelis called a *hamsin*, a word that came, he assured the president, from the Arabic for "fifty." An undoubtedly correct piece of information, but one that Sadat might reasonably be expected to have known already.

My own modest efforts to disseminate an urban legend have so far proved fruitless. Loyal readers may remember that I have a theory that Israeli jellyfish commit mass suicide on our shores during the nine days preceding the Jewish fast of the Ninth of Av, and disappear on the day of the fast. Will my jellyfish go the way of the alligators in the sewers of New York or will they appear this year on schedule?

Watch this space.

10 June, 2005

Lawyers are no Joke

The one-act opera "Trial by Jury" is a minnow swimming in the company of such whales as "The Mikado" in the musical ocean of Gilbert and Sullivan. This half-hour-long *jeu d'esprit* usually serves as a light curtain-raiser for some of its weightier brethren. The entire action of the opera is given over to the trial of an action for breach of promise of marriage. While enjoying a pleasing performance of the opera given by the Jerusalem Encore Theater last month, it occurred to me that such lawsuits have vanished, the unmourned victims of sex equality. We are no longer regaled with accounts of the plight of the abandoned fiancée who, because she paid no heed to the Psalmist's warning that all men are liars, was compelled to seek satisfaction in a court of law.

Even the most hopeless nostalgist, if he retains a speck of humanity in his make-up, should not regret the passing of the breach of promise action, a humiliating reminder of the days when marriage was the only prospect open to a woman, and a broken engagement was a disaster. And indeed I do not regret its disappearance. But as a historical curiosity and as the subject of some fine 19th-century comic writing it merits a digression.

After all, you could hardly accuse George Orwell of advocating murder merely because he wrote an essay on the decline of the English murder. And if, with Orwell, we are to lament a decline, how much more should we rue total extinction. Murders may lack the class they once had, which was Orwell's point, but there is an inexhaustible supply of potential assassins more than willing to keep the homicidal flame burning. In terms of what keeps our policemen occupied, murder is up there at the top of their list of priorities, alongside double parking and French kissing. Like the poor, murder will always be with us, but the action for breach of promise of marriage has, with carbon paper and the passenger pigeon, been relegated to gather dust in the basement of history.

But, though it no longer seems to feature as an attraction in the law courts, the breach of promise case remains alive and well for readers of Victorian literature. Considering the rampant misogyny apparent in their treatment of these lawsuits, it is surprising that the works of Charles Dickens, Rudyard Kipling and W.S. Gilbert have not been blacklisted by the militants of the women's movement. Because, without exception, these writers, in their treatment of breach of promise actions, make us - against our will - laugh at the wretchedness of the jilted woman plaintiff and empathize with the dishonourable behaviour of the male defendant.

Gilbert has the ex-fiancé in "Trial by Jury" glory in his caddishness ("At last, one morning, I became another's love-sick boy. Tink-a-tank! Tink-a-tank!") By his own testimony, a potential wife-beater, drunkard, smoker and womanizer, the rat gets away scot-free when, to the plaudits of all in court, the judge resolves the case by marrying the toothsome plaintiff himself.

In his poem "The Betrothed," Rudyard Kipling unabashedly sides with the heartless defendant. In a breach of promise case of 1885, Maggie, the scorned woman, has unwisely given her former suitor an ultimatum; he must choose between her and his cigar. "For Maggie has written a letter to give me my choice between/The wee little whimpering Love and the great god Nick o' Teen." Eloquently explaining why the callous man opts for his cigars - his "harem of dusky beauties, fifty tied in a string" - the poem climaxes with the deathless line: "And a woman is only a woman, but a good Cigar is a Smoke".

And then there is Charles Dickens. In what is arguably the most celebrated court case in Victorian fiction - the case of Bardell vs. Pickwick in "The Pickwick Papers" - we are left in no doubt as to whose side we must take. Misconstruing Mr. Pickwick's request for advice on whether he should employ a manservant, his landlady, Mrs. Bardell, the archetypal breach of promise plaintiff, believes he has proposed marriage and swoons in his unwilling arms just as his friends - who become reluctant witnesses for the plaintiff - enter the parlour. Judgment for the plaintiff!

The benevolent attitude toward the two-timing male evinced by these writers does not mean that breach of promise fiction lacks villains. We live in an era when satirists must go easy not only on women, but on every group - from Muslims to homosexuals - that feels itself entitled to protection from ridicule. But there is one unprotected class of person that Dickens and Gilbert mocked and that we too can mock with impunity. As consistently as the jilted woman is a figure of fun and the man a cad in literary litigation, the bad guys are always the lawyers. The heavies of Bardell vs. Pickwick are not Mrs. Bardell and her friends, but her attorneys, Dodson and Fogg, and it is his determined refusal to pay their costs that lands Mr. Pickwick in the Fleet Prison. Fortunately for Mr. Pickwick, he is sprung when Mrs. Bardell refuses to pay Dodson and Fogg.

It was certainly not from ignorance of legal practice that Dickens and Gilbert satirized lawyers so mercilessly. Both writers knew the law from the inside. While in his teens, Dickens worked as a law clerk - and hated it. His books are full of references to practitioners of the law, few of them kind. "Bleak House," in my eyes the finest of all Dickens novels, is the ultimate lawyer joke, a savage satire on those that practised in the Court of Chancery. Gilbert's legal career was likewise brief. Averaging five clients a year he was a singularly unsuccessful barrister. Generations of devotees of the operas he wrote with Sir Arthur Sullivan can be thankful that his failure at the bar compelled him to earn his living by his pen. Gilbert was kinder than Dickens to the lawyers that he lampooned, but he never ceased to find them funny. Attorneys and judges appear in at least half a dozen Gilbert and Sullivan operas.

In selecting the legal profession for their barbs, the Victorian satirists could not have found a more popular Aunt Sally. *Plus ça change!* The lawyer joke is today more prevalent than ever. When you Google "lawyer jokes" you will find nearly two million entries to choose from. If you find one in that agglomerated mass that makes you laugh, please let me know because I must have missed it. I concede that, in failing to find funny wisecracks aimed at as fine a body of men and women as ever overcharged a client, I might be accused of bias. I can bear that with fortitude. But more than lack of objectivity, my fear is of being accused of lacking a sense of humour. It is as hard to admit that one lacks a sense of humour as it is to admit that one is a bad driver, but I have to confess that the evidence of my inability to laugh at what the rest of the world finds funny is mounting.

Like George Eliot's Herr Klesmer I perceive of myself as being "very sensible to wit and humour," but I was recently sharply reminded of how hopelessly deficient I must be in that department. Any movie that upsets the Anti-Defamation League of B'nai B'rith cannot be all bad, so I was predisposed to enjoy - to give it its full snappy title - "Borat: Cultural Learnings for Make Benefit Glorious Nation of Kazakhstan." After all, what could whet one's appetite more than a movie that inspired the ADL's po-faced "Statement on the comedy of Sacha Baron Cohen, a.k.a. 'Borat'?" Even the remark that Mr. Cohen is "himself proudly Jewish" could not dull my high expectations for a film that could provoke the ADL to write that "one serious pitfall is that the audience may not always be sophisticated enough to get the joke".

And everyone seems to have loved it. I do not believe that I can match the ADL for humourlessness, but I found the film dull. I sense that it must be a generational thing. Younger people than I certainly found Borat funny. I know, for example, that, were someone to come to the family dinner table holding a plastic bag filled with his own excrement, my two-year-old great-nephew would subside into gales of laughter that would gladden the heart of Mr. Baron Cohen. My own feeling is that Cohen will be very funny when he gets out of the lavatory.

I suppose that I should be thankful that neither Borat not his alter ego Ali G have started on lawyers yet. You can imagine the scene: A wrestling match between two naked overweight Supreme Court judges. But maybe not. As I said earlier, lawyers simply aren't funny.

9 March, 2007

Analphabetics Anonymous

James Watson's best-selling account of the discovery of the structure of the DNA molecule, "The Double Helix," famously opens: "I have never seen Frances Crick in a modest mood." Not, for that matter, that Watson's own Nobel Prize was ever likely to be awarded for humility. But arrogance does not, of necessity, form part of the job description of a great scientist. For the conductor of a symphony orchestra, however, a belief in his own superiority is vital. Charged with imposing his personality on some hundred professional musicians, an ego is as indispensable a part of his bag of tricks as is his mastery over the score. There may be exceptions to this rule, but I am pretty sure that maestro Zubin Mehta is not one of them. Those who have watched and admired him over the years have never had cause to be concerned that he might be suffering from any deficiency in self-esteem.

So you might perhaps be surprised to learn that my first sight of the man who has, like a Colossus, bestrode Israel's musical world for almost 40 years, was when he was almost literally playing second fiddle. The 1969 film of five prodigiously gifted young musicians, each now a legend, performing Schubert's "Trout" quintet at London's Queen Elizabeth Hall, is now so famous that people forget that the same group also played the work in Jerusalem that same year. I remember it well; I travelled from Haifa to hear and marvel.

A piano quintet conventionally comprises, besides the obvious piano, a string quartet of two violins, a viola and a cello, but the "Trout" is scored for a double bass in place of the second violin. As music lovers know, in that historical performance, Daniel Barenboim played the piano, Itzhak Perlman the violin, Jacqueline du Pré the cello and Pinchas Zukerman the viola. And the double bass? The fifth member of the quintet that called itself "the Israeli Mafia" was none other than Zubin Mehta. Outsize though it is, the double bass adds tone and colour, but rarely has a starring role. And nor does it in the "Trout." While the other four virtuosos, with the skill of Brazilian footballers, deftly passed

Schubert's deathless melodies from one to the other, scant attention was paid to the double bassist at the back, essential but self-effacing, who was destined to become so important a part of Israel's cultural life.

If Zubin Mehta was then, for Israelis, the least known of that fabulous five – three of the others being home-grown and a fourth being, as it were, married into the family – we soon got to know him better. No pop diva could have expected half as rapturous a reception as was accorded to the maestro in Tel Aviv last month at the gala concert celebrating his 70th birthday. The music was memorable and the wave of affection palpable.

It is not only that Mehta, in reigning over the Israel Philharmonic Orchestra for close on 40 years, has taken our national orchestra to new heights, but he has so often and so openly shown his great love for this country and its people. And never so notably as when, in the first Gulf War, while we commuters would cautiously leave Tel Aviv each day during the daylight hours, and others decided it was a good time for an extended holiday in Eilat, Zubin Mehta braved the Scuds and came to Tel Aviv to show solidarity with the city that had taken him to its heart.

For me, the gala occasion was mildly marred by the short film that the organizers had prepared to celebrate the event. It was made with the best of intentions, but its English text was replete with errors. It referred to maestro Mehta's great contribution to mosic in Izrael. When we were told of the maestro's celebrated visit to Israel during that titanic struggle between Tiger Woods and Ernie Els – "the Golf War" – I asked myself for the umpteenth time: Why should studying "Julius Caesar" for their matriculation exams implant in the natives of this country the widely erroneous belief that they are competent to write English for public consumption?

I regret that my lifelong inability to collect anything – whether stamps, first editions, butterflies or jokes – has frustrated my periodic intentions of cataloguing the linguistic sins I have encountered during the time I have lived here. But there are offences that are hard to forget or forgive. One is the cavalier treatment accorded to the name of my town. The city of Herzliya is named after the founder of modern Zionism, Theodor Herzl. And that is how he wrote his name. This fact has never deterred the responsible municipal department, in its valiant attempt to exhaust every available phonetic permutation of the letters forming the town's name, from variously writing the name as Herzel, Hertzl or Hertzel.

But then the Ministry of Transportation got into the act. Confusion at the local level was all very well, but when it came to inter-city signs, something more was needed. It was necessary to extend the municipality's equal-opportunity programme for the literacy-challenged from favouring the merely dyslexic to doing something for the pig ignorant. What was required was a sign-writer who not only was unable to spell the name of Theodor Herzl, but who also had never heard of him. The triumphant result can now be seen on the coastal road: a spanking-new sign directing you to ... Hertselia.

I think they derive their inspiration from the stonemason in the 1964 British short "A Home of Your Own." A farcically incompetent construction crew builds an apartment block for the municipality. When the time comes for the inauguration ceremony, the lady mayoress ceremonially unveils the inscription engraved in stone, reading: "The money for this erection was raised by pubic contribution".

Up the coast from us they are also doing their bit in the sacred cause of confounding the foreigner. The town of Caesarea was named by Herod the Great in the first century BCE in honour of Emperor Augustus Caesar and has borne that name ever since. Or rather it did until the demented sign-writers got onto it in the second half of the 20th century. They have decided to give one of the most historically important towns in the Holy Land the name of Qesarya, sometimes called Kesarya, but rarely the name by which it has been known for centuries.

I scent a conspiracy here. If Dan Brown is running out of ideas for his next paranoid blockbuster, I suggest he look into Analphabetics Anonymous ("Fact: Analphabetics Anonymous exists,") an organization financed by a slush fund of Israel's Ministry of Transportation, devoted to putting up signs to deter potential tourists. Merely puzzling the foreigner is not enough, however; to earn a place in the Hall of Fame of Analphabetics Anonymous, you have to be able to fool him completely.

A strong contender for the title of all-time great is the anonymous author of the road sign indicating the route to the airport. This immortal, who surely deserves to have his achievement inscribed on the Tomb of the Unknown Signwriter on Mount Hertsel, succeeded in bamboozling all but the initiated by directing the perplexed traveler to "Natbag" – a transliteration of the acronym used in Hebrew for the name of the airport. Running a close second, by common consent, was the sign (now sadly removed) pointing toward the north Tel Aviv railway station. The sign, in Latin letters, read "Raqevet" – the Hebrew word for a railway train. Go figure.

Menus, on the other hand, are more a source of exasperation than bemusement. The illiteracy of restaurateurs is, of course, a commonplace throughout the world. At the international schools of haute cuisine, innovation is prized as much in spelling a dish as in cooking it but, though a global phenomenon, the misspelling of menus has been elevated to an art in this country. Never go out to eat in Tel Aviv without a ballpoint pen. Anyone who has any regard for the written word should regard it as a solemn duty to deface with corrections the menus that are proffered at even the most expensive of restaurants. What, for instance, can Tzimes Restaurant of Herzliya have meant in its menu of starters: "Gefilte Fish with Slice of Crap"?

It is not as if it is hard to find native English speakers here. I would hazard a guess that there are over 100,000 residents of this country whose first language is English. Take part in a demonstration and you will notice that the slogans chanted by the bearded young man at your side will be in the accents of deepest Brooklyn; throw a cricket ball in the main street of Ra'anana and the odds are that you will bean a South African; cut in front of another car at a traffic light in Jerusalem, and you will be able to add some choice Anglo-Saxon to your vocabulary.

Which is all a long way of saying that the Israel Philharmonic could have honoured Zubin Mehta's contribution to Izraeli mosic more professionally.

Their pubic expects no less.

12 May, 2006

Tastes and Distastes

In the socialist Zionist youth movement on whose periphery I hovered almost 60 years ago, much of our time was spent singing songs. When we were not singing soulful Hebrew songs of toil and yearning, we would sing songs in English of an earthier variety. In reading recently of the crisis facing the caviar industry, I was reminded of one of those songs. The first verse goes:

"Caviar comes from the virgin sturgeon,
The virgin sturgeon's a very fine fish,
The virgin sturgeon needs no urgin',
That's why caviar is my dish".

I have to admit that this song creates problems for the literal-minded. In the first place, the behaviour imputed to the sturgeon seems to be an inadequate reason for enjoying its eggs. Second, there is an internal contradiction. According to a plain reading of the text, the sturgeon is both chaste and promiscuous; you cannot help feeling that mention of its virginity was added for reasons of assonance rather than biological accuracy. The remaining verses of the song, however, explain the attraction of caviar. It is not because it tastes good, but because its consumption can do wonders for your love life. The singer gives some caviar to his girlfriend, who at the start of the verse shares the sturgeon's state of celibacy but who, upon tasting caviar, can teach the author of the Kama Sutra a thing or two. Much the same happens to his 93-year-old grandfather who, once given caviar, pursues Grandma in a manner unparalleled in a nonagenarian since the days of Abraham.

Having never tasted caviar, I cannot attest personally to its aphrodisiac properties. I only observe that while, with the advent of proven chemical substitutes, the bottom has dropped out of the market for rhino horn and Spanish fly, the demand for caviar remains strong. I have to assume that people eat caviar for reasons that go beyond a desire to add a little colour to the lives of their girlfriends and grandfathers. It's not because it's cheap. The best caviar comes from the threatened Beluga sturgeon, which swims in the Caspian Sea. A decent-sized portion of Beluga caviar – which, to protect it from any metallic taste, should be handled with a spoon made of mother of pearl – costs about $300. That is only marginally less than the current price for an equivalent amount of gold.

Any idea of feeding the starving millions of the Third World with caviar is doomed to failure. But the initiated are still clamouring for the stuff. What has caused a flutter among the dovecotes of Park Avenue, Park Lane and the Faubourg Saint Germain is that the Convention on International Trade in Endangered Species of Wild Fauna and Flora, known to its friends as CITES, has refused to approve the export quotas for 2006 for caviar from wild stocks. It seems that if the Beluga sturgeon is not to go the way of the dodo and the passenger pigeon, connoisseurs will have, for a while at least, to forego their favourite nosh.

I believe that caviar is what is commonly referred to as an acquired taste. That usually means that you have to plug away at something that tastes vile until you can stand it, but the uninitiated should recognize that there are those who have been educated to enjoy the best food and wine. It is all very well for those who, unable or unwilling to shell out three hundred bucks for something to spread on their teatime toast, react with indifference to the looming Beluga crisis. You cannot tell a gourmet used to caviar that he should try peanut butter instead.

Not that acquired tastes should always be respected. The English – admittedly not known for their discriminating palates – produce something called Marmite. Like caviar, you can spread it on bread, but that is where the similarity ends. Marmite can best be described as an acquired distaste. The closer one's acquaintance with it, the more repellent it tastes and smells. It is made from the yeast that is left over after beer is brewed. On the theory that you can get the English to eat anything, someone came up with the bright idea that instead of throwing the stuff away, they could sell it in Britain. It is said to ward off mosquitoes, which only goes to show that mosquitoes have better taste than Englishmen.

Those who have been happily and guiltlessly guzzling caviar for years might be surprised to hear that it is an abomination. My source for this seemingly provocative statement is Chapter 11 of the Book of Leviticus, the core legislation for the Jewish dietary laws. The chapter sets out the rules and gives examples of what animals, birds, fish and insects may and may not be eaten.

An animal, for instance, may only be eaten if its hooves are split and it chews its cud. Any other animal is an "abomination." In the case of fish, "all in the seas or in the rivers that do not have fins and scales ... they are an abomination to you".

This might sound clear and unambiguous, and you can now follow why observant Jews do not eat such finless wonders as shrimps, prawns, crabs or lobsters. Obviously oysters are also off the menu, whether or not there is an "r" in the month. But, even accepting that the eggs of an abomination are themselves abominable, what is wrong with the eggs of a sturgeon, a fish that has both fins and scales? Well, it seems that the scales are not sufficiently scaly to satisfy the exacting demands of those charged with deciding what is and what is not an abomination. The scales are technically termed "ganoid," which means that they cannot be easily severed from the skin of the fish and that is enough to make the sturgeon rabbinically abominable.

If you thought that scientific progress would inevitably lead to a rationalization of the Jewish dietary laws, you would be wrong. The resources of zoology, ornithology, entomology, botany and, in our case, ichthyology have been called upon to think up fresh prohibitions. Cutting-edge sages beaver away on the frontiers of knowledge to dream up new things that Jews may not do. Even the most hostile must have found it hard to stifle their admiration of the rabbis who prevented their flocks from drinking from taps in New York City on the grounds that the water pouring from the taps contain copepods – mini-crustaceans which, when looked at through a microscope, turned out, to nobody's surprise, not to have fins or scales. You might well wonder if, before he struck that rock to provide water for the thirsty children of Israel, Moses was able to carry out an analysis to ensure that there were no such nano-abominations in that water.

No doubt to the delight of many children, broccoli and cauliflower are now on the firing line. It seems that there are near-invisible bugs in frozen broccoli and cauliflower that render those often detested vegetables unacceptable in some rabbinic circles.

I readily concede that in an age when abortion clinics are blown up in the name of Jesus and aircraft are made to crash into skyscrapers for the glory of Allah, the lunacies of the Jewish ultra-Orthodox are pretty innocuous. But it is hard not to conclude that, in a world of their own, they are sometimes out to lunch.

And who am I to talk? Food taboos are a relic of the past and yet, although I have no strong objection to anyone else eating abominations – after all, the cooking and restaurant columns of *Haaretz* seem seldom to feature anything else – I myself more or less keep to the dietary laws of my ancient religion. It would never occur to me to seethe a kid in its mother's milk, and although I am not deterred by cauliflower or tap water, I have, all my life, steered clear of flying, swimming and crawling abominations.

I do not find it easy to explain why I, an enlightened, not excessively spiritual child of the 20th century, observe these seemingly outmoded food taboos. Partly, of course, the inertia factor comes into play: it is simpler to keep to the habits of a lifetime, however irrational, than to change them. But it is something more than that. Just as the most freethinking of Jews can be seen observing the Passover seder with no sense that this religious practice is inconsistent with their beliefs, many Jews observe the dietary laws to some degree because that is what Jews have always done. The Jewish aversion to eating the flesh of the pig, the classic dietary prohibition, resonates over the centuries. As the Second Book of the Maccabees tells it, two centuries before the Current Era, Jews were ready to be martyred rather than be forced do eat pork.

Not to sound too pompous, the dietary laws are an affirmation of the Jewish historic identity. That's why caviar's not my dish.

17 March, 2006

Deadly Sins

Malaysia's National Registration Department has published a list of names that parents will henceforth be prohibited from calling their children. You may think that this is an interference with a basic liberty, but I believe they have a point in preventing their citizens from calling their sons or daughters "007," "Male Adulterer," "Smelly Dog," or "Unsound Mind." The trouble with making an exhaustive list, however, is that it breeds inconsistencies. An admirer in Kuala Lumpur of Douglas Adams' "Hitchhiker's Guide to the Galaxy" may choose to name his child "Ford Prefect" – it is not on the list – but he should give up any idea of calling him "Honda Accord" because names of Japanese cars are expressly proscribed.

I do not believe that Malaysia's neighbour, the Philippines, has any such law, but even if it had, it would surely have raised no objection to the naming at his birth in 1928, of the future archbishop of Manila, Jaime Lachica Sin. The difficulty arose later because, in 1976, Pope Paul VI elevated the archbishop to the College of Cardinals, thus making him Cardinal Sin. I quote the po-faced entry on the eminent cleric in the Wikipedia online encyclopedia: "His name should not be confused with 'cardinal sin,' which is a synonym for the seven deadly sins".

And we all know what they are. From Dante Alighieri via Hieronymus Bosch to Bertolt Brecht, the Seven Deadly Sins of the early Christian church – Lust, Gluttony, Avarice, Sloth, Anger, Envy and Pride – have become embedded in Western culture. The achievement of Gregory the Great, in the sixth century, in boiling down the number of sins to seven – a triumph of compression – is what has given the Seven Deadly Sins their particular cachet. Although, to be fair, each has spawned progeny so that you have, as it were, sons of sins which in turn have produced grandsins and great-grandsins.

A characteristic of these cardinal Christian sins is their universality. Regardless of your religion, indeed regardless of whether you even have a religion, these are broad-brush sins with which anyone can identify. Of course, like any other commodity, the Deadly Sins are subject to market fluctuations. On my personal Dow-Jones sindex, Sloth has latterly hit an all-time high, Lust has dived while Anger has held steady.

My own initial exposure to sin was of a more tribal nature. It was in the pages of the then canonical English edition of the service for Yom Kippur – the Day of Atonement. Today, the reader of English may choose from at least three competing translations but, in my youth in London, the "Service of the Synagogue," edited by Arthur Davis, reigned supreme. It was known, and I think is still known, as the "Routledge Mahzor" after the name of its publisher. The work of several turn-of-the-last-century men and women of letters (one of whom was the celebrated author and Zionist, Israel Zangwill,) the already-obsolescent language of the translation was ill-tuned to mid-20th century ears.

A central part of the liturgy for Yom Kippur is a litany, recited no less than eight times during the course of the day, confessing to 44 sins, two for each letter of the Hebrew alphabet. As you go through the confession in translation, you will see that you are required successively to own up to an arrogant mien; haughty eyes; a wanton glance; impure lips; and an obdurate brow. That about covers the facial transgressions; you need not seek absolution for jug ears or a pimply nose.

I do not think that I am being unjust when I observe that, on Yom Kippur, the apparent penitents take an almost sensual delight in the catharsis of confession. The coreligionists of Sigmund Freud wallow pleasurably in guilt. As you get into the swing of the confessional ritual, thumping your chest while pleading guilty to each charge of the 44-count indictment, the flow is interrupted after each dozen or so sins by a petition for forgiveness belted out by the congregation to a melody, the gaiety of which belies the solemnity of the words. But, impressive though it is, and sincere as the breast-beaters assuredly are, I am not sure that this ritualized contrition has a more than limited shelf life.

Although a record is doubtless kept on high, I have never, down here, seen any data on the long-term or short-term effects of mass confession on the presumed penitent. I suspect, however, a high degree of recidivism. It is all very well, as you frenziedly punch yourself, to resolve that your mien will no longer be arrogant and that your eyes will cease to be haughty. But can you really change? Will not your brow revert to its pristine state of obduracy? And, can you be sure that your glance will cease to be wanton or might you not – forgive me for doubting you – echo St. Augustine's prayer, "Make me chaste, Lord, but not yet"?

An almost universal failing that gets top billing on any list of sins that you care to name is the sin of envy, and there is a specific sub-group of that sin to which many are prone. I call it occupation envy. Simply put, we find it hard to accept that there are people who are paid to do a job that we would willingly do for nothing. That dream job changes. At different times of life we have wanted to spend our days tasting chocolate; watching movies; and taking photographs for one of those calendars that you only ever see when you take your car in for a service. And who has not fancied working for Michelin and, god-like, awarding stars to, or withholding them from, top restaurants?

A job requiring you to read books is, I think, less likely to arouse envy than one in which the call of duty compels you to eat and drink in smart restaurants. However, for anyone addicted to the printed word, the idea of spending the day with books is a seductive one. So it is pleasant to record that I have, late in life, achieved what for me is the modest septuagenarian equivalent of my early teenage ambition of being a Nestlé's chocolate taster. Candour compels me to admit that writing a monthly column and the occasional book review for Haaretz does not constitute a livelihood. I am not at liberty to disclose what the paper pays me except to say that it accurately reflects their assessment of my value and is considerately calculated to keeping a tight rein on my self-esteem. If my mien remains arrogant the blame cannot be laid at the door of Haaretz.

Nevertheless my new career has afforded me a pretext for reading what I want whenever I want. I should explain why I feel the need to justify myself at all: I have a weakness for what can be generically called escapist literature. Why this should instil in me the slightest feelings of guilt is thanks to an upbringing – common, I suspect, to most of my peers – that prized study and work over pleasure. To this day I am mildly ashamed that people might think that this kind of perfectly respectable, if time-wasting, literature is all that I read. As this is confession time, I will admit that when I go in to Hatchards, the Piccadilly bookshop, to stock up on my year's supply of thrillers and whodunits, I will add a work of history or philosophy so that the assistant will realize that I am, at bottom, a serious person. When you see me reading a book on a plane, it will probably be one on linguistics or evolutionary biology. You will not catch me holding the latest Robert Ludlum that I will nevertheless be reading when I reach the privacy of my hotel bedroom. Considering that Ludlum died five years ago, it might seem strange to talk about his latest but, giving the term "ghostwriter" new meaning, he still manages to produce a best-seller a year. The Lubavitcher Rebbe is not, after all, the sole evidence for the existence of an afterlife.

But now that I have emerged from the closet, I can read junk in the line of duty. My new persona stood me in good stead two years ago when I conceived of the idea of reading the then top six *New York Times* best-sellers with the vague idea of writing something condescending about popular taste. I started with new books by Stephen King, Michael Crichton and John Grisham, and found that there was nothing dismissive that I could write about these consummately professional works of fiction. Only Dan Brown restored my faith in the basic illiteracy of the reading public and it was on his execrable "The Da Vinci Code" that I eventually wrote an article.

That, in short, is how I overcame the sin of envy. For next year's Day of Atonement, I shall work on that obdurate brow.

13 October, 2006

All in the Family

BSkyB is Europe's largest satellite broadcaster. When the post of its chief executive recently fell vacant, this publicly listed company appointed a nominations committee to find his replacement. An executive-search firm was then hired to produce a list of candidates. The committee conducted "'an arduous search'" in the words of its chairman, the Lord St. John of Fawsley. The search produced only one name: that of James Murdoch who just happened to be the 30-year-old son of Rupert Murdoch, BskyB's controlling shareholder. The satirical magazine *Private Eye* claimed that candidates were required to leave their applications on the breakfast table in an envelope addressed to Dad.

If your father owns a bank, a newspaper or a country, the good news is that nepotism is back. I do not want you to think that this is sour grapes on my part. I muffed my own opportunity for preferment. At the time that the Digger moved his papers from Fleet Street to Wapping in London's East End, the Fox empire – alas not listed on the Stock Exchange – was already well ensconced in that part of the capital. Indeed thanks to the farsighted strategic vision of its founders it had never left there. When the nominations committee consisting of my father and my uncle, who also owned, managed and exclusively staffed their woollens business from its corporate headquarters at 250 Commercial Road E.1, looked for an executive to share their not over-burdensome load, I was told gently that I was over-qualified. I became a lawyer instead.

My interest in the subject of nepotism was aroused some months ago when I read that Saadi Qaddafi, the son of Libyan leader Muammar Qaddafi, had been named to Libya's football squad for the African Nations Cup. Uncharitable thoughts of nepotism seemed ill-founded when young Saadi was signed on by the professional Italian team Perugia last summer. But never fear. Three months into the Italian soccer season, the 30-year-old Qaddafi has not yet played for Perugia and, to add insult to injury, has recently tested positive for steroid use.

Nepotism is, of course, rife throughout the Middle East. When the late unlamented Uday Hussein was appointed president of the Iraqi National Olympic Committee, nobody bothered with a search committee although, had he wanted to, father Saddam would undoubtedly have been able to find an English lord to make it kosher. Uday had a way of stimulating the competitive spirit of his players that would give pause even to Manchester United's Sir Alex Ferguson. Sir Alex, it will be recalled, sent a boot flying to the head of the iconic David Beckham, causing a cut eye which necessitated the insertion of stitches. Uday did better. He executed athletes for fun and would torture his footballers for losing games. These original training methods do not seem to have resulted in improved performances but maybe it was worth a try. Certainly the players who were terminally dropped from the team never complained. One is reminded of the line in Voltaire's "Candide" a propos the execution of the English Admiral Byng for losing a battle: "In this country it is good to kill an admiral from time to time *pour l'encourager les autres*".

Not that nepotism is confined to the third world. It flourishes too in the land of the free and the home of the brave. When reproached for having appointed his brother Robert attorney general, John F. Kennedy retorted that he wanted to give him some legal experience before he went out to practise law. And it is well to recall that the current occupant of the White House was elected thanks to the votes of justices of the Supreme Court who had been appointed by his daddy.

Of course there have been rulers and men of influence who did not practise nepotism. Take for example our own King Herod. History has given him a bad press. With good reason you might say. It seems that he kept a kosher home; but like Uday Hussein he had what you might call anti-social tendencies. It cannot have been much fun being his son. An adherent of the "tall poppy"' doctrine centuries before Stalin, Herod executed two stepsons, Alexander and Aristobulus, and then, for good measure, his own son Antipater. Herod's penchant for filicide coupled with his observance of the Jewish dietary laws prompted the Emperor Augustus to remark that he would rather be Herod's pig than his son.

The story in one of the Gospels that Herod carried out a massacre of children is unfounded but he did give orders – happily disobeyed – that on his own death the heads of the leading families of Judea be killed; that way his death would not be an occasion for rejoicing. Suspicious of his wife Mariamne, the last Hasmonean princess, he had her put to death. But he loved her in his fashion. After her death he had her body embalmed and according to Josephus, repeated in the Talmud, continued exercising his conjugal rights on her corpse.

Nepotism has existed from time immemorial but the expression as such originates from the Italian word for nephew – *nipote*. The notoriously corrupt and venal Renaissance popes referred to their illegitimate children as their nephews and shamelessly advanced their interests. By far the most colourful papal family was the Borgias, leading candidates for the nepotism hall of fame. When people referred to Pope Alexander VI – Rodrigo Borgia before his accession to the papacy – as the Holy Father, they were talking literally. Of his many children by a succession of mistresses, those best known to history are Cesare and Lucrezia Borgia. His father elevated Cesare to cardinal when Cesare was aged 22. The model for Machiavelli's prince, he was an able ruler but his spirituality left much to be desired. Perhaps he never made a graven image but he left none of the other commandments unviolated. His sister Lucrezia shared the family propensity for homicide though her thing was poison. But she certainly loved her family. She is said to have bestowed her favours on her father and her brother, those less than perfect princes of the Church.

Yet the Borgias' nepotism was confined to Italy. For a world-class nepotist we need to wait for Napoleon Bonaparte whose blatant exercise of imperial power in advancing the interests of his family most certainly contributed to his downfall. Europe was his family business and he made three of his brothers kings. He did well by his favourite generals as well. The descendants of Marshal Bernadotte sit on the throne of Sweden to this day.

You might think that an institution with an ancestry as ancient as nepotism would have been the subject of numerous books, theses and doctorates over the years. We are assured, however, by Adam Bellow, the author of a book published only this year entitled "In Praise of Nepotism" that the subject has never before been treated at book length. It is sad to report that this book has not filled the gap. Much of this long and – it has to be said – tedious apologia for an indefensible practice is given over to a history of dynasties and to lists of people who have inherited their genius from similarly gifted forebears. Yet in what sense can, say, Martin Amis or Lucien Freud be said to have benefited from nepotism? They may owe their talents to their genes but surely not to any kind of family preferment. Disarmingly the author claims that he himself is the beneficiary of nepotism. Were he not the son of Nobel prizewinner Saul Bellow, he suggests, he might have found it difficult to find a publisher. It is hard to disagree.

In making his case, the younger Bellow invokes the theory of kin selection, a favoured explanation of the evolutionary problem of altruism. He shows convincingly that it is natural for us to favour our relatives. But you knew that already, didn't you? It is apparent that the author has fallen prey to the naturalistic fallacy: the belief that what is "natural"' is therefore good. As Steven Pinker devastatingly demonstrates in his book, "The Blank Slate," this conflation of "is" and "ought" underlies some of the most pernicious doctrines of modern times. It bedevils any rational study of differences between the sexes and races for fear that if differences were shown to exist they would justify discrimination. Even worse, the naturalistic fallacy is responsible for Social Darwinism, the theory beloved of Nazi ideologues that because nature favours the fittest, might is right.

For Bellow, nepotism "feels good" and "represents a valuable corrective to the extreme tendencies of meritocracy." What next? "The Case for Bribery and Corruption"? "The Pros and Cons of Pedophilia"? Having read the book, it is hard to believe that any objective reader will find himself convinced by this defence of a practice that is reprehensible, inefficient and a scourge of good government.

12 December, 2003

The Trait of Sodom

Older readers may remember a musical from the early 1950s called "Kismet." The action takes place in Baghdad, eleven centuries before Shock and Awe. This is Baghdad of the Arabian Nights, peopled with wazirs, poets, beautiful princesses and colourful beggars. There is a caliph with the usual caliph's equipment: turban, sash, scimitar and well-stocked harem. This mildly pleasing piece of Middle East hokum has been restaged from time to time, mainly, I suspect, because even after "Hair" in the 1960s made its mark as the first full-frontal Broadway musical, the public (or half of it, anyhow) has never tired of seeing oodles of odalisques with death-defying décolletages lolling around in diaphanous pajamas. The 1955 film of "Kismet" had Vic Damone in the role of the caliph. Because I had heard his name long before I saw it in print, I still think of him as Victor Moan. What a perfect name! The Happy Family of Mr. Bun the baker, Mr. Block the builder and Mr. Tuckin the chef can now be augmented by Mr. Moan the crooner.

Whatever the shortcomings of the plot, the score is excellent. It ought to be because, in an act of musical grave robbery, the writers of "Kismet" shamelessly pilfered the work of the 19th-century Russian composer, Alexander Borodin. The show's music is principally derived from Borodin's sublime second string quartet and from his opera, "Prince Igor".

The celebrated "Polovtsian Dances" are the source of a witty number in the show - "Not Since Nineveh," which - in its Danny Kaye version - was at one time a treasured record of mine. According to the song, eighth-century Baghdad was an unprecedented sin city, the axis of an evil far more alluring than George Dubya ever dreamed of. Space constraints prevent me from giving the lyrics in full, but I cannot resist quoting the last lines of one of the verses: "Not since Nebuchadnezzar's hanging gardens went to pot / Not since that village near Gomorrah got (pause) too hot (pause) for Lot / No, not since Nineveh."

I cite this verse because it is, to my knowledge, the only instance in literature that Gomorrah is mentioned to the exclusion of its more colourful Sodomite neighbour. Gomorrah may well have been Sodom's equal in wickedness, but it has always been a stooge, a satellite. Gomorrah is Robin to Sodom's Batman, Watson to Sodom's Holmes. The Lord did a good job of wiping Gomorrah off the map with fire, adding brimstone for good measure and, so far as I know, the town never made a comeback. There is no Gomorrah in the Israeli gazetteer - but, in contrast, Sodom is today a thriving area on the Western shore of the Dead Sea, known usually by its Hebrew name of Sdom. Indeed it is a popular tourist destination, though I agree that saying you are off to Sodom for your vacation might still cause a ripple at a Manhattan dinner party. Disappointingly, Sdom is for the health tourist, not the sex tourist. If your problem is an outsize libido, you are better off going to Thailand. All that a dirty weekend in Sdom conveys is getting caked in mud.

Traditional Jewish sources do not stress the practice with which the world associates Sodom. Although the dictionary definition of sodomy lacks precision, there is no doubt that it has a derogatory sexual connotation. The ninth Marquess of Queensberry left his visiting card at a London club addressed to "Oscar Wilde posing as a somdomite." The aristocratic author of the rules of pugilism may not have known how to spell, but everyone knew what he meant. There is, of course, clear biblical authority for reading the sins of Sodom as offenses of sexual perversity. Only a providential attack of blindness visited on the men of Sodom saved Lot's angelic guests from a fate worse than death. Yet, while rabbinic literature attributes all kinds of misanthropic behaviour to the Sodomites, it is rarely of a sexual nature.

For the sages of the Talmud, what particularly characterized the Sodomites was excessive mean-spiritedness. The Talmudic reference to the "trait of Sodom" is to a characteristic known in Western culture as the dog in the manger. That beast, in Aesop's fable, ferociously prevented the cattle from eating the hay in the stable though he himself was unable to eat it. The ox articulated the trait of Sodom in declaring the moral: that people often begrudge others what they cannot enjoy themselves. The trait of Sodom is so commonplace a feature of modern life that we fail to remark it. The driver of that huge gas-guzzling 4x4 that stops in the intersection in front of you so as to block you when your light turns green, though he himself has gained no advantage, is a Sodomite. The man who wants to prevent you from hearing Wagner though he has never been to a concert in his life is another.

The trait of Sodom often appears in the form of class envy. It was very much in evidence in the zeal that British legislators showed two years ago in passing a law criminalizing fox hunting. I truly have no axe to grind here. Not only have I never taken part in the pastime that Oscar Wilde described as the "unspeakable in pursuit of the uneatable," I have never been anywhere near a hunt. Since the time that Jacob stayed at home perfecting his recipe for lentil soup while Esau went hunting, Jews have never gone in for the chase; they prefer canasta. "Jewish Fox Hunters" surely qualifies for the title of the world's shortest book. The only character who could conceivably appear in that book would be that iconic fox-hunting man, the poet Siegfried Sassoon. But, despite his Jewish ancestry, he was brought up in the Church of England and embraced Roman Catholicism before his death. I find it easy to contemplate a world without fox hunting or, come to think of it, of any other kind of hunting, but I cannot escape the impression that the MPs who passed the Hunting Act, 2004, were less motivated by their concern for animal rights than they were at depriving those red-coated toffs of their pleasures.

And, getting closer to home, I suspect that the yawn that has greeted the imminent closing of Israel's only full-sized golf course, at Caesarea, contains more than an element of the trait of Sodom. The owners of the land, the Caesarea Development Corporation, propose to build luxury houses in the middle of the course. The general public has shown scant sympathy for the plight of the business executives, corporate lawyers, airline pilots, diplomats, media personalities and consultant surgeons who are to be deprived of the game they love. But it is a shame. Personally, though no longer a golfer, I would feel the kind of ache at its disappearance that I would at the extinction of an indigenous species of animal. We can live without golf and we can live without spotted owls, but life is just that bit better with them.

I thought of the Caesarea golf course when I read a couple of weeks ago of the death of that peerlessly funny writer, Art Buchwald. Art played at Caesarea in the early 1960s. He wrote that it was the only golf course in the world where, if you hooked, the ball would drop into the sea and if you sliced, it would fall into enemy territory. He might also have remarked that the course is beautiful. There are so few spots in Israel where you can lose yourself in nature and the thought that such a wild, sylvan area will be covered by rows of villas to be sold as second homes to absentee tourists is a melancholy one.

Robert Browning's Andrea del Sarto believed that a man's reach should exceed his grasp or "what's a heaven for?" When I did play golf I played it spectacularly badly, but the laws of probability decreed that, playing week after week, things would occasionally go sufficiently right for me to catch that glimpse of a golfing heaven beyond my grasp, but within my reach. It was another poet, the bard of suburbia, John Betjeman, who best described the euphoria that a poor golfer feels when the ball runs well for him. In his poem

"Seaside Golf," he describes a rare birdie three. We follow him as he plays an iron to the green:

And spite of grassy banks between
I knew I'd find it on the green.
And so I did. It lay content
Two paces from the pin;
A steady putt and then it went
Oh, most surely in.
The very turf rejoiced to see
That quite unprecedented three.
Ah! Seaweed smells from sandy caves
And thyme and mist in whiffs,
Incoming tide, Atlantic waves
Slapping the sunny cliffs,
Lark song and sea sounds in the air
And splendour, splendour everywhere.

Splendour indeed! Don't let the Sodomites take it away.

9 February, 2007

*M*ichael's Memoirs

I move in literate circles – most of my friends can both read and write – but I still find it mildly surprising that so few of my acquaintances have managed to reach pensionable age without burdening the world with their memoirs. I have a shelf in what I like to call my library that is entirely devoted to the self-published reminiscences of people I know. I exclude from this virtual book club anything written by professional authors. Any book that has been brought out by a reputable publisher with an eye to making money will not find its way to this shelf.

I have been obliged, for this reason, to relegate to another section of my library the books of friends who tainted themselves by accepting filthy lucre for their memoirs. The distinction between amateurs and professionals – between gentlemen and players, in cricket's supremely snobbish parlance – has been blurred in recent years, but I apply it rigorously. To qualify for admission to this shelf, you have to have written for love, not money.

I suppose I have a score of these books. I have read all of them, something I cannot say about the lengthening line of weighty biographies vying for my attention on my other shelves. The books come in all shapes and sizes. At one end of the spectrum you can see the results of vanity publishing at its finest: hard-backed volumes with attractive covers, replete with photographs and complete with an index. At the other end are the no-frills samizdat versions consisting of photocopied folio pages in spiral bindings. The memoirs reflect a diversity of experience: business success, military exploits, family life, friendships with the great and the good.

These are not works of the imagination. They tell of events and of people. They tend not to be contemplative. The memoirs tell it as it is. If any of these writers waited anxiously for a goodnight kiss from his mother, as Proust notoriously does over 30 pages, he omits it in his memoirs. Nor are the books remotely confessional. There are no cringe-worthy incidents, no guilty secrets,

111

Michael's Memoirs

we are not made privy to any skeletons in any cupboards, and there are no failures – or none, at any rate, that are not retrieved by subsequent triumphs.

The public clamour for me to publish my own memoirs has so far proved resistible. Not that I would be unwilling to hazard the handsome sum that such an enterprise would cost me. I am not immune from narcissistic impulses but, for the life of me, I cannot think of anything that has happened to me that might be remotely interesting to anyone. Unlike one of my memoirists, I was never on a first-name basis with either Lord Rothschild or Sir Isaiah Berlin. Nor, as another memoir reports, did I give King George VI a ride in a Bren-gun carrier. The king then said, "Thank you. I enjoyed the ride" – a fair example of His Majesty's reputed powers of conversation. Nor did I make a daring escape from a German prisoner-of-war camp as did another memoir-writing friend.

My memories of my own spectacularly undistinguished military career are of the almost-unrelieved monotony that I believe to be the lot of the average soldier. The aftermath of the Yom Kippur War saw me on the far side of the Suez Canal, reading "War and Peace" while ostensibly guarding anti-aircraft installations that seemed to me well able to look after themselves.

A commercial currently being aired on the radio – imbecilic even by the less than exacting standards of the Israeli advertising industry – asks you where you were when some important event took place. It seems that, due to the lack of the pill the ad is peddling, you were probably in the lavatory. Stupid, yes, but it gave me an idea. Could my memoir perhaps describe my interaction with the world-shattering events of which I was a contemporary? I have, after all, lived, in the words of the apocryphal Chinese curse, in interesting times. True I was a bit late for the invention of moveable type and the publication of the "Origin of Species," but the dropping of the first atomic bomb, the discovery of the structure of the DNA molecule and Israel's gold medal for windsurfing all occurred on my watch.

What, for instance, was I doing at the time of the Munich Agreement? In September 1938, I was four. I cannot boast of my precocious scepticism over peace for our time, but while Mr. Chamberlain was cozying up to Hitler, I, in unsuccessfully attempting to placate a wrathful parent, was discovering the inefficacy of appeasement.

I and my friend Judy were left alone upstairs in our house. We went into the bathroom and having first taken the precaution of plugging the bath, ran both taps, predictably causing a flood. The first inkling the adults downstairs had that anything was amiss was when a damp patch appeared in the kitchen ceiling. Judy, who was almost three at the time, though I recall her as being the instigator, got away scot-free on the grounds of diminished responsibility. I, on the other hand, though I put forward the oldest male defense in the book – "The woman gave me of the tree and I did eat" (Genesis 3.12) – received the back of a Mason Pearson hairbrush, a punishment I regarded as, to use the current buzzword, disproportionate.

As my recollections of the battle of Stalingrad, the assassination of President Kennedy and the fall of the Berlin Wall are equally irrelevant, I have had to consider another approach for my memoirs. True I have left no footprints in the sands of time, but I could, at least, write of my life in a parallel universe, in a private world that I suspect most people inhabit – the world of Walter Mitty. Walter has escaped the bounds of the James Thurber short story in which he originally appeared and, thanks mainly to the Danny Kaye film of the same title, has become a name deeply embedded in popular culture. Thurber's "The Secret Life of Walter Mitty," tells of a meek, hen-pecked suburbanite who has a fantasy life in which he successively becomes the commander of a navy hydroplane, a brilliant heart surgeon, a debonair killer and a World War I fighter pilot.

Inspired by Walter Mitty, the opening chapter of my memoirs will read something like this:

"It is with not a little hesitation that I set pen to paper to chronicle an exceptional life. Hitherto, my unwillingness to write my autobiography has stemmed from the life-long modesty that my friends have long regarded as my besetting sin. In overcoming this reluctance, I am inspired by the example of our teacher Moses who, in the fourth of his five books, wrote of himself: "Now the man Moses was very meek, above all the men that were upon the face of the earth" (Numbers 12.3). I, too, am renowned for my meekness.

The year that I was awarded three Nobel Prizes – for Literature, Physics and Peace was admittedly unusual. The physics prize was something of a fluke. While I was waiting to bat against Australia in the Lords Test, I relaxed by reading a book on quantum mechanics. As I piled up a double century, I found myself worrying about a discrepancy in what I had been reading. I had, it became clear, spotted a flaw in quantum theory, which enabled me a week or two later to come up with the long-sought "Theory of Everything," the Holy Grail of theoretical physics.

I suppose that I cannot avoid mentioning my six gold medals at that summer's Olympic Games, remarkable principally because I broke four world records in the process. I passed the drug test summa cum laude, of course. No one had yet devised a method of detecting the substance that was responsible for my extraordinary athletic prowess: chicken soup with noodles. I should add that during the Games, I received a phone call from Pinchas Zuckerman inviting me to bring my clarinet that evening and join him and some friends (Itzhak Perlman, Yo Yo Ma and a violist whose name escapes me) in the Brahms Quintet. The exalted feeling that lingered from that performance inspired me to new heights in the next day's 1,500-metre finals.

Similar fortune attended me when, while waiting to escort Julia Roberts to the Academy Awards ceremony, I was idly reading a grammar of Inuit. It struck me that there was a close connection between the Eskimo-Aleut languages and ancient Etruscan. Serendipitously, I had solved the mystery of the origins of the Etruscan language.

I have the feeling that all this may sound like bragging, so I shall leave it to others to recount my victory the following week over the IBM chess computer Big Blue only a month or two after it had made mincemeat of Gary Kasparov".

On second thought, I won't write my memoirs. I'll take up bellringing instead.

11 August, 2006

HEAVILY HISTORICAL

Was Lopez Guilty?

In the rigid stratification of Shakespeare's dramatic works into tragedies, histories and comedies, "The Merchant of Venice" is classified as a comedy. And in the Aristotelian sense that is what it is. After trials (in more than one sense) and tribulations, its three pairs of star-crossed lovers unite and presumably live happily ever after.

Have I left out anything? Yes, I have. I have not mentioned the brooding presence in the play of one of the most memorable characters in literature – the tragic figure of Shylock, the Jewish moneylender. By the end of the play he is compelled to convert to Christianity and his beloved daughter has stolen his money in collusion with her Christian lover. Some happy ending! Like loving Levy's Rye Bread, you don't have to be Jewish to wonder why this play is a comedy.

"The Merchant of Venice" without Shylock is the proverbial Hamlet without the Prince of Denmark. He is omnipresent; he is the ghost at the feast. Without him the play is another "feel-good" romantic comedy. With him it acquires a malevolent spirit that makes it immortal. He so dominates the action that one is surprised to learn that Shylock appears in only five of the play's twenty scenes and that the merchant of the title is not Shylock but Antonio.

In the preface to his absorbing study "Shylock: Four Hundred Years in the Life of a Legend" (Chatto and Windus, 1992), John Gross writes that each Shakespeare play is a self-contained world and that to concentrate on a single character is to risk losing sight of the whole. He then goes on to assert that Shylock is a special case. His myth works independently of the play in which he appears.

From Kean to Dustin Hoffman via Irving, Gielgud and Olivier, the part of Shylock has attracted the great actors. In America the role had been played by a real-life villain, John Wilkes Booth, the assassin of Abraham Lincoln, although it was his brother Edwin Booth whose 1867 performance in New York stands out as one of the great Shylocks. These days, Shylock is usually played sympathetically but, in the past, he was often an anti-Semitic caricature. In Vienna in 1943, Werner Krauss, who had played Jew Süss in the infamous 1940 film of that name, predictably played Shylock as a "Der Stürmer" cartoon.

Seen through the prism of the Holocaust, Shylock's insistence on extracting his pound of flesh is unhappily redolent of the charges of ritual murder that have dogged the history of the Jews since the early Middle Ages. But Shakespeare, though arguably the greatest writer that ever lived, was a man of his time. He knew no Jews. For him, they were as exotic as the ghosts and witches that people his plays. To impute anti-Semitism to him for his creation of Shylock is as anachronistic as to accuse Maimonides of not prescribing antibiotics in his medical practice.

But Shakespeare would certainly have known of at least one reputed Jew, Dr. Roderigo Lopez. Lopez had been the personal physician to Queen Elizabeth I and on June 7, 1594, about two years before Shakespeare completed "The Merchant of Venice," Lopez was hung, drawn and quartered on Tyburn Hill for conspiring to poison the queen.

Lopez, though a practising Protestant, was a Marrano of Portuguese origin, part of a small community that lived in London at the time. The Marranos, it will be recalled, were the crypto-Jews of Spain and Portugal who had been forcibly converted to Christianity in the 14th and 15th centuries. The term Marrano has pejorative connotations and historians writing in Hebrew have in recent years avoided the word. Those writing in English have retained the term Marranos, perhaps because the more politically-correct Hebrew term *anusim* does not read happily in English.

Because the play was completed soon after the Lopez trial, it is commonly assumed that, in writing "The Merchant of Venice," Shakespeare was influenced by the case. In most annotated editions of the play Lopez rates a mention. James Joyce certainly made the connection when writing in "Ulysses": "Shylock chimes with the Jew-baiting that followed the hanging and quartering of the queen's leech Lopez".

Played against the backdrop of the struggle between the Protestant England of Elizabeth I and the ultra-Catholic Spain of Philip II, the Lopez Affair is a convoluted tale of espionage and counter-espionage, involving an international Marrano spy network (it seems likely that the Marranos were the first to bring to England the news of the embarkation of the Spanish Armada), bitter factional fights in the court of the queen and the efforts of Portuguese Marranos to supplant Philip II and put their own candidate on the throne of Portugal.

Until recently Dr. Lopez had, for me, remained a marginal note in the

"Merchant of Venice." I was sure he was innocent. This was certainly the received opinion in the standard histories of Anglo-Jewry. So I was unprepared for my encounter with Professor David Katz, who, over dinner at the home of mutual friends, stunned me by declaring that he had come to the conclusion that Lopez was indeed guilty of treason. I recall protesting that he would be telling me next that Dreyfus had passed those secrets. But Professor Katz has to be taken seriously. Chairman of the Department of History at Tel Aviv University, he is a formidable scholar of Anglo-Jewish history and has written a fascinating account of the Lopez Affair in his book "The Jews in the History of England 1485-1850" (Oxford University Press, 1994).

The Lopez Affair suddenly became hot. The professor's case against Lopez had put the Katz among the pigeons and champions of Lopez were not slow to react. An attack on Lopez was seen by some as an attack on the Jews. It is easy to understand why. Of all the false accusations that have been levelled against Jews over their long history, the poison myth is the most potent and the most enduring – and it frequently features Jewish physicians. In mediaeval times the Jews poisoned the wells to spread the Black Death; Stalin's Jewish doctors plotted to poison him; and Jewish doctors have been accused by Louis Farrakhan of deliberately spreading AIDS in the ghettos. Furthermore, staged in London contemporaneously with the Lopez trial, Christopher Marlowe had his "Jew of Malta" poison a whole nunnery.

So it is not surprising that defenders of Jewish honour took up the cudgels on behalf of Lopez. The counter-attack on Katz came in 1996, predictably in *Commentary*, the house organ of America's neo-conservatives. In an article entitled "Shakespeare, Shylock and the Jews," William Meyers declared Lopez innocent and accused Katz of having an "agenda," a bit rich coming from that most agenda-heavy of journals. Even a 400-year-old trial becomes a bone of political contention in the cultural wars of the Jews. Meyers further claims that Shakespeare, on the back of the Lopez case, intentionally did harm to the Jewish people through his creation of Shylock. Katz is in distinguished company.

Having been virtually neglected for centuries, the Lopez Affair has generated unprecedented literary activity in the past decade. David Katz appeared in a BBC documentary on the subject and there have been two recent full-length books, one in English, finding Lopez guilty and one in Hebrew, by a prominent Israeli lawyer, absolving him.

Was he guilty? I pass. I don't think Lopez really intended to poison the queen; she herself did not believe it and sought to delay his execution until political necessity compelled her to sanction it. But he had accepted a valuable jewel from England's great enemy Philip II for services that, by definition, were inimical to the interests of England. Up to the neck, as he was, in the murky world of espionage, he was very likely guilty of treason according to the laws of that time.

Guilty or innocent, Lopez was not the victim of an anti-Jewish conspiracy. True the trial must have influenced the creation of Shylock, but his Jewishness was not central to the trial. It was not a kangaroo court, though it was certainly a show trial. Reported by none other than Francis Bacon, it was prosecuted by the great jurist Sir Edward Coke and the commission that adjudicated the case was a roll call of the highest of the land.

As for the unhappy Lopez, he even screwed up his own last words. According to a contemporary report he declared on the scaffold that he loved the queen as well as he loved Jesus Christ. The reporter, William Camden, adds "which coming from a man of the Jewish Profession moved no small Laughter in the Standers-by." He was being sincere, but oh, how he got it wrong! It must have put the mob, standing in serried rows at what is now Marble Arch, in a fine mood to watch his public disembowelment.

They were now ready to enjoy Shylock.

23 July, 2004

The Strangest Man to Play Baseball

Historians have long speculated on the surprise trip of the German physicist Werner Heisenberg to German-occupied Copenhagen in September, 1941. Heisenberg had travelled from Germany to make an unheralded visit to his half-Jewish Danish mentor Niels Bohr, but what was said at the meeting between these two colossi of 20th-century physics has never been conclusively established though Bohr lived on until 1962 and Heisenberg to 1976. Each of them later gave conflicting accounts of the meeting, which ended their friendship and which, nearly sixty years later, became the subject of Michael Frayn's brilliant and, given the recherché nature of its subject matter, surprisingly popular play, "Copenhagen".

Why the meeting interests historians outside the arcane world of particle physics is that Heisenberg was, at the time of the meeting, the head of the German atomic programme and, two years later, Bohr escaped to the West, where he advised on the Manhattan Project, the Allies' successful programme to develop an atomic bomb. That the Nazis did not succeed in developing the bomb, or indeed getting near one, is history – and much has been made of how the Führer shot himself in the foot by driving the ablest of his physicists into exile where they worked for the Americans and the British – but Frayn's play brought to a boil a simmering controversy as to why Germany had failed so spectacularly in the race for the bomb.

Heisenberg is best known to the general public for his "uncertainty principle," one of the cornerstones of quantum mechanics. According to this principle, the more precisely you measure the position of a particle, the less you are able to measure its momentum, and vice versa. And it is uncertainty that is the principal theme of Frayn's play. As Heisenberg says in the play: "Everyone understands uncertainty. Or thinks he does. No one understands my trip to Copenhagen. The more I've explained, the deeper the uncertainty has become." They did talk about the feasibility of manufacturing an atomic bomb, but Bohr later maintained that Heisenberg was trying to pump him for information whereas Heisenberg claimed that he had raised the issue of the morality of making such a weapon.

In 2002, a battle royal raged in the columns of the *New York Review of Books* between the partisans of two irreconcilable historical views of the German bomb effort. Put crudely, one camp maintains that the Germans did not get the bomb because Heisenberg and his team got their sums wrong; their opponents' version – gingerly supported by Frayn – is that Heisenberg did not really try because he was deeply ambivalent over handing over to the Nazis a weapon of such power. In a postscript to the play, Frayn writes that there is material in the affair for several more plays and films. Certainly there is one related story positively screaming for dramatic treatment: had Heisenberg been further along on the trail of the bomb, his career would have been prematurely terminated by an extraordinary American spy rejoicing in the name of Moe Berg.

When I say that Moe Berg was one of the most unusual spies ever to feature in the annals of espionage, I speak with authority. I cannot claim ever to have risked my own neck at the Great Game – the only person I ever knew with licence to kill was our local *shohet* (ritual slaughterer) – but I have a lifetime of experience as an armchair spy. The literature of espionage has been my constant companion. But not even the most fanciful of spy novelists could have invented Moe Berg.

The first surprising thing about Moe Berg (1902-1972) was that he was a professional athlete. He played for 15 seasons in major league baseball. So, before I focus on Moe Berg I propose, for non-American readers, to provide some British disinformation on baseball. The game has an honourable ancestry, being mentioned even in Jane Austen's "Northanger Abbey." It derives from an English children's game called rounders (Americans also play basketball, which is based on the British girls' game of netball, and American football, which is a thuggish version of a thuggish British sport called rugby). Although its championship event is known as the World Series, baseball is not today played widely outside America.

I expect that I shall go to my grave without understanding baseball but I have acquired, through regular exposure to American culture and literature (much like inhaling secondhand smoke), a smattering of baseball lore. Many American authors, like Stephen Jay Gould, a minor literary idol of mine, write lovingly of the game and I have a friend – otherwise normal in every respect – who has converted a room of his house into a shrine to the New York Yankees.

So I find that I can recite the names of a score of baseball stars. Unlike in England, where Jewish professional cricketers are about as common as Belzer

Hasidim in the Sahara, in the U.S. a number of Jews have played professional baseball and some of them have played it rather well. Who does not know of Sandy Koufax, who famously refused to pitch for the Dodgers on Yom Kippur, or of Detroit's Hall of Fame slugger Hank Greenberg? I would have liked to have added to my list the name of the great Hank Aaron – surely of the priestly tribe – but learned that his ancestors did not, as did mine, leave Africa by walking across the Red Sea (since when, Jews have had bad feet), but – even more uncomfortably – sailed westward from the dark continent packed in the hold of a ship.

And somewhere from the recesses of my memory I conjured up the name of a ballplayer called Moe Berg, though I knew nothing of his accomplishments. To be regarded as the brainiest ballplayer ever does not sound much of an accolade – professional sportsmen are not normally noted for their intellects – but Moe Berg truly was a prodigy of learning. He graduated magna cum laude in modern languages from Princeton and finished second in his class at Columbia Law School while playing professional baseball for the Chicago White Sox. It is sad to report that he was no great shakes as a ballplayer – the best known remark about him was by a teammate who said, "Moe Berg can speak seven (or 12 or 15, depending on which of his three biographies you read) languages and can't hit in any of them." Which is why it was curious that in 1934 he should have been selected to tour Japan with a team of all-stars including Babe Ruth and Lou Gehrig. The hypothesis is that Berg, who spoke fluent Japanese, was already moonlighting in what has been called the second-oldest profession – espionage.

Not only was Berg a linguist, he was a polymath who could grasp complex scientific ideas. This made him uniquely qualified to carry out the mission that by rights should have earned him a place in the espionage Hall of Fame. Late in World War II, his superiors at the Office of Strategic Services entrusted Berg with the task of determining how far the Nazis had advanced with their atomic project. If necessary, he was to assassinate the head of the programme, Werner Heisenberg.

Berg, who spoke perfect German, caught up with Heisenberg in 1944 in Zurich. From a conversation with him, Berg concluded that the Germans were nowhere near a bomb, whereupon he decided not to shoot Heisenberg. Berg continued to look for evidence and spent the last months of the war behind German lines on its trail. It was Moe Berg who provided the Allies with the first substantial account of the German nuclear project. He became, in fact, a very important spy.

In contemporary intelligence parlance, Berg was HUMINT, human intelligence. HUMINT has, in recent years, been largely displaced by satellites and computers. We can thank the replacement of human agents in espionage by electronics for such intelligence triumphs as the reports of large stocks of weapons of mass destruction in Iraq and the failure to conjecture why a number of young Saudis were taking lessons in Florida to fly passenger jets, without investing in the additional expense of learning to land them.

Brave, dedicated linguists like Moe Berg are a rare commodity in intelligence today. Had he killed Heisenberg, Berg could have acquired the same kind of dubious immortality that posterity has conferred on John Wilkes Booth and Lee Harvey Oswald. But he didn't shoot and, prodigiously gifted as he was, he died in 1972 an almost forgotten figure. His body was cremated and his ashes were brought to Israel. In keeping with his shadowy life, no one knows the whereabouts of his remains, though, according to one source, the ashes are scattered somewhere on Mount Scopus.

The great manager of the Yankees, Casey Stengel, called Moe Berg "the strangest man ever to play baseball." No doubt he was, but it is somehow an inadequate epitaph for this remarkable man.

15 April, 2005

Stampede of Folly

Enguerrand de Coucy VII (1340-1397) was one of the great nobles of France, the son-in-law of Edward III, king of England, and a major figure in the Europe of his time. Yet, although I have learned, to my cost, never to underestimate the erudition of my readers, I think it unlikely that many would be familiar with Enguerrand's name had he not been the protagonist of Barbara Tuchman's 1978 tour de force, "A Distant Mirror." Tuchman hit on the idea of using Enguerrand's life as the peg on which to hang her fascinating account of what she epitomizes in the book's secondary title as the "The Calamitous 14th Century." The Sire of Coucy, whose life spanned much of the century, was a good choice. He was personally involved in much of what went on and he lost a parent in each of the two defining events of that terrible century. His father was killed at the battle of Crécy, an early encounter of the terrible Hundred Years War between France and England. His mother, along with one in every three of the inhabitants of Europe, died in the worst plague in recorded history, the Black Death, that tragic scourge that put its stamp on that and succeeding centuries.

I have read virtually all of Barbara Tuchman's books. Her interests were eclectic. She wrote of ancient, medieval and contemporary events with equal facility. In the writing of history for non-specialists she has, in my view, no rival. You read her as you read a novel, and a well-written one at that. She once said that she tried to create movement in every paragraph she wrote, and her books are evidence that she succeeded. I single out "A Distant Mirror" because I find it the one that best represents her enviable ability to revitalize the past. You could say that she brings the Black Death to life.

However, it is another book of Tuchman's whose title and central thesis have achieved iconic status. In 1984, she published "The March of Folly: From Troy to Vietnam." The book describes a phenomenon she identifies in history: the perennial pursuit by governments of policies contrary to their own interests. The bulk of the book consists of four hugely entertaining case histories that bear out her theory. Starting with the Wooden Horse of Troy, she proceeds to tell of the Renaissance popes whose purblind policies led to the Protestant Reformation; the cack-handed actions of the British toward the American colonists, bringing about the secession of the colonies; and, finally, the tragic entanglement of the United States in Vietnam.

The stories are splendidly told but, to my mind, the thesis is banal. It is not that governments sometimes act against their own interests; they seldom do anything else. The book is like one of those portmanteau films that used to be popular, featuring disparate stories vaguely connected by some faint unifying theme.

Still, Tuchman's book became a byword for the inability of governments to see beyond their noses, and it was inevitable that reviewers of Gershom Gorenberg's recently published book, "The Accidental Empire: Israel and the Birth of the Settlements, 1967-1977" (Times Books) should trot out the march of folly to account for the Israeli government's actions – "policy" would be too positive a word – conniving at, but rarely approving outright the colonization by Jewish settlers of the areas unexpectedly conquered by the Israel Defence Forces in the Six-Day War.

Like Buridan's ass that died of starvation because, placed between two bags of hay, he could not decide from which one to eat, Israel's leaders, faced with the territorial windfall that their victorious armies had left on their doorsteps, neither annexed the newly conquered areas nor returned them. Instead, they dithered and, in the course of their dithering, they permitted the construction of settlements in the occupied territories, accidentally, as Gorenberg argues, acquiring an empire and painting the country into the corner in which it now finds itself.

Gorenberg's story ends in 1977, the year that the Likud party first came to power and turned the march of folly into a stampede. But it was the previous Labour government that had legitimized it. At that time, there were only 11,000 settlers. From then on, construction proceeded apace and new non-ideological settlers, attracted by a standard of living they had no hope of attaining in Israel proper, started to populate the new West Bank towns as cheap subsidized housing became available to them. The settlements were no longer reversible and the empire could no longer be regarded as accidental.

Not that there was ever anything accidental in the single-minded actions of the new breed of religious nationalists who, to this day, form the ideological core of the settlement movement. For them, disdainful of the rights of the people who inhabited the land and unhampered by any commitment to democracy and the rule of law, settling the land was God's work. The conquest of the territories was the climax to a divinely directed process, and settling the land was a further step on the road to redemption. Don't thank the Israel Air Force; it was all a miracle wrought by God. For that matter, don't blame Hitler; he, too, was part of the divine plan. There was a time when, if you expressed such ideas aloud, a plain white van would shortly arrive at your door to take you away. Nowadays, it is the rationals who are on the defensive throughout the world.

But those intoxicated by a perverse pietistic ideology were not alone in espousing irrational views on the settlements. The British Empire is famously said to have been acquired in a fit of absentmindedness. The secular politicians, whose fecklessness Gorenberg blames for creating the accidental empire, were not being absentminded. To extend the Trojan analogy, there was no shortage of Cassandras to warn them of their folly. As social democrats, they should surely have realized that imposing one's will on a hostile population has no long-term future in a post-colonial world. And as Zionists, they well knew that – as even Ariel Sharon realized 30 years later – the idea of settling the whole Land of Israel was, because of the demographics, incompatible with the existence of a Jewish state. They seem to have believed that a Jewish majority could be preserved for the long term by mass immigration from North America, a chimera as groundless as the dream of the settlers that one day they will wake up and find that all the Palestinians have decamped overnight. If Eshkol, Dayan and Allon were alive today, they would surely be aghast at what they so recklessly set in motion. And what of the founder of the early settlement, Elon Moreh, Shimon Peres, he of the Nobel Peace Prize and the New Middle East? Does he not regret his part in bringing about the situation that he so much deplores today, but did more than his bit to promote?

But Barbara Tuchman herself would not have applauded the analogy that has been so glibly drawn between her march of folly and the Israeli government's toleration of the settlements. She would not have added a chapter to the book to encompass Gorenberg's accidental empire. She was a romantic about Israel, which she admired almost uncritically. A passionate Zionist, she was proud that the coastal city of Netanya was named after her grandfather, Nathan Strauss.

Her first major book, "Bible and Sword," which culminates in the Balfour Declaration, is an enthralling study of a historical attachment felt by Englishmen to the Jews and to the Holy Land. In her introduction to the 1983 edition of the book, she explains why she could not have extended it to cover the birth of the State of Israel: "As regards the fortunes of the Jews and of Israel, I am not detached but emotionally involved. That ... invalidates the work of a historian." And, in the same introduction, she defends the settlements against their American critics: "Israeli settlements in occupied territory have been virtuously denounced by Americans with short memories of how Texas was settled and then annexed when no question of survival was at stake".

In 1983 when Tuchman wrote these words, the accidental empire of the settlements was expanding apace. As she said, she loved Israel too much to be detached, but she was too good a historian not, if put to the test, to have judged the settlement enterprise to be ultimately a futile one. In an essay entitled "Israel's Swift Sword," published after the 1967 war, she reflects on a speech of Yitzhak Rabin in which he said that the Jewish people was not accustomed to conquest and received it with mixed feelings. Her concluding comment is: "What they will make of it and what conquest will make of them is the question that remains".

It still remains.

18 June, 2006

A *Doctor in the Quai d'Orsay*

France's Ministry of Foreign Affairs publishes the names of over two hundred French statesmen who have served as the country's foreign minister since 1589. It is an impressive roster. Early on you meet the great ministers Richelieu and Colbert. Later on you come across Talleyrand, history's great survivor who, over a period of over 40 years, served in succession the Ancien Regime, the Revolution, Napoleon and the Bourbon restoration, ending up, in his dotage, as France's ambassador to London under the "Citizen King," Louis Philippe. Then you encounter the Romantic poet Alphonse de Lamartine, followed closely in 1848 by Alexis de Tocqueville, author of the classic text "Democracy in America." And so they continue – names that reverberate over the centuries.

So any French politician who aspires to head the foreign ministry knows that he has large shoes to fill. The final name on this illustrious roll of honour is that of Philippe Douste-Blazy, the latest incumbent of the Quai d'Orsay. Recently, Minister Douste-Blazy visited Israel. Like every other distinguished visitor, he was taken to Jerusalem's Yad Vashem Holocaust memorial and museum. As quoted by the French satirical magazine *Le Canard Enchaîné*, when shown the maps of the areas where communities had been destroyed, the minister asked whether British Jews had also been murdered. Since the time that German Chancellor Schroeder accidentally extinguished the Eternal Flame (did it have to be a German?), the staff at Yad Vashem has become relatively inured to the vagaries of important foreigners, but Douste-Blazy's question was greeted with incredulity. After all, you don't need to be a postgraduate student in modern history to know that the Germans did not invade Britain. When tactfully reminded of this, the minister persisted, asking, "Yes, but were no Jews deported from England?"

M. Douste-Blazy, perhaps wisely, has refrained from commenting on the press reports, but the story is so astonishing that well-wishers have, unsolicited, sprung to his defence. It is not only untrue, according to these apologists, that the minister is as stupefyingly clueless as might first appear but, on the contrary, his questions demonstrate his rare grasp of the history of World War II. In short, he was thinking of an episode so obscure that it had even slipped the minds of his Holocaust-savvy Yad Vashem interlocutors. Because, although it is a fact that the Nazis could not have deported Jews from Britain, there were indeed deportations from British possessions.

A little-trodden byway in the history of World War II is the occupation by German forces of the Channel Islands. Geographically, the Channel Islands are not part of the British Isles, being closer to the coast of Normandy than to England, but constitutionally they are dependencies of the British crown. For years the islands were only known for the dairy cattle that bore the names of their principal islands: Jersey, Guernsey and Alderney. Today they are familiar to the cognoscenti for the banks and trustee companies that proliferate there, to look after the hard-earned savings of public-spirited foreigners who decline to put temptation in the way of their home governments by paying them income tax. Due to the proximity of the islands to France, the British, after the fall of France in June 1940, decided that the islands were indefensible, and by early July 1940, all the inhabited Channel Islands had been occupied by German forces without encountering resistance.

In recent years there have been books and documentary films about the occupation, including a monograph by a leading member of the Jersey community, Frederick Cohen. There was ample warning of the German invasion and most of the Jews forming the small communities of Guernsey and Jersey had fled to the British mainland by the time the Germans arrived. But a few isolated Jews remained. These were either infirm or so removed from Judaism that they no longer looked upon themselves as Jews. The paucity of Jews did nothing to dampen the zeal of the Germans (regular Wehrmacht, incidentally, not SS) in hunting down, with some local help, the few remaining ones. Their efforts produced the grand total of eleven Jews on Jersey and two on Guernsey. In April 1942, three women, Jews born in Poland and Austria, were deported; they perished in Auschwitz. Eight more Jews were deported in February 1943 as part of a general deportation, and subsequent internment in Germany, of 2,000 residents who held British citizenship, but had not been born in the Channel Islands. They all survived the war. These seem to have been all the deportations of Jews from the Channel Islands.

If Douste-Blazy was indeed thinking of the Channel Islands, he has been misjudged. Yet, in a way, it makes his question stranger. Millions of Polish and Russian Jews were exterminated. And, yes, some 80,000 Jews were deported from France to their deaths. In that context, to inquire about the fate of the pitiful handful from the Channel Islands betrays not only a perverse insensitivity to the scale of the Shoah, but what looks like a Gallic Anglophobia that verges on the paranoid.

As the minister himself has been silent on the matter, I shall adopt the more charitable explanation: Douste-Blazy, who was born years after the war ended, simply did not know. I am talking off the top of my head here, but it occurs to me that French schools may touch only lightly on a chapter of history that, after all, was not France's finest hour. In plumping for ignorance as the likeliest explanation of the minister's gaffe I now bring, ladies and gentlemen of the jury, corroborative evidence for the charge that he had not the faintest idea what he was talking about.

Tucked modestly away in the final paragraph of the *Haaretz* report of the story is a sentence that, to the prejudiced, might provide an explanation for the minister's apparent ignorance: "A cardiologist by training, he served until a year ago as health minister."

That's it! The minister is also a doctor! Without necessarily endorsing it, I repeat here the widely held belief that the more a physician knows about medicine, the less he knows about anything else. If I offer the minister's former profession as an explanation for that otherwise inexplicable lacuna in his education, I rush to say that, though it may be that there are brilliant diagnosticians who have yet to learn to read without moving their lips, it would be grossly unfair to stereotype a profession in whose ranks are numbered such unarguably outstanding intellects as Maimonides, Freud, Schopenhauer, Roget (he of the Thesaurus) and writers like Chekhov, Keats and Schiller. Still, belonging as I do to a profession that has long been the target of more jokes than have blondes, commercial travelers and Irishmen put together, it is with a distinct feeling of *Schadenfreude* that I repeat, with relish, the monstrous canard – dear, oh dear! – about the general lack of literacy of physicians.

And, while I am at it, I cannot resist adding a couple of entertaining facts I have stumbled upon. The first is that you can be diagnosed with something called an iatrogenic condition. This refers to a state of ill health or adverse effect caused by medical treatment. Let your imagination run riot here. Your doctor, in treating you for your iatrogenic condition could make a mistake, thus causing a second iatrogenic condition and so on, to the growing detriment of the patient, but to the unquestionable advantage of the medical profession.

The second example is even more fascinating. It has been the subject of learned articles in medical journals throughout the world, but originates in the country that also gave the world the Bible, Ogen melons and the Uzi submachine gun.

In 1983, and again in 2000, the Israel Medical Association took industrial action and applied sanctions in public hospitals, cancelling thousands of outpatient visits and elective operations. Did people – cruelly deprived of medical treatment – drop in the streets like flies? Actually, no. The result was a measurably significant drop in the death rate for the duration of the strike. It seems that medical inactivity is a sure-fire prophylactic for iatrogenesis.

Like many people, I have personal horror stories to tell about doctors. There was, for example, the distinguished consultant who disposed of me, during a dark time of my life, in three short sentences: "I am sorry you had to wait an hour and a half. You have twelve months to live. That will be 1,000 shekels please." But I would be biting the hands that cured me if I were to end there. Almost seven years after that unfortunate experience, I am still around and in tolerable health, thanks to the skill and devotion of the surgeons and physicians with whom I came into contact at the time.

So let me close by recording my unconditional admiration of doctors. Some of them even know that there was a war between 1939 and 1945.

28 October, 2005

Meinertzhagen – Such a Strange Bird

Unless you are an Australian, you are unlikely to have seen "The Lighthorsemen." The film, made in 1987, tells the thrilling story of the charge on Beersheba on 31 October, 1917, of the Australian 4th Light Horse Brigade. Unlike the disastrous charge of the Light Brigade at Balaclava immortalized by Tennyson, the attack, though a frontal assault on Turkish artillery and machine guns, was successful and Australian casualties were gratifyingly low. Some military historians credit the ultimate victory of General Allenby in Palestine to the Australian achievement at Beersheba. The key to success was surprise - achieved by what came to be known as "the Haversack Ruse."

The haversack in question was the property of an extraordinary character, a British intelligence officer named Richard Meinertzhagen. Despite his German name, Meinertzhagen was as English as they come and is played in the film by the exquisite Anthony Andrews (chiefly remembered for his part as the doomed Lord Sebastian Flyte in the television adaptation of Evelyn Waugh's "Brideshead Revisited.") The Australian filmmakers cannot have relished giving a Pom even a smidgen of credit for their triumph but, in truth, it was unavoidable. The insanely brave Meinertzhagen, who had a habit of roaming alone on horseback behind enemy lines, permitted himself to be pursued by a Turkish patrol and, in his apparent haste, "dropped" a haversack containing what purported to be the British plan of battle. The plans, in an easily deciphered code, indicated that the British were going to attack Gaza rather than Beersheba. The plans had been expertly forged by Meinertzhagen. The ruse worked; the Turks committed their main forces to the defense of Gaza, leaving a small garrison to protect Beersheba.

When I saw the film at a private screening in a garden in Herzliya, Meinertzhagen was already a name familiar to me, a fact that I was anxious to divulge to anyone who would listen. I own to a tendency - one that I have, without success, tried to eradicate all my life - to share with others nuggets of information in my possession. I am the boy in the class with a darting hand, who cries: "Please sir: Ask me sir. I know the answer sir." It is of a piece with an unconquerable desire to correct perceived grammatical solecisms and factual errors. I have a habit of reading a book with a pencil at the ready, poised to scrawl my improvements in the margin. I even had the gall to start a correspondence with the (as I discovered) astonishingly courteous Colin Dexter, the author of the splendid Inspector Morse novels, on the meaning of a Latin term that I believed he had misused. My motive for attempting to overcome this unselfish desire to educate others is that I have found that, in general, the recipients of my generosity show no sign of appreciating my efforts.

That evening I was bursting to tell the assembled throng a few of the facts that I had gleaned about Meinertzhagen. He was an eccentric, of a type that, over two or three centuries, has come to be seen as a speciality of the British ruling class. What set him apart from other English oddities was that, like that other lunatic British soldier, Orde Wingate, he liked Jews and, from an early date, he advocated the establishment of a Jewish state. In a remarkable letter to the British prime minister, David Lloyd George, of 25 March, 1919, Meinertzhagen contrasts "the virile, brave, determined and intelligent" Jews with the "stupid, dishonest" Arabs. He prophesies that a national home for the Jews must develop sooner or later into sovereignty. In the inevitable resultant clash, he urges the British government, in its own interest, to side with the Jews. But while Wingate's name appears in numerous locations throughout Israel, it was only in 1997 that Meinertzhagen Square was dedicated in Jerusalem - the first and, so far, sole concrete recognition of Meinertzhagen's contribution to Zionism.

But it was in respect of his lifelong passion for rare birds that Meinertzhagen would have liked to have been remembered. He became known as one of the greatest of all amateur ornithologists. His vast collection of stuffed birds was world famous. I should say that, in general, I have a profound distrust of collectors and hobbyists. Grown-ups should do grown-up things. As a child I caught mumps, measles, scarlet fever, chicken pox and a bad dose of philately. I got over them all and when I became a man, in the words of my coreligionist, Paul of Tarsus, I put away childish things. And some of those things beggar the imagination.

According to Wikipedia, you can become a lotologist by collecting lottery tickets, a sucrologist by collecting sugar sachets or a notologist by collecting banknotes. I didn't know they were called notologists, but there are plenty of them around.

But, little as I am attracted to hobbies in general, I do understand the fascination of birds. Alfred Hitchcock, who had a pathological hatred of birds, might not have agreed, but the thought of a world without birdsong is, to my mind, intolerable. That is what made the title of the book that launched the whole environmental movement - Rachel Carson's "The Silent Spring" - so potent. It is hard not to have some interest in birds in Israel. Israel may be poor in natural resources, but it is a birdwatcher's paradise and I challenge anyone who believes himself indifferent to the attraction of birds not to be infected by the enthusiasm of the charismatic Dr. Yossi Leshem, Israel's birding guru.

It was Yossi who inspired us to look round our own suburban garden where we see and hear dozens of species, few of which we can identify. Of the ones I do recognize, I have a handful of favourites: wagtails, hoopoes, the occasional kingfisher - resplendently blue in flight - and my own favourite, the diminutive and so beautiful, sunbirds. A pair of them decided to nest in our pergola this year; we spent weeks watching the tiny parents fly in and out of the nest, little larger than a ping-pong ball, clutching morsels to feed the chicks that we never actually succeeded in seeing.

If Meinertzhagen loved birds - and I suppose he did - he had a funny way of showing it. He slaughtered them in large numbers so as to add their skins to his collection. Why his name was fresh in my mind at the time I saw him glamorized on the screen by Anthony Andrews was that only two or three weeks before, I had read a magazine article on his ornithological activities. The article, in the 29 May issue of *The New Yorker*, was by a staff writer, John Seabrook, and was entitled "Ruffled feathers," subtitled "Uncovering the biggest scandal in the bird world".

It seems that Meinertzhagen was a serial thief. He persistently stole bird skins from London's Natural History Museum and from private collections such as that of Lord Rothschild at Tring. Yet although it was a fairly open secret in ornithological circles, the strange British code remained unbroken. In Britain, morality is a vice of the middle classes. Members of the ruling class can, with impunity steal or lie. Or worse. When Sir Anthony Blunt was unmasked as a major Soviet spy, it was felt to be bad form to deprive such a fine scholar of his post as Curator of the Queen's Pictures.

But Meinertzhagen committed a much greater scientific crime than larceny. He did the scientifically unforgivable. The man who had forged the British war plans to bamboozle the Turks faked ornithological data to fool fellow ornithologists. Tags on the feet of birds showing where and when they had been collected had been replaced with tags, forged by Meinertzhagen, indicating a false provenance that served the purposes of Meinertzhagen.

There have, to date, been three biographies of Meinertzhagen, all of them flattering. That is now about to change. To use an avian analogy that he might have appreciated, the revisionist vultures are now about to pick at Meinertzhagen's carcass. A new book on Meinertzhagen is about to be published. "The Meinertzhagen Mystery: The Life and Legend of a Colossal Fraud" by Brian Garfield is unlikely to be another hagiography. The publisher's description of the book does not bode well. It discredits the haversack ruse; it casts doubt on many of the exploits that Meinertzhagen claimed for himself in his diaries; it repeats *The New Yorker's* charges of theft and forgery in greater detail; it suggests that he might have murdered his wife and, for good measure, it claims that, although he was a genuine Zionist, he flirted with Nazism in the thirties.

Please may we have our Square back?

PARTIALLY POLITICAL

Vive la Difference

On balance I think that my classical education, such as it was, was wasted. I can translate a passage of Thucydides today about as well as I can the Bhagavad Gita. Nor is my Latin much better. On the whole I find I can live with it. Shakespeare, according to Ben Jonson, had "small Latin and less Greek" and he managed just fine. To me it is a mystery how anyone should have ever thought that such an education would prepare one for life in the 20th century. My own headmaster, a classicist himself, often said that a classical education enabled one to despise the riches that it prevented one from attaining.

But there remain with me faint echoes of the glories of Greece and Rome. I remember, for instance, the Satires of Juvenal. Juvenal lived in Rome in the first century of the Common Era. He wrote caustic verse satires so bitter that they provoke astonishment to this day. In my schooldays – maybe it is still the case – school editions of the classics omitted passages thought indelicate for youthful minds. It is hard to conceive of a policy less conducive to achieving its object unless that policy had the subtle intent of encouraging extra-curricular research. Almost as soon as a bowdlerized textbook hit the streets, unexpurgated versions would be circulated in samizdat. Juvenal is an especially earthy writer and our versions were spattered with the telltale rows of asterisks that indicated the absence of a juicy fragment. But thanks to a thirst for knowledge as assiduous as it was prurient, I was well informed of the hair-raising sexploits of the Empress Messalina years before her television appearance in "I Claudius".

The third Satire of Juvenal contrasts the corruption of Rome, with the older and simpler way of life still found in the Roman countryside. A rampant xenophobe, Juvenal puts it all down to the influx of immigrants to Rome. "I cannot abide," he writes "a Rome of Greeks." A later right-wing satirist, the famed Dr. Samuel Johnson, was much taken by Juvenal. His poem "London" is an imitation of the third Satire. In Johnson's poem, 17th century London takes the place of Juvenal's Rome. Instead of Greeks, London is infested by that evergreen bugbear of the English – the French. "Forgive my transports on a theme like this" says Johnson, "I cannot bear a French metropolis".

Dr. Johnson was neither the first nor the last Englishman to express his hostility towards the French. Anglo-Saxon francophobia has a long pedigree. It probably dates back to the Norman conquest of England in 1066, the last time – as every British schoolchild knows – that a foreign invader set foot on British soil. Although the Normans spoke French and thus greatly enriched the English language, they were, as their name implies, Norsemen who seized territory in France at the beginning of the 10th century. From their base in Normandy, these Scandinavian Rambos plundered, pillaged and ravished their way across Europe. The First Crusade owed its astounding success to the unconquerable desire for their own fiefdoms that drove the dispossessed younger sons of the Norman nobility to create kingdoms for themselves in Palestine.

Henceforth, according to the triumphalist form of history taught in British schools, wars between England and France – and there were many – were fought on the continent of Europe or at sea. By the 14th century the kings of England, now fully anglicized Normans, cast covetous eyes on France.

The long and bitter Hundred Years War between England and France is the background to Barbara Tuchman's vivid depiction of the brutal 14th century – "A Distant Mirror," to my mind her finest book. This century of the Black Death also witnessed a string of English victories in France. Crécy and Poitiers were followed in 1415 by Agincourt. The English were victorious thanks to their archers' devastating use of the longbow, a technological innovation to which the French had no answer. The English even captured the French king, who for years lingered, unransomed, in England in comfortable captivity and eventually died there. For three brief years, inspired by Joan of Arc, the French drove the English back. The English burnt Joan at the stake for heresy, which did nothing to further the future *entente cordiale*. Not that the English, whose national vice according to George Orwell is hypocrisy, would admit to any enmity towards France. When Princess Katherine asks Shakespeare's Henry V how she could love an enemy of France, he replies: "I love France so well that I will not part with a village of it".

A particularly singular British habit, and one that testifies to the ancient nature of English francophobia has its origin at Agincourt. The semioticians among you will know that many nations use a gesture of contempt that imitates the sexual act and is the non-verbal equivalent of the most common of all obscenities. In America they "give the finger" – what the Romans called the *digitus impudicus*. The more phallically endowed Europeans give the *bras d'honneur* which involves energetically jerking the right forearm upwards with the left hand restraining it at the elbow. The British, however, raise the middle and index fingers in the form of a "V." This anatomically misleading gesture originates from the battle of Agincourt. The French had boasted that they would incapacitate the English bowmen by cutting off their index and middle fingers. After the battle the triumphant archers raised those two fingers as a sign of defiance.

But it is almost 200 years since Britain last faced France on the field of battle and it is unthinkable nowadays that armed conflict of the most limited kind should occur between these countries. Admittedly World War II left some bitterness. On the British side there was a feeling that their supposed ally had shown little backbone in resisting the German blitzkrieg. France for its part had cause for complaint against Britain. On 3rd July 1940, the British navy attacked and destroyed a large part of the French fleet moored at Mers-el-Kebir, killing 1,300 French seamen. The British, of course, believed that the French navy, answerable to the German puppet regime of Vichy, might hand over its strategically important ships to the Germans; but it was hard for the French to come to terms with this disaster wrought by their erstwhile allies.

Where there was once enmity there is now little more than mutual irritation. But there remains a profound difference of cultures, not a clash of civilizations in the Huntington sense, but two totally disparate ways of looking at the world that go beyond the side of the road that each nation drives and the temperature of their beer.

The French love ideas and idolize intellectuals. Even their footballers are cerebral. The English, on the other hand, are uncomfortable with theories. They are allergic to systems and this is reflected in their main contribution to philosophy; empiricism. It would be unfair to accuse the English of philistinism but, as we have seen with that quintessential Englishman George Orwell, they have a heartfelt dislike of intellectuals. The English poet W. H. Auden, though himself an intellectual, put it into words:

To the man-in-the-street, who, I'm sorry to say,
Is a keen observer of life,
The word "Intellectual" suggests straight away
A man who's untrue to his wife.

Today the French are once again unpopular. Without justifying it, it is not hard to see why. The better class lunatic asylums always contained at least one patient who thought he was Napoleon. The Elysée Palace seems to perform the same function. Some kind of delusion of grandeur enters the head of a president of France the minute he takes office. How else do you explain a president who preaches morality to the world while hosting Mugabe and doing business with Saddam Hussein?

But nothing excuses the mindless anti-French hysteria that has seized much of the English-speaking world. What reaction except disgust can you have for the *Sun*, the house organ of England's football louts, which brands President Chirac, "Saddam Hussein's whore"? Ill-natured jokes about the supposed French lack of military prowess – as if that were how a nation should be judged – and insulting formulations like "cheese-eating surrender monkeys" are wholly contemptible. Much the same goes for such chauvinistic enormities as "freedom fries." The French, who love their food almost as much as they love their language, must have been relieved to lose the attribution to their nation of this culinary barbarity.

The yahoos who disseminate such vulgarity are sneering at the most civilized nation on earth. Despite sporadic bouts of hostility to the French, the English know that. The French excel in all that makes life worth living – food, wine, love, painting, literature. Yes, the French are different from the British and the Americans but – *vive la difference*!

14 November, 2003

*T*he Age of Unreason

On the eve of the 1981 Knesset elections, a senior Likud politician, Ya'acov Meridor, announced that he was sponsoring an invention that would solve the world's energy problems. With the aid of his machine the energy currently (sorry!) required to power a single light bulb would be sufficient to light up the whole city of Ramat Gan. Television viewers were treated to the sight of a delightful Heath Robinson (Rube Goldberg to Yanks) contraption going putta-putta-putta, with bells jangling and whistles whistling.

Meridor, like many before and after him, had disregarded David Hume's maxim. The Scottish philosopher propounded a maxim that retains its relevance in an age that, for gullibility, far surpasses Hume's 18th century:

> *That no testimony is sufficient to establish a miracle, unless the testimony be of such a kind, that its falsehood would be more miraculous than the fact which it endeavours to establish.*

Hume was saying that if you are confronted with something so extraordinary that it is in conflict with the known laws of nature you should require equally extraordinary evidence to accept it. Meridor's infinite energy machine violated one of the most fundamental of physical laws, the first law of thermodynamics: energy is conserved. Put simply, the law says that you can never get more energy out than you put in. Indeed, because of the "entropy" of the second law, you will always lose something in the process of converting one form of energy to another.

It transpired that the laws of nature had not, after all, been suspended for Mr. Meridor. But, by the time the hapless politician was revealed to have been the victim of a confidence trick, his Likud party had been voted in by an electorate that didn't care a fig for the laws of thermodynamics. So mark another victory for ignorance over reason.

Despite almost universal literacy and massive scientific and technological progress, the West is today prey to irrational beliefs and superstitions that are reminiscent of the Middle Ages. Isaiah Berlin, in an interview published shortly before his death, stated that what had surprised him most in the second half of the 20th century was the reversion to the irrational. Faith healers, psychics, miracle-working rabbis, scientologists and charlatans of every description prosper in a way that Hume, in the Age of Reason, could never have foreseen. We are flooded by New Age claptrap. Decisions of President Reagan, with the world's fate in his hands, were influenced by the horoscope readings of his wife's astrologer.

"The most common of all follies," wrote H. L. Mencken, "is to believe in the palpably untrue." For a case of stupefying credulity, you could not do better than look at the so-called Bible Code. The Bible Code is a code allegedly embedded in the Hebrew Bible. Based on work carried out a few years ago by a group of Israeli mathematicians, a computer is used to identify equidistant letter sequences. This hi-tech version of *gematria* can reveal, in hindsight, astounding predictions.

A book making supernatural claims for the Code written by Michael Drosnin became a runaway bestseller in the United States. It certainly proved H.L. Mencken's adage that no one ever went broke underestimating the intelligence of the American public. In Drosnin's book, published in 1997, two years after the assassination of Yitzhak Rabin, he claimed that the assassination was foretold in the Code. Drosnin finds advance predictions a little tougher than retroactive ones and, happily, the dates for his predictions of an atomic holocaust in Israel and the assassination of Benjamin Netanyahu have already passed

The Code's critics pointed out that, with literally billions of possibilities, it is not difficult to find patterns in a vast mass of raw data. Drosnin unwisely challenged the sceptics to find similar prophecies in "Moby Dick." They did. Like Pharaoh's magicians they duplicated the miracle – finding in Melville's novel predictions of the assassinations of Indira Gandhi, Leon Trotsky, Martin Luther King and Robert F. Kennedy.

One wonders why they bothered. The American humourist Bill Bryson, in explaining his decision to return to the United States after living in Britain for 20 years, writes that, when he read that a Gallup Poll had revealed that 3.7 million Americans believed that they had been abducted by aliens at one time or another, he came to the conclusion that his people needed him. So what can you say about people who believe that you can tell the future with a Bible and a laptop? Extra-terrestrial kidnappings look sane by comparison.

One should not be surprised that distinguished mathematicians should have lent their weight in support of the Bible Code. There has not been a dotty theory – spiritualism, creationism, psychic phenomena, you name it – that has not had adherents from the ranks of professional scientists. The great Isaac Newton himself was a mystic who dabbled in alchemy and the occult. A number of physicists were for years impressed by the fork-bending Uri Geller, an Israeli prestidigitator who poses as a psychic with telekinetic powers. Richard Feynman, one of the great scientists of the 20th century, admitted to being baffled by Geller. But, perhaps mindful of Hume's maxim, he did not jump to the conclusion that the laws of physics should therefore be rewritten. Feynman was smart enough, as he said, to know that he was dumb. He realized that the right people to investigate so-called psychic phenomena are professional magicians. Geller, who still has a following of diehard believers, was exposed by the Amazing Randi as a fellow magician of average competence with no more supernatural powers than you or I.

As Meridor discovered, credulity can be good for you. An outstanding example is the placebo effect, which underlies the vast and prodigiously lucrative field known as alternative medicine. It is a euphemism scientists employ to describe a cynically offensive view of human intelligence. The placebo effect means that if you are stupid enough to believe that a particularly worthless remedy is doing you good, it just might do you good.

Nowhere is the violation of Hume's maxim more apparent than in alternative medicine. Ranging from the plausible to the outlandishly loony, alternative medicine is a term that covers a multitude of sins. Its many forms claim untold numbers of adherents but I have yet to meet the most fervent believer who will not give his sick child an antibiotic regardless of his faith in a particular nostrum.

Perhaps the greatest success story in alternative medicine – a triumph for the placebo effect – is homeopathy. At the end of the 18th century, a German physician by the name of Samuel Hahnemann developed what he called a "law of similars." According to this scientifically unsubstantiated theory, natural substances that produce symptoms that are similar to the symptoms of a particular disease can be used to cure that disease. As such substances are frequently toxic, Hahnemann started to dilute the substances. You will not be surprised to hear that the more he diluted the toxic substance, the better his patients fared. Eventually, he diluted his potions to such an extent that not a single molecule of the original substance remained in a homeopathic dose. What remains is a "memory." In fairness it should be said that if you take homeopathic remedies you get a concoction that, due to its total blandness, can do you no harm. Legend has it, however, that a homeopathic patient died of an overdose when he mistakenly took ordinary water.

Others have jumped onto the dilution bandwagon, or rather waterwagon. Some years ago recipients of Purim parcels from their local branch of Lubavitcher hasidim found, together with the cookies, candies and sweet wine, a small vial of water with instructions attached. The vial contained water from the ritual bath of the Lubavitcher Rebbe. Ingested or applied externally, it would cure your ailments. You could dilute the contents as much as you wished without diminishing its effect – surely a wholly justifiable claim. Like homeopathy, it was sufficient for the solution to retain the memory of the Rebbe's mikveh water to confer the desired benefit.

None of us is immune from falling prey to irrational fears and superstitions. We exaggerate many risks and minimize others. We blithely accept the danger of injury on the roads while frantically seeking to avoid the far less probable risk of being victims of a terrorist attack. Why are we like that? Cognitive scientists have speculated on a "belief" gene which is built into us and which causes us to discard reason and go for the supernatural and the paranormal. As in the case of the placebo effect, stupidity may even confer an evolutionary advantage.

It is easy to laugh at superstition and credulity but it is far from laughable. That same capacity that we have for accepting the impossible and the improbable in defiance of reason and commonsense makes others accept the most outlandish of conspiracy theories. Believe in faith healers and you can believe in the "Protocols of the Elders of Zion." You disregard Hume's maxim at your peril.

As for me, my horoscope tells me that I should be careful not to offend people today. But I am a Pisces and, as you know, Pisces do not believe in astrology.

19 September, 2003

*B*oycott the Boycotters

The boycott business is flourishing and if you are into boycotting, ours is a golden age. Never before has the aspiring boycotter been faced with such an embarrassment of riches. The Internet reveals a veritable Aladdin's cave of boycotts. Google – itself the object of a boycott for refusing to take advertisements for guns – lists about 850,000 sites. There is hardly a Fortune 500 company that you cannot boycott if you wish. Patriotic Americans boycott French wine and rename French fries "Freedom fries." The English cricket team boycotts Zimbabwe. Arabs boycott Coca-Cola. Consumer activists boycott Nestlé. Israel boycotts the BBC. You can ostracize the Boy Scouts, the Oscars, genetically modified foods, fur, hunting, World Bank bonds and Beijing 2008.

With the vigilance of kashrut authorities these websites list the products to avoid. The German site that provides alternatives for American products finds itself without a substitute for Viagra and – *faute de mieux* – proposes tea. Oh, those passionate British civil servants!

Boycotters tend to be paranoid and humourless. Benetton is to be boycotted because the company places hidden sensors in clothing and this could "fuel a global surveillance network." Californian Latinos have been asked to boycott the magazine *Vanity Fair* because its spoof agony aunt "Dame Edna" asked by "Torn Romantic" of Palm Beach if he should learn Spanish; she replies: "Forget Spanish. There's nothing in that language except Don Quixote and a quick listen to the CD of Man of La Mancha will take care of that".

Captain Charles Cunningham Boycott shares with Nicolas Chauvin, the Reverend A.W. ("the Lord is a shoving leopard") Spooner, Etienne de Silhouette and the fourth Earl of Sandwich, the linguistic immortality of having inspired an eponym, a word derived from the name of a person or place. The Internet lists hundreds of eponyms, many of dubious derivation, but a sequential segment taken at random reveals how this particular figure of speech has enriched the

English language. "Galvanize," "gamp," "gardenia" and "gargantuan" are all eponyms. Did you know that the word "dunce" was a derogatory term given by their opponents to the Schoolmen, the followers of the Scottish Franciscan theologian John Duns Scotus?

Captain Boycott himself was the victim rather than the instigator of the activity that bears his name. He served in Ireland in the 19th century as a land agent for an absentee English landlord. He refused to reduce the rents of his distressed tenants and was consequently ostracized by his neighbours. He was also memorialized in film. In the British movie "Captain Boycott," which starred Stewart Granger, the eponymous captain was played by Cecil Parker, best remembered by film buffs as the perfect screen butler.

Boycotts have been used seriously and effectively; witness the Montgomery bus boycott and the sports boycott on South Africa. These have their place in history as have others that have a defined and attainable political objective.

But it is the boycott as revenge fantasy that dominates the websites. Boycotters feel themselves impotent victims in the face of a perceived but untouchable enemy. A boycotter identifies with King Lear when he says: "I will do such things, what they are, yet I know not; but they shall be the terror of the earth".

There is something mean-spirited about the boycotter. When the Rabbis referred to *midat sdom* – the trait of Sodom – they were not referring to that vice that has given the world yet another eponym. They meant that it is the desire to mar the pleasures of others at no corresponding cost to oneself that epitomizes the boycotter. I do not believe that those patriotic American boycotters poured more than one bottle of expensive French wine into the gutter. I doubt if any of the members of the Education Committee of the Knesset who called for a boycott of Daniel Barenboim cared a fig for music.

Daniel Barenboim's crime was that he performed the music of Richard Wagner. Wagner was a rabid anti-Semite and a wholly repulsive man. He was Hitler's favourite composer and his odious descendants were among Hitler's greatest friends and supporters. But his operas contain no overt anti-Semitism. If you are looking for anti-Semitism in music, listen to Bach's St. John's Passion; yet no one has proposed a boycott of Bach and the work is performed here without protest.

On Wagner I claim to be disinterested. I once sat through "Das Rheingold" without any burning desire to repeat the experience. I rather sympathize with the man who defined "Parsifal" as the kind of opera that starts at 6 pm and after it has been going for three hours, you look at your watch and it says 6.20. Mark Twain maintained that Wagner's music is better than it sounds.

But banning Wagner is not a trivial matter for he is an important figure in Western culture and, by keeping him out of our concert halls, we deprive many of a profound and irreplaceable musical experience. You can listen to Wagner and be inspired by none but the noblest sentiments. Theodor Herzl was a fervent admirer of the music of Wagner and was inspired to write "The Jewish State" while listening to a performance of "Tannhauser." We can normally dissociate a work of art from the personality of its author. Some of the great writers, painters and composers were far from admirable human beings and more than a few were anti-Semites. But we read Dostoyevsky and enjoy the paintings of Degas without being unduly troubled by their fanatical anti-Semitism.

And yet it is not that simple. To those of us who did not experience the Holocaust directly, its memory remains central to our identity. It is seared on our collective consciousness. There are still many among us who experienced the Holocaust at first hand. They cannot be ignored and their sensitivities must be respected. If those who are principally troubled by Wagner concerts are Holocaust survivors rather than a rabble of professional killjoys it is inadequate to reply that they can always stay at home.

So why should a non-Wagnerian such as myself find this proscription so profoundly disturbing? It is not only that I suspect the motives of some of the boycotters. What discomforts me is that I scent a faint whiff of the bonfire. The gap between banning music and burning books is too close for comfort. I was brought up on Milton's "Areopagitica" and Mill's essay "On Liberty" and I am frightened by the too ready willingness that I see today to cast out the disagreeable: books, plays, films or broadcasting corporations. Wagner is not a special case. He is a test case for the freedom of expression. Wagner is not a borderline issue on the limits to that freedom.

It will surprise no one that it is Israel that is the most popular target of the boycotters. I find the boycott of Israeli academics and academic institutions especially objectionable. Its victims tend to be, by and large, critics of the policies that the boycott purports to attack.

It is not the fact of Israel's unpopularity that is so difficult to understand as its intensity. The academic boycott is not anti-Semitic in intent, but it attracts anti-Semites and understandably so, because only Jews are its victims. The visceral dislike of Israel – so prevalent today in Europe – is, in my view, principally proxy anti-Americanism, part of a ragbag of beliefs, often laudable but inconsistent because egregiously selective, that form the world-view of the modern liberal.

Those who subscribe to these views appear to absolve themselves from thinking about them. The case of the wretched Professor Wilkie of Oxford

University, who refused to consider the application of a doctoral student because he was Israeli, is only the most recent example. When faced by the inevitable outcry he withdrew his objection. What strikes me is how often offenders like Professor Wilkie find themselves apologizing for their impulsive reaction to Israel and Israelis. A hatred of Israel is now so deeply imprinted in their psyches that they have become incapable of reflection. Why is it not apparent to them that their blanket antipathy to all Israelis is not far removed from the racism they profess to detest?

No survey of boycotting, however cursory, would be complete without at least a passing reference to the part played by religion in employing the boycott as a means of suppressing dissent. Admittedly the rabbinical *herem* pales into insignificance besides the Catholic Index and the *fatwa*. The ayatollahs' idea of literary criticism is to terminate the author with extreme prejudice. But the rabbis have proved no slouches at banning and their victims over the centuries have included such towering figures as Maimonides and Spinoza.

That the herem is alive and well today is illustrated by the recent treatment of a biography of his late father by Rabbi Nathan Kamenetsky. The book, which – thanks to the effectiveness of its opponents in the yeshiva world – is now unobtainable, offended the canons of Haredi good taste by presenting an actual life rather than a hagiography. It was enough for the book to describe how Rabbi Ya'acov Kamenetsky, a revered Torah scholar, enjoyed English and Russian literature, for the book to be viciously attacked in Lithuanian yeshiva circles and removed from circulation.

Boycotting and suppression are two sides of the same coin. The message is clear: "Boycott the boycotters".

25 July, 2003

Untruth in Advertising

I do not want to give you the impression that the life of a law student is an exciting one. It is not. The way we staved off monotony was to read case reports. Lined up on the shelves in rows of identical bindings, the law reports appear forbidding, yet they contain vivid stories, plots for a thousand novels. Better than any archive, these volumes encompass hundreds of years of social history.

In our extracurricular thirst for knowledge, there was at times an element of the prurient. You could pick up a book that would spring open unbidden at a case that had been pored over diligently by generations of heavy-breathing undergraduates. Such a case was the tale of the singing teacher whose unconventional, though for all I know efficacious, method of improving the voice of an unusually gullible female pupil landed him in court on a rape charge.

Other cases, less titillating but no less absorbing, claimed our interest. A leading case in criminal law featured two shipwrecked seamen named Dudley and Stephens who killed and ate a cabin boy; a groundbreaking case on the tort of negligence involved a pregnant lady who miscarried after she had drunk ginger beer from an opaque bottle that turned out to have a snail in it; there was the sailor who, intending to make a will, wrote "All to Meg" on an eggshell.

And the dramatis personae of this pageant that spanned the centuries made up a cast list worthy of a Dickens novel: sovereign states; great corporations; murderers; thieves; confidence men; maharajahs and fishwives; fertile octogenarians and precocious toddlers – equal citizens in the great democracy of litigation.

But there is one lady that no law student will ever forget: I refer, of course, to Mrs. Carlill who emerged from obscurity in 1893 to bring a lawsuit against the splendidly named Carbolic Smoke Ball Company. The company inserted an advertisement in the *Pall Mall Gazette* of 13 November 1891, promising

100 pounds to any person who contracted influenza after using the company's smoke balls in the specified manner. Despite dosing herself as directed, Mrs. Carlill contracted influenza and claimed her 100 pounds. The company refused to honour its promise and, in defending itself in the ensuing action, raised every objection known to the law of contracts. But the court ruled against it. Mrs. Carlill, immortalized by her flu, won her case. The law had championed truth in advertising.

To find fault with advertising in the pages of a newspaper is akin to preaching temperance in a distillery, but it must be said that truth and advertising are awkward bedfellows. Advertisers, like lawyers, teachers, rabbis and politicians, are in the business of persuasion. They should not, of course, tell barefaced lies, but to be successful they must sometimes be economical with the truth.

There are people who habitually lie, who will only tell the truth when all else fails. But most of us flounder in the twilight zone between truth and falsehood. White lies are, after all, the fabric of social intercourse. You admire someone's baby though you know that they all look the same; you praise a friend's new hairstyle though you hate it; you pretend to like a painting that means nothing to you; you flatter, you cajole. You indulge in what lawyers term *suppressio veri* or *suggestio falsi*; you suppress the truth or you mislead. Even the most honest advertisers do that. A literal adherence to truth in advertising would result in something like the spoof ad I recently saw on the Internet: "John Kerry: Dumber than Gore, More Exciting than Mondale".

The advertising industry would find itself in harmony with the School of Hillel in its 2000-year old dispute with the School of Shammai. When dancing before a bride, Hillel, according to the Talmud, requires us to sing of her beauty and grace even if this would be a departure from the literal truth. The followers of Shammai demand that we tell it as it is.

Shammai, an uncompromising truth hawk, would have been a dead loss in an advertising agency. Much as we may admire the sea-green incorruptibles of this world we are uncomfortable with them. George Orwell, something of a Shammai himself, wrote in his essay on Gandhi that saints should always be judged guilty until they are proved innocent. No one should be surprised that later generations have almost always favoured the more worldly school of Hillel in its many disputes with the stern, unbending school of Shammai.

The advertising industry, flying the flag of truth in advertising, has in the past century indulged in an orgy of self-regulation, so it is comparatively rare these days to encounter a blatant lie. But, in Israel, there is one class of advertisement, as mendacious as it is pervasive, that arouses in me feelings of moral outrage. I refer to the advertising for the national lottery.

The lottery, I should explain, is a device that enables the government to profit from its failure to educate its citizens in numeracy. By creating the totally false illusion that the purchaser of a lottery ticket may achieve riches beyond the dreams of avarice, the state – in sponsoring the lottery – takes money from those least able to afford it. It is hard to think of anything more immoral.

A typical television advertisement shows a benevolent patriarch giving to each of his several adult children, tears of gratitude in their eyes, the keys to a new apartment. This could be you, says the ad, if only you had purchased a lottery ticket. That advertisement is a lie. You will not be that kind gentleman. Even if the big prize in the series for which you bought your ticket is still up for grabs – and the lottery will happily urge you to buy a ticket though there is no longer a jackpot to be won – your chances of winning are over eight million to one for each column you fill in. To anyone but an astronomer that means zero. You have no chance at all. You have been lied to.

Just think for a minute. If you play roulette or blackjack in a casino, the odds are plain. Not so with the lottery. Visit the Web site of the national lottery (*Mifal Hapayis* in Hebrew) and you will learn nothing of your chances of winning a prize, though you will read of all the charitable works that your weakness supports. But you didn't go in for the lottery in order to build the Cameri Theatre in Tel Aviv or a multipurpose sports centre in Jerusalem. You could have given the money directly to those causes. You bought a ticket because you wanted to be the gentleman handing out the apartment keys. You will not be that gentleman.

There is a private member's bill before the Knesset for a law that will compel the lottery to publish the odds of winning a prize. It is shameful that a law is needed. The lottery is sponsored by the state and you would think that it would not want to be a party to a flagrant deception. But it is. Not that I am sure that publication of the figures would help. Large numbers confuse people. Most of us can understand that a chance in a hundred is a long shot and our eyes already glaze over when we think of a chance in a thousand. Yet we are talking of a chance in more than eight thousand times a thousand. Rather, the lottery should produce some graphic illustration to bring out the remoteness of the likelihood of a prize. Think of a full football stadium with 50,000 spectators. Then think of 80 of such stadiums. You now have 4,000,000 spectators out of whom one will win a large prize for his five-shekel investment in two columns of the lotto.

There is nothing worse in Israeli popular perception than to be a *freier*, Hebrew slang for a dupe. A *freier* is ranked somewhere in the minds of Israelis between a paedophile and a serial murderer. I am sorry to tell you this, but if you fall for the advertisements for the lottery, you are a freier. Of course, I know that the second cousin of your sister's hairdresser knows someone whose gardener made a killing, but that is the kind of anecdotal evidence that permits innumeracy to thrive.

Cigarette packages and advertisements carry a legend that smoking kills or is injurious to your health. If you smoke three packs of cigarettes a day, you are very likely to contract lung cancer or heart disease. But it is not certain; you might die of old age. If you buy a lottery ticket, on the other hand, you will not win a big prize. That is certain, if that word has any meaning. So, I propose placing on every lottery ticket and advertisement the following legend: "Waste your money if you must, but buying a lottery ticket does not give you the slightest chance of winning".

1 October, 2004

Presidential Menagerie

It has probably not escaped your notice that the United States is in the throes of a presidential election. American readers may be sorry to learn that they must go elsewhere for guidance on how to cast their votes in this vitally important election. This column has elected to adopt a policy of benevolent neutrality. My disinterestedness has not been emulated by the normally high-minded London newspaper the *Guardian*, which has launched a campaign, complete with website and email addresses, urging its readers to bombard the unsuspecting voters of Clark County, Ohio (a precariously marginal district) with hortatory emails. Being the *Guardian*, you can assume that the emails are not intended to benefit President Bush.

And every little bit counts. Chaos theory would have you believe that the fluttering of the wings of a butterfly in the Amazonian jungle can bring about a hurricane in the Pacific. On that analogy, the opinion of one obscure Israeli columnist could sway the result of the U.S. presidential election. After all, the last election was decided by one solitary opinion, though admittedly a more authoritative one than mine. In the case of Bush v Gore, you will recall, the 2000 presidential election was determined in favour of the Republican candidate by a 5-4 vote of the United States Supreme Court.

Cynics among you might not have found it surprising that the five justices who constituted the majority on the Court were all appointees of a Republican president. Moreover, these traditionally conservative justices adopted, for the purpose of this decision, a policy of judicial activism that, in other circumstances, they would have found repugnant. The Supreme Court is one of the most admired institutions in the world. This blatantly partisan decision did nothing to enhance its reputation.

Had I endorsed a candidate, I would have needed to disclose a conflict of interest. I have a bottle of single malt Scotch whisky riding on the result. My wager signifies no partiality for the candidate I backed but follows a strategy

– one that has served me well in the past – of betting against a friend with a long, virtually unblemished record of losses. I draw this fact to the attention of the pollsters, who are still refusing to give us a clear winner.

My reluctance to endorse a candidate does not signify indifference. The US presidential election matters to us all; the West faces a crisis of historic dimensions that only the resolute leadership of the United States can resolve. With so great a responsibility, you would think that the electorate of the United States would respond by turning out to vote. Yet only one in two eligible Americans bothers to vote in a presidential election. Having looked into the matter, I am convinced America's voter turnout is low because voting in America is such a daunting experience.

For one thing, you are expected to vote for candidates for every office from the president down to the legendary dogcatcher. Voting in America is not a right; it is an occupation. It has been calculated that there are more than 176,000 elective offices in the United States. Americans indulge their passion for democracy by voting for someone or other on the first Tuesday in November of every single year. The seriously inclined will also vote in referenda and primaries. However small your town, you cannot escape your civic obligation. Greenhorn, Oregon has a population of three but regularly goes to the polls to elect a mayor.

So the American voter has his work cut out when he enters that polling booth. Even when he knows for whom he wants to vote as governor, district attorney or dogcatcher, he has also to know how to cast that vote. From what I can make out, you need to have a doctorate in computer science or to be one of the brighter kinds of brain surgeon to navigate the American voting system. In Florida, the home of those notorious floating chads, you can now go to a course to learn how to use the voting machines. Dummy machines will be installed at polling stations to enable those brave ones who plan to vote to practise on the equipment before undergoing the terrifying experience of actually voting.

There are as many different ways of voting in the United States as there are of executing criminals. A recent edition of the *Economist* provided a map showing seven totally disparate voting systems scattered haphazardly over the U.S. Now that we are in the 21st century we would expect electronic systems to prevail. But Luddites take heart. The pencilled cross on a printed list still has the edge. In one election in Virginia, the touch-screen voting machines subtracted votes from the candidates' total instead of adding to them. And there was a district of Indiana, where, thanks to their state-of-the-art equipment, 5,352 voters cast 144,000 votes.

Self-imposed neutrality aside, had I been an American I am not sure how

I would vote. In the last election, in those prelapsarian days before 9/11, the choice was easier. During the campaign, Al Gore declared his favourite book to be Stendhal's "The Red and the Black." That tale of an amoral social climber might have been a surprising choice for a presidential aspirant, but, at least, it implied that the candidate, the *soi-disant* co-inventor of the Internet, was literate. For the bookish he should have won hands down against George W. Bush, whose favourite book was "The Very Hungry Caterpillar." It probably still is.

In this election, I find both candidates unappealing. Senator Kerry's principal attraction appears to be that he is not George W. Bush. Yet it is hard to warm to him. He claims that his pursuits are hunting, ski boarding, windsurfing and motorcycling. Ugh! On his campaign tour of Ohio, he has been out killing geese with a 12-gauge pump-action shotgun to show that he is one of the guys. Deer would have been better, but only Republicans slaughter deer.

Kerry is very rich and is a Boston Brahmin patrician on the distaff side. On his father's side, his lineage is far more ancient. The Senator's paternal grandfather acquired the surname of Kerry in the belief that he would be regarded as Boston Irish. But his original name was Kohn; the Democratic candidate has the blood of Aaron the peacemaker coursing through his veins.

I confess to being troubled by the part played by religion in American politics. Senator Kerry has said that his faith is personal and private – a sentiment that I find wholly admirable – but in a recent speech in Tempe, Arizona, he succeeded in calling on the Almighty no fewer than ten times. In general, however, Kerry (who is a Roman Catholic, as if that mattered) keeps his faith where it should be – in the closet.

President Bush, on the other hand, brandishes his newfound evangelical Christianity at every opportunity. It is his religiosity that leads him to espouse a host of illiberal and irrational views on a variety of social issues. Except that he is the most hated man in France it is hard to find much to say in his favour. He is, by any standard – apart from his willingness to spend federal money – a right-wing conservative and, as governor of Texas, presided over more executions than any governor in history. Like the late Senator Joe McCarthy, he uses the word "liberal" as a term of abuse and his polarizing rhetoric has made this election one of the most poisonous in living memory.

If Bush is re-elected it will be principally because of his unequivocal position on Islamic terror. Enlightened liberal opinion, with its belief – despite all evidence to the contrary – in the essential goodness of man, finds it as hard to come to grips with the reality of terror as it did in the last century with Nazi and Soviet totalitarianism. The question that many who abhor everything that

President Bush stands for are asking is whether Senator Kerry, a liberal even though he shoots geese, grasps this issue. The symbol of the Democratic Party is the donkey and Senator Kerry too much resembles the donkey of mythology that had a sack of hay on each side of him but died of starvation because he could not decide which sack to choose.

Having given you hungry caterpillars, geese and donkeys, allow me to exhaust my bestiary with two more creatures, the hedgehog and the fox. Isaiah Berlin in a famous essay uses as his theme a line from the ancient Greek poet Archilochus. The fox, according to the poet, knows many things but the hedgehog knows one big thing. President Bush does not know many things but perhaps he knows one big thing.

By name and nature I am a fox, but my bottle of whisky is riding on the hedgehog and his friend the very hungry caterpillar.

29 October, 2004

*S*ongs of Zion

I have been observing, with an emotion approaching awe, the relentlessly dynamic activities of the settler activists in their spirited opposition to Israel's withdrawal from Gaza. No one can fail to be impressed by their vitality, power of organization and discipline. Whether you agree with them or not, these are people who believe fervently in the justice of their cause and whose certainty that they are the possessors of the absolute truth gives them a strength that those who take more nuanced positions cannot match. And their ingenuity is equal to their vitality.

Their latest fancy is that their struggle is a struggle for democracy. With an irony that would have appealed to George Orwell, these young nationalists – the implementation of whose ideals would necessitate the perpetual denial of civil rights to the Palestinian inhabitants of Gaza and the West Bank – sport the colour orange in imitation of the democratic movement in Ukraine.

What immediately strikes the observer about the demonstrators is their homogeneity. Almost without exception, the demonstrators wear the uniform, sing the songs and chant the chants of the modern religious. Support for the retention, indeed for the expansion, of the settlements in the areas occupied by Israel after the 1967 war has become the orthodoxy of the Orthodox. The synagogues are full of anti-government posters and pamphlets; the religious schools and yeshivas take the same uncompromising political stance. Dissent is rare; how could it not be when parents, teachers and fellow pupils are united in imposing a single worldview? I find this strange. There are surely valid political and strategic arguments to be made for and against a peace based on a two-state solution, yet opposition to such a solution has been turned, by the near unanimity of Zionist rabbinical opinion, into a religious imperative. It would be a mistake to regard this synthesis of religion and militant nationalism as self-evident. Nothing in Judaism precludes a softer approach to the challenges that face this country; indeed, the official national religious line, prior to 1967, was more in tune with the dovish views of the Israeli left than with those of the more nationalist parties of the right.

The year 1967 was a watershed for religious Zionism because, as a result of its remarkable military victory in the Six-Day War, Israel's forces found themselves in occupation of the whole of the historic Land of Israel, including cities and sites that had strong biblical associations for the Jewish people. In religious circles the victory was regarded as miraculous; the Redemption was nigh, and a new, nationalist ideology was brought into the open, out of the cloistered confines of the source of that ideology, the Mercaz Harav Yeshiva in Jerusalem. The young rabbis who taught this ideology were teachers and leaders in the religious youth organization Bnei Akiva, and what happened to Bnei Akiva after 1967 mirrors what happened to the whole National Religious movement.

I was never a member of Bnei Akiva but, in my early teens, when I still lived in England, I was on its fringes. The organization was then a softer, paler version of Habonim, the youth movement to which I was attached. Like Habonim, it was a socialist organization that encouraged its members to emigrate to Israel and, ideally, to settle on kibbutzim. Bnei Akiva was, of course, religious but not obtrusively so. Boys and girls sang together, danced folk dances together and went together to summer camps.

Bnei Akiva, in Israel at any rate, has today moved away, religiously and politically, from the moderate left to the not-so-moderate right. Single-sex dancing is de rigeur and members dress in a way that differentiates them from their non-religious compatriots. Most significantly of all, Bnei Akiva has become politically militant.

And the songs have changed. One of the features of the modern revival of Hebrew poetry was a newfound love of nature and landscape. Bialik, the great national poet of a century ago, wrote of birds, fields, trees; the poet Rachel sang of the beauties of the Galilee. And, in common with Hebrew poetry through the centuries, the new Hebrew poets sang of the love of a man and a woman. These were our songs in Habonim, and so they were in Bnei Akiva before it caught a bad dose of the Redemption. No longer. The songs of the anti-disengagement protesters are of an exclusively religious nature. They speak of our entitlement to the entire Land of Israel; they long for the restoration of the Temple and the sacrificial cult. A recent article in *Haaretz* by Yair Sheleg reports on a new phenomenon among the national religious: songs of vengeance – Samson's prayer for revenge on the Philistines, the killing by Moses of the Egyptian slave-driver. Love is out; hate is in.

Songs matter. From its beginning, poetry and music have played a central role in the Zionist enterprise. "Sing to us from the songs of Zion," writes the psalmist as he longs for Zion on the banks of the rivers of Babylon. "My heart is in the east, and I in the uttermost west," sighed the great Hebrew poet of the Golden Age of Spain, Yehuda Halevi. There is a law on Israel's statute books called – to give it its important-sounding official title – the Law for the Encouragement of Songs in the Hebrew Language (Statutory Amendments), 5759-1998. The statute is a short one and the operative section provides that at least one half of all songs broadcast on Israeli radio in any month must be in Hebrew. You may think this is the height of musical jingoism but the point I want to make is that Hebrew song is at the core of our national identity. I am not being totally frivolous when I say that it had a far from insignificant part in my own decision to settle in Israel.

I was reminded of this recently when, in carrying out a major reorganization of my bookshelves, I came across a book that I could not recall having seen in upwards of 40 years. The title of the book, echoing Psalm 137, was "Songs of Zion" and it opened the wellsprings of memory for me as effectively as did that tea-soaked madeleine for Proust. I have no recollection of when I acquired it, or how, but it was certainly a prized possession of mine by the end of the 1940s. Published in the United States in 1942, the book contains the words and music of more than 200 Hebrew songs and, at one time, I knew nearly all of them. A glance at the chapter headings will give you the flavour: "Of Our Land and Our People," "Aliyah, Songs of Striving," "Songs of Hope and Courage," "Songs of Toil," "Pastorals".

I loved those songs; I was captivated by the romance of this faraway country that I had not yet visited. I yearned to drain the swamps of the Huleh and play the flute for the tone-deaf sheep of the Galilee. To this day, if you ask me – something nobody ever did – to sing to you of what happens when rest comes to the weary in the Valley of Jezreel, I can render at least three stanzas in an exceptionally fine baritone. Sad to report, the only person who can testify to this talent is she who has shared a bathroom with me for 48 years.

It should perhaps be no surprise that music should so powerfully affect one's emotions. Religion, Philip Larkin's "vast, moth-eaten musical brocade," has known this for centuries. But it is in the political sphere that it is most palpable. For me, one of the most memorable moments in the movies is the scene in the beer garden in "Cabaret." A fresh-faced boy with a pure treble voice starts singing a lovely song entitled "Tomorrow Belongs to Me." The other patrons gradually join in and, as the camera pans down to the swastika armband that we suddenly realize the boy is wearing, the ballad slowly segues into a powerful and stridently nationalist anthem. This, you feel, is how Nazism took hold on the imagination of millions. Music can have that effect on you.

The cliché goes: you are what you eat. It might be more correct to say that you are what you sing. It is easy to be cynical about the songs that we used to sing in our youth movements: the pastoral songs, the songs of yearning, toil, hope and courage. "Bliss was it in that dawn to be alive, but to be young was very heaven." Wordsworth eventually became disillusioned with that dawn of his youth, the French Revolution. The dream of Zion was never that simple but when we sang, we sang of an ideal that had no place in it for the subjugation of others.

Perhaps, for many of us, the dream of Zion has not worked out in the way we had hoped, but there was nothing ignoble in those dreams or in the songs that expressed them.

20 May, 2005

The Wisest Fool

Like the proverbial dustcart that comes after London's Lord Mayor's show, any monarch that succeeded Elizabeth I was going to be an anti-climax. James I was already a king, having become James VI of Scotland at the age of one when Elizabeth deposed his mother, Mary, Queen of Scots. As James I of England he will go down in history, if for nothing else, as the man who inspired that treasure of English literature, the King James translation of the Bible. The archetype of the ineffectual intellectual – he spoke fluent Greek, Latin, French, English and Scots, and was schooled in Italian and Spanish – he was a poor ruler. Henry IV of France, no fool himself, called James "the wisest fool in Christendom".

The epithet has stuck. In memory of King James, the *Economist's* Christmas issue offered a Bible to each of the three best entries in a competition to nominate the wisest fool of recent times. Not for nothing does the *Economist* call itself a liberal newspaper, and one can only hope it will not regret this act of spontaneous generosity. There are, incidentally, easier ways of acquiring a Bible. I am not suggesting for a moment that after your next stay at a hotel, when you sweep the sewing kit and body lotion samples into your briefcase, you include a Gideon Bible, but the Internet is full of offers of free Bibles. To be eligible all you have to do is provide your e-mail address, pick a password and convert to Christianity.

I am not entering the *Economist's* contest as I already have a Bible, but I hope I shall not be abusing the hospitality of this newspaper by submitting a phantom entry here. The results of the competition will only be published on January 29, but, to my mind, the linguist Noam Chomsky will romp home in both compulsory categories.

I do not subscribe to the widespread superstition that the views on politics of scientists, philosophers and authors have any special sanctity. Chomsky is a distinguished scientist but, outside his sphere of expertise, his opinions should carry as much weight as those of David Beckham (although I must admit to being appalled that my spell-checker recognizes Beckham, but not Chomsky!) Yet Chomsky's opinions have been granted an attention that has no relation to their merit.

Chomsky-baiting has become such a popular blood sport that it seems unsporting to join the pack, but he systematically talks ineffable nonsense. According to his rigidly simplistic ideology, a demonic America and its mega-corporations are pitted against the Third World, which he uncritically admires. In his view, the American 1998 raid on a pharmaceutical factory in the Sudan, which may have cost the life of a single security guard, was far worse than 9/11, which cost no fewer than 3,000 innocent lives; he persistently denied that the Khmer Rouge was carrying out genocide in Cambodia, and when he could deny it no longer, he blamed America for it. According to Chomsky, Roger Faurisson, a notorious Holocaust denier, was not anti-Semitic, but "an apolitical liberal." In the words of George Orwell, whom Chomsky frequently cites, "One has to belong to the intelligentsia to believe things like that: no ordinary person could be such a fool".

But I come to praise Chomsky, not to bury him. Serial crackpot though he is, his formidable mind must surely put him ahead of the competition when it comes to the second leg of the *Economist* biathlon. Noam Chomsky is a very important scientist. According to the Arts and Humanities Citation Index, he is the most frequently cited living intellectual, and rightly so, for in his field of linguistics, he has brought about a conceptual revolution. Chomsky's subject is language. It is man's possession of language that has enabled him to master nature, to fly to the moon, to communicate across vast distances. Language is unique to man and there is no form of Homo Sapiens, however primitive, that lacks language. Chomsky noticed something important about language. Children, at an early age, utter sentences that they have never heard before. Chomsky argued convincingly that the capacity of children to acquire languages naturally – a capacity they lose around the age of puberty – is wired into their brains. Language is an instinct. Whatever the language, it obeys deep rules of grammar that are common to all human languages. Chomsky has devoted much of his career to discovering the rules of that universal grammar, one that forms the basis of every language.

That makes Chomsky pretty interesting but, for me, what makes him additionally interesting is his close relationship with the Hebrew language. Chomsky is not friendly toward the State of Israel. Despite his Zionist upbringing – he even once went to work on a kibbutz with the intention of staying – Chomsky's attitude to Israel is in tune with his world view and he has little good to say about this country. But, as you might guess from his quintessentially Hebrew first name, he grew up in a Hebrew environment, immersed, as he says, in Hebrew culture and literature. His early ideas on linguistics were developed in his master's thesis, which bore the catchy title of "Morphophonemics of Modern Hebrew."

I have long thought that, while we Israelis preen ourselves for being the only democracy in the Middle East, draining swamps, winning wars and all that jazz, we have short-changed ourselves on the one truly remarkable aspect of our return. The revival of the Hebrew language has no historic parallel. Let me invite a Chomsky, Noam's father, William Chomsky, in his book "Hebrew: The Eternal Language," to do the flag-waving: "Can there be any question as to the vitality of the Hebrew language? None of the modern attempts to revive old languages, such as Gaelic, Welsh and Indi, can boast of anything approximating the progress made by Hebrew. Yet the Irish, Welsh and Indians have been rooted on their own soil and are free from political, physical and economic difficulties with which the young struggling Jewish community in Israel has had to cope".

The story of how this came about deserves a history of its own. A significant link with the revival of Hebrew was recalled last week with the death, at the age of 103, of Dola Ben Yehuda. Her father, Eliezer Ben Yehuda, is credited with being the father of modern Hebrew. Ben Yehuda was, like many revolutionaries, a half-mad obsessive – Dola would later recall that when she was a child in the early years of the last century, she was only allowed to play with the few children who could speak Hebrew – but, thanks to him and a few fellow fanatics, Hebrew became the first language of millions; it became a mother tongue. What better example of Chomsky's theories is there than that of the Israeli child who laughs, cries and jabbers in a language that, for centuries, Jews only knew in their prayers?

Hebrew is, of course, the language of the Bible, and you will rarely see a popular account of language without finding mention of the biblical account of the Tower of Babel. It is not hard to understand why. The legend seeks to account for two of the most interesting things about language: its power and its diversity. As told in Genesis 11, the possession of a single language made the sons of men so powerful that they conspired to build a tower that would reach the heavens and thus rival God. There seemed no limit to what they could do, so God came down to earth and confounded the tongues of the sons of men so that they could no longer understand each other.

As Umberto Eco described in his recent book "Serendipities", medieval Christian scholars who, of course, took the Bible literally, devoted much time to speculation on the nature of the pre-Babel language. This was a critical question for theologians because creation itself arose through an act of speech. The language of creation was not only the first language; it was, according to their lights, the perfect language. The theologians grudgingly conceded that the primordial language was Hebrew – Latin and Italian were unfortunately out of the question – but it was an uncorrupted Hebrew that disappeared with the destruction of the Tower of Babel and, being a perfect language, was a kind of linguistic matrix that formed a basis for all the languages of the world: in short, a universal grammar.

And so we return to Chomsky, linguist, Hebraist and the cleverest of fools. He would not see it that way but, in searching for the rules of a universal grammar, Noam Chomsky is, if we are to believe those scholars of the Middle Ages, occupied in a quest for the language used by God for creating the world. Perhaps he will find that it is Hebrew.

21 January, 2005

Roll Over Beethoven

E.M. Forster opens a chapter of his novel "Howard's End" with an arresting sentence. "It will be generally admitted," he writes, "that Beethoven's Fifth Symphony is the most sublime noise that has ever penetrated into the ear of man." Forster clearly intended to startle, but was too civilized a man to be preposterous for no reason.

The Fifth is indeed one of the great Beethoven symphonies. It was familiar to me long before I developed a liking for classical music. In World War II the stirring opening of the symphony preceded BBC news broadcasts; its three short notes and one long note signified in Morse code the letter "V" (for victory). Britain's propaganda chiefs seem to have seen no irony in harnessing a German composer (albeit one of impeccably progressive sentiments) to the war effort against his fellow Germans.

Still, although Forster's pronouncement was uncharacteristically bombastic, had he written of the Ninth Symphony rather than of the Fifth, I would have been bound to agree. Because the Choral Symphony truly is a sublime noise, and last week the Israel Philharmonic Orchestra under the baton of Zubin Mehta proved it for me. It is a work I know tolerably well but this performance knocked my socks off. The symphony, culminating in Schiller's inspiring "Ode to Joy" is the pinnacle of Western culture; in listening to it, I experienced that rare spine-tingling feeling the feeling that, as the contemporary cliché goes, it can't get better than this.

I had returned early for the concert from a short trip to London, and I was reminded that there are forces that would deprive us of such pleasures. There is no place for Beethoven in the pan-Islamist utopia envisaged by the deluded young men who blew up themselves and their fellow citizens on the London transport system. I realize that I am not exactly a lone voice crying in the wilderness when I sound off against terrorism in an Israeli newspaper. But to strike at great cities like London, New York and Madrid is to strike at civilization itself and at all that the culture of the West has built up over the millennia. The barbarians who bombed those great cities were not intent on redressing grievances, real or perceived, but sought to destroy a culture they envied and of which they did not feel a part.

And yet, in the face of all this, London's *bien-pensants* persist in refusing to confront the reality of Islamist terror. Most mornings I read online the *Guardian* newspaper of London. It is and I say this without irony a fine liberal newspaper: humane, intelligent, the epitome of the Western civilization that the jihadis seek to destroy. Yet the *Guardian* is emblematic of a certain school of liberal opinion that finds it difficult to believe that there are people who are prepared to spread wanton destruction for an irrational cause.

Examples of the *Guardian* at its best and worst could be seen in the issue of July 27. Alongside a trenchant article by Jonathan Freedland punching holes in the moral equivalence implicit in recent pronouncements of London's mayor, Ken Livingstone, is an insanely fatuous article by Jonathan Glover, who teaches "human values and contemporary global ethics" at King's College, London. The heading of the article says it all: "Dialogue is the only way to end this cycle of violence." Together with "root causes," "cycle of violence" is one of the most overused terms in the *Guardian* lexicon. It seems that if you react to violence, as the United States did after 9/11 and Israel did at the outbreak of the armed intifada, you create a cycle of violence. Voltaire put the views of the violence cyclists in a nutshell: "This animal is dangerous. When attacked, it defends itself."

As the title to his article implies, Prof. Glover's solution is to institute a dialogue with the Islamists. What you have to do is to talk reasonably to these chaps and all will be well. Employing his expertise in human values and contemporary global ethics, Glover would be the ideal person to represent the West in the dialogue. If past demands of Islamists are anything to go by, he should be prepared, in exchange for an Islamist undertaking to travel by Egged instead of London Transport, to agree to the foundation of a worldwide pan-Islamic republic; the imposition of *shari'a* law throughout the Western world; the stoning of adulterers, homosexuals and uppity women; a free hand in killing Jews wherever they are; compulsory female circumcision; and the closing of all non-Islamic concert halls, museums, theatres and cinemas.

If I could compel all contemporary global ethicists to read one book, I would send them a copy of Paul Berman's "Terror and Liberalism" (W. W. Norton, 2003), the best book I have read on the thorny subject of Islamist terrorism. This short book analyzes the ideological underpinnings of radical Islam and the equivocal response by many Western intellectuals to the monstrous atrocities perpetrated in the name of Islam. It will, in my opinion, become a classic of anti-totalitarian literature to put aside for rereading with Karl Popper's "The Open Society and its Enemies," Isaiah Berlin's "Essays on Liberty" and the works of George Orwell. Berman shows that, in the tradition of the spineless reaction of the intelligentsia to the totalitarian ideologies of the last century, many liberals in the West today are in a shameful state of denial over the Islamist threat.

Berman gives a full and fair-minded summary of the philosophy of the Egyptian Sayyid Qutb, the thinker who has most influenced the ideology of modern radical Islam. Qutb calls for martyrs to die in a war of conquest to restore the pan-Muslim civilization that existed in the seventh century. He followed his own advice, though perhaps inadvertently; he was executed in Egypt in 1966. Berman argues convincingly that Qutb's Islamism, with its cult of death, is a totalitarian movement that follows directly upon the totalitarian movements of the 20th century, left and right. The ideal was always the same; it was the ideal of submission to the kind of authority that liberal civilization had slowly undermined.

While anti-liberal extremism is not exclusively religious – communism and fascism are striking examples of that – Islamism is only the most recent instance of the depressing history of the misuse of religion to justify intolerance and violence. Berman cites Norman Cohn's classic book "The Pursuit of the Millennium," which graphically tells of the violent religious millennial cults of the Middle Ages, but Berman goes even further back, tracing this ideological paranoia, he calls it the ur-myth to the book of the Revelation of St. John the Divine.

The abuse of religion for political ends has a special contemporary resonance for Israelis, but you should not compare the practices of the Islamists with the kosher black mass, the *pulsa denura*. In Iran, you laugh at fatwas at your peril, but here people appear to find something diverting in a group of born-again psychopaths praying for the Angel of Death to pay a professional call on the prime minister.

My prayer book is reprehensibly deficient in this valuable component of the liturgy, but I gather that you have to play some kind of Russian roulette with the dark forces. According to a press report, if the Angel of Death does not take out Ariel Sharon within 30 days of the ceremony, the participants in it will themselves die. Talk about a boomerang; I would not take that kind of risk even for Osama bin Laden.

The pulsa denura fits much better into the death-loving philosophy of Sayyid Qutb than into the Jewish religion. Qutb writes that "The Quran points to another contemptible characteristic of the Jews: their craven desire to live." I don't know about craven, but Jews certainly like life even though Qutb and his ilk want to deprive us of it. However fervent his belief in the next world, a Jew will always rather bear those ills he knows, than fly to others that he knows not of. What's wrong with that?

This unhappy marriage of religion and politics is very much on the minds of Israelis today. It is obscene to liken our anti-disengagement protesters to the demented jihadis, but we should not forget that our foulest ideological murderers, Baruch Goldstein and Yigal Amir, acted in the name of the Jewish religion. And we have our own imams and our own madrasas. There are valid political arguments against the withdrawal of Israeli troops from Gaza. Protest may be justified, but it should not be made a religious duty.

Of course the young religious Israelis in orange have nothing in common with the homicidal maniacs of the London underground, but there is one lesson to be learned. The job of rabbis is to teach people how to live their lives. They have neither skill nor authority in deciding how nations should conduct themselves. To believe otherwise is to slide down the slippery slope to theocracy.

And then, roll over, Beethoven.

5 August, 2005

Sacred Cows to the Slaughter

In my book, the furor over the Mohammed cartoons is a no-brainer. I hold a simplistic, perhaps naïve, view of the right to freedom of expression. I was raised on the classic texts of English liberalism – Mill's essay "On Liberty" and Milton's "Areopagitica." I regard free speech as axiomatic, and I view with suspicion any attempt to restrain it.

In September 2005, *Jyllands-Posten*, a Danish daily newspaper, published twelve cartoons depicting the Prophet Mohammed. Although most newspapers pusillanimously refrained from reproducing the cartoons, you can see them for yourselves on the Internet. They are not particularly good cartoons, nor is it hard to see why they would offend the sensibilities of devout Muslims. The very depiction of the prophet is forbidden under Islamic law, but the cartoons go beyond that. One shows Mohammed with a bomb in his turban, another has him wielding a scimitar. To portray the founder of their religion as a terrorist cannot but hurt the many Muslims who neither practise terrorism nor advocate it.

Still, shocking to believers as the cartoons undoubtedly were, it was only in January 2006, after a group of Danish imams had spent the intervening months hawking them round the Middle East, that the proverbial excrement hit the proverbial fan. Saudi Arabia, Syria, Libya and Iran withdrew their ambassadors from Denmark; Danish goods were boycotted and crowds rioted in the streets of Arab capitals, where Western embassies were attacked and torched.

No one should be surprised that, in countries where any kind of freedom is an alien concept, enraged mobs should, egged on by their imams, embark on an orgy of mayhem, arson and murder. Why, after all, should blasphemous cartoonists fare any better than heretical novelists or hostile filmmakers? What I was unprepared for was the supine attitude in the West to this appalling assault on the cherished principle of freedom of speech. Only France, to its credit, saw the hullabaloo as the black-and-white issue of liberty of expression that it surely is. The French have a clear-headed approach to the clash of cultures. They have the largest population of Muslims in Europe and extend to them full citizenship. But France expects its citizens to adhere to its customs, and those customs include the practice of tolerance and free speech.

In the U.S. and Britain, informed progressive opinion almost invariably allied itself with the forces of darkness. Without telling Denmark how, short of the imposition of state censorship, it could have prevented this "insensitive" and "unnecessary" (to quote Britain's pathetic foreign secretary, Jack Straw) insult to the feelings of the murderous mullahs, the progressives of the West – media and politicians alike – fell over themselves in deploring the affront to religion that the cartoons presented. You would have thought that it was the Danes who were setting fire to Arab embassies.

A good example, taken at random from the tedious Western chorus of political correctness, was furnished by the heir to the British throne. Prince Charles has recently returned from a visit to the Middle East, where he distinguished himself by wearing a variety of silly hats. At Cairo's Al-Azhar University, an institute of higher learning not particularly noted for its devotion to the virtues of tolerance, His Royal Highness said – to the obvious delight of his listeners: "The recent ghastly strife and anger over the Danish cartoons show the danger that comes of our failure to listen and to respect what is precious and sacred to others".

That's not what the anger shows at all. It shows the danger of indulging a system that seeks to impose on the world the subjugation of women, the stoning of adulterers, the hanging of homosexuals and the suppression of free enquiry. Why did the prince not tell them that in Denmark, as in Britain, you can say what you like if it does not harm others, and that he deplored the trashing of buildings and the murder of innocents in the name of the Prophet?

Blasphemy is no longer a crime in Western countries. If God is insulted, he can unleash his own thunderbolts unaided. I have no doubt that blasphemy is hurtful to the feelings of true believers. Jezebel's prophets were probably pretty miffed at the nasty things Elijah said about Baal. When, in one of the funniest scenes of Monty Python's "Life of Brian," a planned judicial stoning turns chaotic, devout Jews surely winced as the Ineffable Name was bandied about. But they did not attack a single embassy.

The cartoon affair passed virtually unremarked in Israel. It is regrettable that we Israelis are so occupied with cultivating our own garden that we pay insufficient attention to what is going on in the world around us. If you listen to a news broadcast here, you will be hard put to learn of what is happening in Darfur or northern Uganda. If you hoped for some mass expression of solidarity with the Danes – a people to whom the Jewish people owe a great debt of gratitude – you would have been sadly disappointed. Instead, to the extent the affair was mentioned at all, Israel's *bien-pensants* joined the woolly western consensus.

Haaretz, the standard-bearer of Israeli liberal opinion, in the ranks of whose contributors I am proud to number myself, while deploring the violence, condemned the "hurtful assaults on religion" that the cartoons represented. The argument, a leitmotif of the liberal media, that attacks on religion – any religion – are somehow out of bounds, needs examining. In an open society, sacred cows are there to be slaughtered. If anything is in need of sending up, it is religion. The Crusades, the Spanish Inquisition and countless wars and massacres have been perpetrated in the name of religion; the religion of the jihadis and the suicide-murderers needs satirizing more than most. Like the "root causes" argument used notoriously by the progressive European press to "explain" Islamic terror, the liberal tut-tutting over the perceived affronts to religion go some way towards legitimating the demented reaction to the Danish cartoons.

There should be no half-measures here. We must be intolerant of the intolerant. The West must believe passionately that its values, the values of the open society, are superior. Denmark is a democratic country and we need to support it wholeheartedly against the bullies who seek to fetter its cherished freedoms. Nothing else will do.

Freedom of speech is not an absolute right, of course. There is a line that may not be crossed. To quote the classic example given by the United States Supreme Court, you do not permit a man falsely to shout "fire" in a crowded theatre. And you cannot permit incitement, but, although the Danish cartoons resulted in horrific violence, the inciters were the imams, not the cartoonists. You might as well blame Rushdie for his own fatwa or the Dutch filmmaker, Theo van Gogh, for his own murder.

If we are to test ourselves over our dedication to free speech, we should bear in mind George Orwell's dictum that if liberty means anything at all, it means the right to tell people what they do not want to hear. And, of course, its obverse: the need for us not to object to others telling us what we do not want to hear. Knowing what anti-Semitic speech led to in the last century, Jews have a right to be thin-skinned; but if it falls short of incitement, we may not like it and we do not have to listen to it, but we should not seek to prevent it.

The tough one is legislation against Holocaust Denial or, as it is known in its sanitized and slightly more sophisticated version, Holocaust Revisionism. Those who deny that the Holocaust occurred, or who maintain that the numbers given for the victims are grossly exaggerated, or that there were no gas chambers at Auschwitz are not arguing over questions of historical fact, but are perpetuating lies of the same order as the Blood Libels and the Protocols of the Elders of Zion. It is nothing more than a particularly nasty form of anti-Semitism. There are anti-Semites who are not Holocaust deniers, but there are no Holocaust deniers who are not anti-Semites.

On the whole, I am against criminalizing denial of the Holocaust. If it crosses the line into incitement, existing laws will take care of it. Austria, the country of Hitler's birth, the country that has never atoned for its part in the Holocaust, has recently sentenced the best-known of all Holocaust revisionists, David Irving, to three years in prison. There has to be something wrong with a law that permits a fascist like Irving, the hero-worshipper of that great apostle of liberty, Adolf Hitler, to pose as a martyr of free speech.

Call me an innocent, but I still go with Milton who, in "Areopagitica", his great 17th century onslaught on censorship, wrote: "Let [Truth] and Falsehood grapple; who ever knew Truth put to the worse in a free and open encounter?" In the long run, we must believe that he was right.

21 April, 2006

Out of Court

History seldom rewards the deserving. When it comes to immortality the sinners have it over the saints. Assassins and mass murderers achieve everlasting fame while the virtuous die uncommemorated. Captain Boycott, Joseph Guillotin and Nicolas Chauvin were not estimable characters but their names live on because they, albeit unwittingly, introduced new words to the language. So if I tell you that the name of Robert H. Bork has entered the dictionary, I am not thereby conferring on him any kind of accolade. The verb "to bork" has become part of the American language. It means, according to the latest edition of Webster's New Millennium Dictionary of English, to seek to obstruct a political appointment or selection.

Bork acquired his everlasting fame when, in 1987, he was nominated to the Supreme Court of the United States by President Reagan and was – well – borked by the Senate. His legal and intellectual qualifications were not in issue; in fact they were outstanding. His crime was that he was an outspoken conservative and espoused views that seriously breached the prevailing liberal consensus. Senator Edward Kennedy's speech voicing the liberal objections to the confirmation is still quoted. He raised the spectre of back-alley abortions, segregated lunch counters, book censorship and religious fundamentalism if Bork were to be elevated to the Supreme Court.

Unfair, but not excessively so. As is evident from his books, Bork is an active soldier in America's culture wars, smiting the liberal elites under the banner of God and morality. The world, and especially the United States, is going to the dogs. His is not the mild quietism of the common or garden conservative. He is a dyed-in-the-wool reactionary who decries progress of any form, who yearns for the good old days when women and blacks knew their place, when homosexuality and abortion were crimes, when old-time religion held sway. A Catholic convert from Protestantism, Bork blames the civil rights movement and the sexual revolution for what he perceives as a serious moral decline in

America. He inveighs against everything modern: multiculturalism, racial and sexual politics, rock and rap and, of course, against the club he was precluded from joining – the United States Supreme Court.

In the United States the appointment of a new justice attracts a level of attention that is only exceeded by the election of a president. The political and social opinions of the candidate are scrutinized meticulously. Everything about him attracts intense media attention. You might well ask why the personal political views of a judge are of interest to anyone but the judge himself so long as that judge conscientiously performs his paramount obligation of dispensing justice. In most countries of the world, a judge's politics are indeed irrelevant to his appointment. But in the United States, the right of the Supreme Court to disallow state legislation as being against the Constitution of the United States confers enormous power on it; witness the much disputed decision in Roe v Wade establishing a woman's constitutional right to have an abortion.

There is perhaps only one other country where the identity of a judge and the politics of that judge are so hotly debated – Israel. This has not escaped the notice of Robert Bork. In his book "Coercing Virtue: The Worldwide Rule of Judges," Bork, in attacking "the recent ascendancy almost everywhere of activist, ambitious, and imperialistic judiciaries," selects three Supreme Courts for special criticism – those of the U.S., Canada and Israel. Bork has no doubt as to which of the three courts he criticizes is the most imperialistic. "Pride of place in the international judicial deformation of democratic government," he writes, "goes not to the United States, nor to Canada, but to the State of Israel".

It goes against the grain to agree with a moralistic dinosaur like Bork but he has a point. In a striking parallel to Bork's rejection by the Senate, Israel is currently in the throes of its own Bork affair. The candidacy of Professor Ruth Gavison for a seat on the Supreme Court of Israel has been opposed by the President of the Supreme Court, Justice Aharon Barak. By virtue of his intellectual supremacy and sheer force of personality, Justice Barak effectively controls the committee that makes appointments to the bench. Although Prof. Gavison's legal and intellectual qualifications for appointment to the Israeli court are as unassailable as were Bork's for the U.S. court, Barak does not want Gavison on the court and, unusually, has said as much in public. In a prize-winning example of the pot calling the kettle black, Barak explained that he was borking her because she had an "agenda." What the learned justice meant was that her agenda was not the same as his.

Gavison is no Bork. She is secular and progressive. It is not her political or social views that make her unacceptable to Barak – after all, there are religious members of the court well to her right – but her outspoken criticisms, and in this she does resemble Bork, of the judicial activism of the Barak court. Put simply, what Gavison says is that it is the job of a judge to interpret the law, not to make it. She also considers, in contradistinction to Barak, that there are areas of activity that are not within the purview of the courts and that, as was the case in pre-Barak days, only a person with a direct personal interest in a case may be a party to it. These are Bork's points too but, unlike Gavison, his principal objection to activist courts is that they promote the enlightened agenda he detests.

The consequences of judicial activism are usually congenial to liberals. The American court has to its credit landmark decisions enforcing desegregation, limiting capital punishment, overturning sodomy laws, legalizing abortion. The Israeli court has made decisions upholding freedom of expression; it has rerouted the separation fence to accord with the requirements of international law; it has forbidden the use of force in interrogating terror suspects; it has exercised control over the activities of the security forces in the occupied territories; it has ordered the dismissal of ministers under indictment in the name of quality of government.

But you can applaud the outcome yet deplore the manner of achieving it. There is one principle that unites all democracies; indeed there is nothing more basic: a country's laws are made by its democratically elected legislature. You do not have to adhere to the antediluvian social views of Robert Bork to find something profoundly troubling in legislation from the bench. Karl Popper in his classic attack on the enemies of the open society singles out Plato as the principal ideological precursor of fascism. Plato believed that political power should not be in the hands of the rabble but in the hands of the few who are suited to make decisions on behalf of the community – philosopher kings. Justice Aharon Barak and his acolytes are would-be philosopher kings. That is the road to totalitarianism.

It is an error to conflate judicial activism with social progress. Judicial legislation is a two-edged sword. The U.S. Supreme Court consistently overturned Roosevelt's New Deal legislation until he put a stop to it by packing the court with liberal appointees. In 1857, in the Dred Scott case, the court invoked the Constitution to uphold the right to own slaves, thus paving the way to the Civil War. And, recently and notoriously, in the case of Bush v Gore, a bare majority of five justices, each of whom had been appointed by a Republican president, used the arguments of judicial activism to hand the presidency to the Republican candidate.

According to Justice Barak, a judge "must sometimes depart the confines

of his legal system and channel into it fundamental values not yet found in it."
On that theory what would prevent a court composed of religious judges from
overturning a long overdue law of the Knesset permitting civil marriage on
the grounds that it violated Jewish "fundamental values"? It could happen and
then what would the progressive advocates of judicial legislation say? Like the
U.S. liberals who rightly screamed blue murder over Bush v Gore, the judicial
activists would be hoist with their own petard.

There are arguments in favour of judicial activism in the United States
that are not available to the Israel Supreme Court. The United States has a
written constitution and it is the constitutional duty of its Supreme Court to
interpret that constitution. Israel's Supreme Court, on the other hand, has no
constitutional authority to overrule legislation.

Churchill famously said that democracy is the worst form of government –
except for all the others. There have been enlightened despots and progressive
dictators but anyone who has a concern for democracy cannot but be worried
at the unfettered powers of an unelected body, however wise, however
benevolent.

20 January, 2006

Pride and Prejudice

Shakespeare's 18th Sonnet ("Shall I compare thee to a Summer's day?") and W. H. Auden's "Lullaby" ("Lay your sleeping head, my love") are among the most beautiful love poems in the English language and no man who has ever loved a woman can fail to be moved by them. Except for one thing: Each was written by one man to another man. Times have changed, but had either poem described the loved one more explicitly, the lingering prejudice against homosexual love would affect the way people read them.

There are few people in the West who today believe that what people get up to in the privacy of their own bedrooms is of concern to anyone but themselves. Even the apologists for fundamentalist Islam who proliferate on the European left must have felt uncomfortable at the spectacle of the teenage boys recently executed publicly in Iran for homosexuality. The Iranian regime can at least claim to be even-handed – straights can also get topped there: In August 2004, a 16-year old girl, Atefeh Rajabi, was hanged in the Caspian port of Neka for having sex before marriage.

But the West no longer treats homosexuality as a crime. This was not always the case. As recently as 1986, Chief Justice Warren Burger in a majority opinion in the United States Supreme Court ruled that "to hold that the act of homosexual sodomy is somehow protected as a fundamental right would be to cast aside millennia of moral teaching." In 2003, the court reversed itself and, despite its conservative reputation, ruled as unconstitutional a law of the state of Texas that made sexual relations between two consenting adults a crime. Still, three justices dissented, Justice Antonio Scalia complaining that the court "has largely signed on to the so-called homosexual agenda." The learned justice must have been referring to the Protocols of the Elders of Greenwich Village.

In Britain too, homosexual acts between men were prohibited until relatively recently. When, in 1885, legislation ("the Labouchere Amendment") was introduced to criminalize all sexual activity between persons of the same sex,

Queen Victoria is said to have initially refused to sign the bill. She refused to accept the possibility of female homosexuality. She is alleged to have said that "ladies do not do such things." Whether the tale is true or not, the eventual statute was confined to proscribing sexual acts between males. Notoriously, this was the Act under which Oscar Wilde was convicted, following the ill-advised libel suit he brought, and lost, against the Marquess of Queensberry.

Despite Justice Scalia, the criminalization of private homosexual acts is no longer given serious consideration in the Western world. But public discussion of the legal rights of homosexuals will not go away. President Bill Clinton's first crisis after coming into office had nothing to do with trivial matters like the Middle East, Russia or the economy. It was a dispute with the Joint Chiefs of Staff over whether gays could serve in the military. Today, the minds of America's judges and politicians are exercised over an equally marginal issue: Can someone contract a marriage with someone else of the same sex? There is even a proposal to amend the Constitution so as to prevent bolshie states from passing laws authorizing such relationships.

Homosexuals are victims in the United States of the so-called "culture wars" that pit liberal opinion against an increasingly assertive, predominantly religious, right-wing camp. Issues that in other countries are peripheral – sexual preferences, the teaching of evolution, stem cell research, abortion – have turned into matters that occupy the foreground of national debate.

Not all the issues are no-brainers, but the attempt to deny full rights to gays surely is. Religion has no right to compel nations to dictate to people how to live their lives if their practices, however repulsive to some, do no harm to society. Gays should be entitled to marry, join the military, teach children or do anything else they choose that does no injury to others.

Still, it is perfectly legitimate for a religion that bases its legitimacy on written texts to be antagonistic to a practice that is expressly forbidden by those texts. If you want to belong to a club you must abide by its rules. Male homosexuality is regarded as one of the gravest offenses under Jewish law. The late polymath, Yeshayahu Leibowitz, the most unorthodox of Orthodox Jews, conducted a wide correspondence with admirers who sought his opinion on a variety of subjects. A collection of his letters has been published (so far only in Hebrew, I regret to say) under the title "I Wanted to Ask You, Prof. Leibowitz" .

In two instances in the book, his advice is sought by young religious Jews who, in the depths of despair, write that they are irresistibly attracted to members of their own sex. They ask how they can reconcile this with the religion that they so desperately want to observe. For a man with a reputation as a curmudgeon, his replies are outstandingly compassionate. Writing as a religious Jew, he cannot condone what he freely asserts to be a transgression, but he is at pains to console his correspondent by assuring him that his prayers are valid and that he remains part of the Jewish people. A similar point is made in a documentary film "Trembling Before God," which movingly portrays the heartbreaking experiences of young Orthodox Jewish homosexuals, men and women, who cling to the ancestral faith that treats as sinful the sexual orientation that they are unable to abandon.

I have only the dimmest idea of what they do. I believe it comes, like Haagen-Dazs, in a variety of flavours. There is still much scientific discussion of whether the roots of homosexual behaviour are genetic or psychological. It looks as if it is a bit of both but, if the reason is biological, perhaps a geneticist reader could explain to me why a characteristic that, in general, militates against producing offspring should not, on purely Darwinian principles, have disappeared over the generations.

Still, I know of at least one case where nurture rather than nature was blamed. On a wall outside a London pub was a graffito: "My mother made me a homosexual." The effect was spoiled by the wag who scrawled underneath: "If I gave her the wool, would she make me one, too?" If, as I believe to be the case, homosexuality is now accepted as normal, I fail to see why members of the gay community should stress their abnormality by putting on Gay Pride parades. Gay Pride seems to me as illogical as Gay Shame. Your sexual preferences are matters of prosaic fact. They don't warrant a procession with a band, except perhaps in New York where there are parades of every description: Thanksgiving Parades, Italian parades on Columbus Day, Irish parades on St. Patrick Day. Only the Jews don't go for parades in New York; they have bad feet.

Though I have an aversion to parades of any kind, including Gay Pride ones, I would not go as far as Rabbi David Basri. In honour of last year's Gay Pride event in Jerusalem, this prominent kabbalistic rabbi was quoted as saying that homosexuals are "subhuman" and will be reincarnated as rabbits. No, I checked; it was not a misprint. He did not say that they would be reincarnated as rabbis, even kabbalistic ones. Anyhow, why rabbits? Had he wanted to underscore the heinousness of their offense, he might have reincarnated the subhumans as mosquitoes or cockroaches. I am not sure I would like to be reincarnated as anything, but a rabbit is surely not the worst thing to be.

Of course, in Israel we have become conditioned to hearing rabbis say things that would, were it not for the great respect that we show to the cloth, qualify them for immediate incarceration in a padded cell. There must be something in the rabbinical education that sends so many of its graduates to la-la land.

Thus, the rabbi who attributed a dreadful railway accident some years ago to the fact that the cinemas in Petah Tikva are open on Shabbat; the prominent settler rabbi who blamed a rise in road accidents on the Oslo Peace Process; the recent pronouncements of one of the most eminent rabbis of them all to the effect that the devastation wrought by Hurricane Katrina was due to the disengagement from Gaza. He added, it is reported, that African Americans were particularly singled out as victims because blacks don't learn Torah.

Not that the rabbis have a monopoly in this inability to follow the elementary rules of causation. Pat Robertson, the popular American television evangelist put the blame for Katrina on America's permissive attitude to abortion.

The idea of homosexuals being reincarnated as rabbits worries me. I too belong to an unjustly maligned group of people: lawyers. When my turn comes round next time, am I going to be a shark? On the whole I'd rather be a rabbit.

16 September, 2005

The Anti-Americans

The London boys' day school that I attended 60 years ago awarded an annual prize called the School Declamation Prize. To compete, a boy had to stand up in front of the whole school and declaim a speech that he himself had written on a subject of his own choosing. Though the prize carried a certain prestige there was always a paucity of entrants because the prospect of standing in front of 800 of your fellow pupils, each with a single burning desire to watch you fall flat on your face, was enough to daunt all but the foolhardy.

In this respect, 1951 was a typical year; there were a mere two entries. Of those two speeches, one was good, the other was bad and the judges had no difficulty in awarding the prize to the good one, an elegant disquisition on the life of Richard Wagner. But there was a serpent lurking in the prizewinner's Garden of Eden. One of the young listeners thought the speech sounded familiar, and the next day appeared brandishing a back copy of the Reader's Digest with an article on Wagner. There could be no doubt that the prize speech was a word-for-word copy of it.

The story has a moral, though not the one you would imagine. They took the prize away, of course; how could they not, when the rules of entry to the competition had been so blatantly infringed? But the reactions were puzzling. The boy who had shamelessly pilfered someone else's work and passed it off as his own became the object of sympathy, almost a hero. The one who had courageously exposed this outrageous theft was, for a time, ostracized. He had violated the code.

There is a code, common to almost all societies, according to which an informer is despised. Look at the epithets that are used – all derogatory: stool pigeon, nark, rat, snitch, sneak, blabber, squealer, grass, telltale, talebearer, tattler. English infants taunt the tell-tale tit whose tongue shall be slit, while American schoolchildren sing of the equally disagreeable tattle-tail who, inexplicably, hangs on a bull's tail. This code has a sound ethical base. When spies informed the Spanish Inquisition of the Judaizing practices of new Christians; when zealous young Komsomol members reported their parents for unpatriotic remarks; when a kindly neighbour of Anne Frank disclosed her hiding-place to the Gestapo – the informers deserved all the opprobrium to which history subjected them.

But, what if the authority to whom the information is entrusted is a just one? What if the information is given to right a wrong or to expose an evildoer? Closed societies deal harshly with informers, yet were it not for the lone courage of the whistle-blower, Roman Catholic priests would continue buggering young boys undisturbed, the larcenous heads of multinational corporations would have no one to prevent them from robbing their shareholders blind; and wife-beaters, child abusers, rapists and blackmailers would, unpunished, flourish like the green bay tree.

Someone's scale of values is screwy. The boy who plagiarized another's work was a thief and a cheat, yet was feted as a hero; the boy who exposed the theft became a pariah. A code that is unable to distinguish between information given for venal or vindictive purposes and information given to right a wrong is a perverted one and is due for an overhaul.

But, while I admit I intended to moralize, this sermon on stool pigeons is not the reason that I have dragged up the dreary tale of the Declamation Prize. For my main message I need to continue the story. The second speech, the bad one, did not win the prize by default, the judges wisely deciding not to award the prize at all that year. It was just as well because the second speech was richly undeserving of any kind of prize. Delivered haltingly by a boy who had not committed his words to memory, its subject was the United States.

I doubt if any copy of the speech is extant, but I remember the speech in general terms. It was a jejune attempt at satire, affecting to praise the United States, but being in reality one long sneer, full of the tired tropes of anti-Americanism. The would-be orator declaimed of Coca-Cola, Hollywood, chewing gum and skyscrapers. It was the kind of performance that I expect would make the boy who delivered that speech cringe for years afterward. In fact, I know that he still cringes, because I was that boy and I sometimes think that I would like to kick the behind of the boy that I was.

When we talk of anti-Americanism we refer to more than a reasoned opposition to American policy or a principled distaste for its culture. There was much to criticize about the United States when I wrote that lamentable speech for the Declamation Prize. In 1951 we were seeing the beginning of the unlovely McCarthy era when it seemed that America, in its zeal for hunting communists, had, as a nation, gone quite mad. Today, too, America's foreign policy causes discomfort to many of its friends as does the strident religiosity that is so much a feature of American society. And few foreigners are able to understand America's strange addiction to firearms or its zest for executing criminals, a predilection it shares only with those bastions of freedom: Iran, China and Saudi Arabia.

But anti-Americanism is something of a different order. As seen in Western Europe and in the Islamic world it is nothing less than a hatred, as irrational as it is ineradicable. And it is rife. A striking example is the British dramatist Harold Pinter whose virulent anti-Americanism earned him last year's Nobel Prize for Literature and whose America-obsessed poems verge on the pathological.

If you want to determine whether a person is a rational critic of America or a paranoid, the acid test is that person's stand on the atrocities of September 11, 2001. Pinter's take on 9/11 was that it was "an act of retaliation against constant and systematic manifestations of state terrorism on the part of America over many years, in all parts of the world." Where do you start to counter such tripe? Salman Rushdie, who knows a thing or two about state terrorism, but of the Islamic variety, made the perfect riposte to that kind of anti-American balderdash: "To excuse such an atrocity by blaming US government policies," he wrote, "is to deny the basic idea of all morality: that individuals are responsible for their actions".

Anti-Americanism has a long, and often surprisingly distinguished pedigree. From "Martin Chuzzlewit" onward, English literature abounds with American characters that conform to a certain stereotype of uncouthness and naiveté. But it is in France that anti-Americanism has been for centuries a cultural tradition shared by all sections of the intelligentsia from Stendhal to Sartre. A recent French writer called this consensus *la pensée unique*. Still, one cannot help being shocked afresh by the intensity of French anti-Americanism. Using 9/11 again as the touchstone, a book called "Le 11 Septembre 2001, l'effroyable imposture," topped the French best-seller lists for several weeks. It argues that the attacks were organized by the US administration and that Osama bin Laden is a CIA agent.

But, because in France ideas are taken seriously, it is in France that a reaction has set in. A new group of French intellectuals – the "anti-anti-Americans" – has started to have its say. They point to the inconsistent nature of anti-Americanism. America is over-materialistic and over-religious; it is on the verge of collapse and too powerful; it is a nation of warmongers, but is afraid to risk the lives of its soldiers; it is racist, but excessively politically correct. And so on.

If the incoherence of anti-Americanism, the vitriolic hatred that America inspires in so many, strikes any chord, the anti-anti-American writers have spelled it out. There is another pathological hatred that has striking parallels with anti-Americanism. The distinction of being at the root of everything that goes wrong in the world, of being the target of fantastic conspiracy theories, is one that Americans share with one other people: the Jews. Anti-Americanism in its rabid form, as several writers have pointed out, resembles nothing so much as anti-Semitism.

Time tempered the adolescent anti-Americanism of that boy. Now, as then, he is disturbed by much of the rhetoric that emerges from the United States. But, just as reading Orwell and Koestler cured him of relativism in the Cold War – in the struggle between the USA. and the USSR, it was simply not true that one side was as bad as the other – he is today in no doubt that, in the struggle with global jihadism, neutrality is not an option and if you are not for America you are against it. European fence-sitting did not wash then and will not wash now. Were that boy to write that speech again today it would be very different.

In short, that boy grew up.

10 November, 2006

Two Cheers for Democracy

Considering his deserved reputation as a master of the English language, Winston Churchill's much-quoted maxim on democracy is surprisingly inelegant. In a debate in the House of Commons in 1947, Churchill said: "... it has been said that democracy is the worst form of government except all those other forms that have been tried from time to time." But the saying, however clumsily phrased, is incontrovertible. The dustbin of history is crammed to overflowing with ephemerally successful attempts at alternative forms of government that have in the end proved disastrous. We only have to look at the calamitous totalitarian experiments of the 20th century to be reminded of what awaits those who depart from the democratic paradigm. Yet there has never been a time that Churchill's adage has been more sorely tested. As the United States attempts forcibly to foist the blessings of constitutional government on a hitherto undemocratic and demonstrably ungrateful Middle East, the newly enfranchised of Iraq and Palestine respond by disobligingly electing parties that vilify the system that gave them power.

Democracies come in all shapes and sizes and electoral systems vary radically among them. In its purest form, a democratic system should give equal weight to the vote of each elector. That is patently not the case in the United States and Great Britain. Their "winner takes all" system for the election of legislatures effectively disfranchises those who voted for a losing candidate in a particular district. But it ensures stable government.

If your idea of an ideal democratic electoral system is one that accurately reflects the percentage of votes cast for a party in an election, you should be looking for a country with a single-chamber legislature and a system of nationwide, single-constituency proportional representation. There is one such country – the country whose language gave the world the ultimate word for chaos, *tohubohu*. In Israel, you get what you vote for. Proportional representation anywhere involves government by coalition; in the Jewish state it is a recipe for anarchy. In order to cobble together a government, a would-be prime minister must yield to the demands of diverse special-interest groups, who command much-needed votes in the Knesset. The process is ruinously expensive because each potential partner has demands, financial and legislative, favouring his own sector. The stranglehold of the religious parties over legislation has resulted in Israel – a country that, whatever its faults, has a Western-style, open society – having laws of personal status that would shame the Taliban.

Israeli elections are said to be dull. I am not sure that I share that view. For one thing the voter is faced with an embarrassment of choices. Earlier this year, over thirty parties presented lists of candidates for election to the Knesset. You could, for instance, choose to vote for such exotica as the Green Leaf Party whose sole platform was the legalization of cannabis. This list received over 40,000 votes, 1.3 percent of the popular vote. With a little more luck it would have passed the two percent threshold and would have put into the Knesset three members who would have joined any coalition that permitted them to smoke pot.

Frivolity on the part of voters is not confined to Israel but it is only under a system such as Israel's that it can actually make a difference. In Britain the Official Monster Raving Loony Party, founded by the wildly eccentric rock singer, the late Screaming Lord Sutch, has contested numerous constituencies over the years, but never got near to getting a candidate elected to Parliament. Yet, in a by-election in the constituency of Rotherham in 1994, the Screaming Lord succeeded in getting 4.2 percent of the vote. That percentage, translated into Israeli terms, would have earned the raving loonies six seats in the 120-member Knesset. Six seats! They would have been worth gold when the time came for negotiating the coalition. The party whose ideology is "Insanity, Satire, Pragmatism and Existentialism" could have demanded, as a condition for its joining the coalition, that the new government adopt the Loony manifesto demanding the abolition of income tax; the introduction of a 99p (make that agorot) coin to save on change; and the retraining of vicars (rabbis) or traffic police too stupid for normal police work. Of course, you could add some really mad ideas that might catch on in Israel. This may sound farfetched but you could, for example, propose a law forbidding any man called Cohen from marrying a divorcee.

Getting the Loonies into the Knesset is something of a pipe dream. But, in 2006, something similar did happen to another single-issue party. A perennial no-hoper in Israeli elections was the Pensioners' Party. Its programme was to improve the lot of senior citizens, an estimable enough cause, but, in the many previous elections in which it had run, the electorate had chosen to cast its vote for parties with less sectoral aims. But something happened in 2006. Against all expectations, the pensioners' list received almost six percent of the popular vote, bringing the party seven seats in the Knesset and taking a group of dazed dodderers to Jerusalem where they found themselves, thanks to the vagaries of the electoral system, wielding a power that they can never have dreamed of as they sat at home dozing in front of their television sets.

How did a party that had in every previous election had meagre support, suddenly produce 185,000 votes? This was not a revolt of the aged. It was not that the elderly, however ill-used, had changed their party affiliations to vote en masse for their special interests. This was a vote for a lark by people who would otherwise not have voted at all. It was a classic instance of the social epidemic, a phenomenon analyzed in a much-discussed 2000 book, "The Tipping Point." According to its author, Malcolm Gladwell, a staff writer for the *New Yorker*, there is a stage that an idea or trend crosses a threshold, tips and spreads like a brushwood fire. This is the tipping point and how it happens is the subject of the book. Here, the word got round that the cool thing to do was to vote for the pensioners. In a matter of days the tipping point was reached.

The beneficiaries of this epidemic, the Pensioners' Party, were not unworthy but the motives for voting for them were essentially irrational. The "connectors" and "mavens" who, according to Gladwell, produce social epidemics could equally have pushed the Raving Loonies or their local equivalents, the War Against the Banks list or the party for men's rights, over the tipping point. Israel's electoral system encourages this type of irresponsibility on the part of the voters.

It is apparent to any reasonably objective observer that reform of Israel's electoral system is long overdue. The difficulty has been that the very interests whose baleful influence gives rise to the need for reform wield that same disproportionate influence to scupper reform. There has been no shortage of proposals for reform. Indeed, there have been as many such proposals as there are party lists in the elections. In the 1980s, a movement for reform spearheaded by prominent law professors actually culminated in a new law: the direct election of the prime minister. Hard though it must have been to achieve, the reform – giving each voter two votes, one for a party list and one for a candidate for prime minister – resulted in even greater chaos than had prevailed hitherto. Fragmentation of government increased and the already outrageous bargaining power of splinter parties was enhanced. The whole sorry experiment was cancelled after the elections of 2001 and the old system was restored. So much for law professors.

Electoral reform is once more in the air in Israel. One who has a proposal for reform is Avigdor Lieberman. The head of a party commanding a powerful eleven seats in the Knesset, he has recently joined the ruling coalition. A principal feature of his platform is the redrawing of Israel's boundaries so as to exclude, in favour of a future Palestinian state, areas of Israel that are chiefly populated by Arabs. He has also advocated the death penalty for Arab members of the Knesset that he regards as collaborators. The fact that liberal-minded ministers find it possible – *faute de mieux* – to sit in the same government as Lieberman is itself the most eloquent criticism of the state to which Israel's electoral system has reduced us. Lieberman's own proposal for reform is for a "presidential system." The strong man he has in mind to lead the country under this system is generally assumed to be the one whose face he sees in the bathroom mirror every morning.

It was an unhappy day for Israel when it adopted its unique, nation-wide electoral system. Ben-Gurion himself favoured a two-party system with constituencies on the British model. Thanks to pusillanimity on the part of the major parties, this is not likely to happen soon. But one day something like it will have to happen if Israeli democracy is to survive.

8 December, 2006

SLIGHTLY SACRED

*L*ost in Translation

Much of what we read, we read in translation. It is commonplace that however good the translation – and a translator must be loyal both to the meaning and to the style of the original – something of the author's original intent is inevitably lost. But one exception is always trotted out; one translation into English that is said to be true to the original yet transcends it. The book that is commonly regarded as the peak of English literary achievement, the work that has most shaped English culture, is itself a translation. With a confidence born of total ignorance, the literati have decreed that the Bible in English is superior to the work from which it is derived. How else can English pride accept that what has been called the greatest work in the English language was not originally written in English?

The culture of ancient Israel is so far removed from that of 17th century England that there is little value in comparing the English translation of the Bible with its Hebrew original. Still, it should be said that a comparison is not always detrimental to the Hebrew. Take the justly celebrated passage of Isaiah that the Authorized Version, as the King James Bible is commonly known, renders as: "They shall beat their swords into ploughshares, and their spears into pruning hooks." Poetic and eloquent, yes. But the original Hebrew has something that any translation must surely lack: *Vehitetu harvotam le'etim vehanitotehem le'masmerot*. You can hear the sound of the weapons being struck in the smithy with the repeated "t" sound of this perfect example of onomatopoeia.

There can be little doubt that the standard translation of the Old Testament into English is a literary masterpiece. Not even the plays and sonnets of Shakespeare have so left their mark on the English collective consciousness. Yet this Everest of literature confounds the theorists; by rights it should be an inferior work. Not only is it a translation, it is the product of many hands. The King James Bible was composed between 1604 and 1611. The English language was at its zenith. Shakespeare was still active and had yet to write Othello, King Lear, Macbeth and The Tempest. James I, no mean scholar himself, had a hands-on approach to the translation that he sponsored.

Two new books – "In the Beginning" by Alister McGrath, and "God's Secretaries" by Adam Nicolson – vividly, though from slightly different perspectives, tell the story of the King James Bible. Some fifty scholars were divided into six "companies," each of whom was allotted different parts of the Old or New Testaments. Each company compared its translations with those of the others so as to achieve a cohesive style. The old joke about the camel being a horse designed by a committee did not apply here for the result was virtually seamless.

Reading the English Bible makes it easier to understand the legend preserved in the Talmud of the miraculous origin of the Septuagint. According to this story the Egyptian king Ptolemy had seventy-two scholars shut in separate rooms. Each emerged weeks later having produced identical Greek texts of the Bible.

There have been many subsequent editions and translations of the Bible into English, but they have all taken the Authorized Version as their starting point. Of the innumerable editions of the English Bible, none is more notorious than the version published in 1631, later known as the "Wicked Bible." The printer omitted the word "not" from the seventh commandment, which consequently read "Thou shalt commit adultery." The unamused authorities imposed a massive fine on the hapless printer.

Judaism has always had an indulgent attitude to translations of the Scriptures. Jewish translations into Greek and Aramaic precede the Christian era. But religious authorities have always regarded greater accessibility to sacred works as a mixed blessing. The ultra-Orthodox community of the United States has long felt the need for translations into English that reflect its worldview. The lavishly backed Artscroll publishing house is there to meet that need. Its excellent English version of the Babylonian Talmud is a massive project. (A Hebrew Talmud is now also being produced.) If you live in a bedsitter, the Artscroll Talmud is not for you. Because of its quirky way of laying out the text, it will comprise when it is completed no less than seventy-three large volumes. With that amount of shelf space, you could house the Vilna Talmud, the Oxford English Dictionary and the Encyclopaedia Britannica – and still have room to throw in the collected works of Agatha Christie.

It is when it gets to translating the Bible that Artscroll comes seriously unstuck. It has no feeling for the poetry of the Bible. Artscroll seems offended that the Bible is not only sacred, but also a fine work of literature. The King

James Bible does not make that error. It echoes the rhythms of the original Hebrew, Aramaic and Greek with its own mellifluous Jacobean English. Few later translations have seen fit to alter its treatment of the recurring theme of the Book of Ecclesiastes: "Vanity of vanities; all is vanity." Artscroll, however, translates it as: "Futility of futilities! All is futile!" Even disregarding the suspect plural "futilities," it is evident that the translator has a tin ear. There is no music in futility.

In stamping out heresy, the Artscroll in its translations is not above tampering with the text. Contrast with the standard translations its treatment of the Song of Songs, a powerfully erotic set of poems with no apparent religious content. The book was admitted into the canon of the Bible as an allegory and perhaps, one would like to think, for its literary quality. At any rate Rabbi Akiva called it the holiest of all books and the liturgy of the Hasidim calls for it to be read every Sabbath eve. By means of marginal notes the King James translators present the book as an extended metaphor of the love of Christ for the Church. The line "a bundle of myrrh is my beloved unto me, he shall lie all night betwixt my breasts" is annotated "The Church and Christ congratulate each other," but the translation itself is literal; the translators, though clerical, seldom resort to euphemism in their translations.

Artscroll, however, is not content to leave to its commentary an allegorical interpretation. Religious correctness has compelled it to ignore the literal meaning of the book entirely. See where Artscroll has placed that bundle of myrrh: "But my Beloved responded with a bundle of myrrh ... the fragrant atonement of erecting a Tabernacle where His Presence would dwell amid the Holy Ark's staves".

Sometimes the demands of orthodoxy make the Artscroll translators give up in despair. Chapter XI of Leviticus contains a list of twenty birds that may not be eaten. The King James Version speaks of eagles, ospreys, vultures, owls, hawks, cuckoos, cormorants and kites. Subsequent versions have altered some of these translations in the light of later scholarship. But Artscroll's house ornithologist must have been on leave when the avian abominations were listed as: "the nesher, the peres, the ozniah; the daah and the ayah according to its kind; every orev according to its kind; the bas hayaanah, the tachmos, the shachaf, and the netz according to its kind; the kos, the shalach, and the yanshuf; the tinshemes, the kaas, and the racham; the chasidah, according to its kind, the duchifas, the anafah according to its kind and the atalef".

Well, thank you for "and" and "the." It's like the sign on the Ayalon highway (since removed) that directed non-Hebrew speaking drivers to Tel Aviv's central railway station with the word *Raqevet* in Latin letters.

Artscroll's problem is that this list of unclean birds is an exhaustive one. Any bird not appearing on the list is not forbidden by the written Torah, so they keep you in the dark for your own good. Were it not for their concern for your moral health, you might be tempted to barbecue your pet parrot.

There are occasions when Artscroll totally loses its always tenuous grip on the English language. I have taken at random, and transcribed verbatim, selections from their translation of this week's Torah portion. Jacob is on his deathbed and is blessing his sons. To Reuben he says: "Water-like impetuosity... you cannot be foremost, because you mounted your father's bed; then you desecrated Him Who ascended my couch." As for Simeon and Levi: "O my honor! For in their rage they murdered people and at their whim they hamstrung an ox." Judah's hand, however, "will be at your enemies' nape." Is this the best Artscroll can do with the language of Shakespeare and Milton?

O, my honor! I am going to get it in the nape for my water-like impetuosity.

9 January, 2004

*N*ot my Passion

Much has been written on the Sixties, that decade of social change and political turbulence. The "Baby Boomers" who made it happen are now approaching retirement. For Philip Larkin, "Sexual intercourse began/ In nineteen sixty-three/ Which was rather late for me/ Between the end of the Chatterley ban/ And the Beatles' first LP".

It was rather late for me too; Larkin's *annus mirabilis* saw me already married and practising law in London. But I was young enough to enjoy the satire boom that swept the English-speaking world at the time. A new form of humour, intelligent and sardonic, was pioneered by Mort Sahl at the "Hungry I" in San Francisco and by shows like "Beyond the Fringe".

And then, of course, there was Lenny Bruce. My clearest and most exhilarating memory from that time is of an act by the already notorious Bruce at "The Establishment," a sadly short-lived satirical nightclub in London's Soho. For an hour he regaled the audience with a performance that is hard to describe to anyone who never saw him. It was akin to a session with a psychiatrist; but it was Lenny who was the patient on the couch and the audience was the shrink.

To the acute embarrassment of the grandees of Anglo-Jewry – a grovelling diaspora if ever there was one – the favourite Aunt Sally of the iconoclastic, blasphemous and brazenly Jewish Bruce was Christianity. Lenny openly admitted that his family killed Jesus: "Alright, I'll clear the air once and for all, and confess. I did it. I, Lenny, nailed him up... and if he came back I'd do it again".

To paraphrase the comment of Sir Thomas Beecham, when an elephant misbehaved on the stage during an awful performance of "Aida," Sir Thomas Beecham is reputed to have commented: "Bad manners, but what a critic!" Lenny may also have had bad manners but – in demonstrating, in his own irreverent way, the absurdity of Jewish guilt for the Crucifixion – he was right on the money.

I have no desire to enter into the overcrowded field of "The Passion of the Christ" criticism, but I would like to add one comment on the feeding frenzy surrounding Mel Gibson's film. What I find bizarre in the storm generated by the movie is that, in arguing, undoubtedly with full justification, against its historical accuracy, its critics lend legitimacy to a preposterously irrational proposition: that the statement "Jews killed Jesus" is identical with the statement that "The Jews killed Jesus".

In the title to his devastating essay on genteel English detective fiction, the literary critic Edmund Wilson famously asked "Who Cares Who Killed Roger Ackroyd?" It would be needlessly offensive to a great religion to ask the same question as to the killing of Jesus but, in truth, the identity of those responsible for the Crucifixion should be of nothing more than mild historical interest. The perpetrators, Jews or Romans, are long dead. It is not that the historical question is an uninteresting one. But in the context it savours of apologetics.

The Gospel of St. Matthew attributes to the Jewish crowd at the Crucifixion the cry "His blood be upon us, and on all our children." To put it gently, it is improbable that any assembly would exclaim anything remotely as coherent. But assume for the sake of argument that Matthew, writing forty or so years after the Crucifixion, correctly recorded the episode. What kind of perverted logic can impose guilt on the unborn? What person with a glimmer of intelligence would believe that Jewish DNA carries a Christ-killing gene? Neither I, nor anyone I know, killed him. We have a cast-iron alibi; we weren't near the place at the time. Whether or not my ancestors did it, it is grotesque to suggest that I bear any kind of guilt.

With Lenny Bruce in mind, and with Steve Martin having a crack at the movie in the pages of the *New Yorker,* it seemed obvious to me that the brouhaha over the film was an ideal subject for satire. In a piece on the movie on the op-ed page of *Haaretz* a couple of weeks ago, Yossi Sarid, a man of known satirical talent, did what I initially assumed to be a send-up of the kind of bluenose who pontificates on a work of art without seeing it. In an unbridled attack on the film, he said that he had no intention of seeing such an "inferior" movie – just like a Boston Cardinal opining on a film too blasphemous or obscene for him to view. But it seems that Yossi was being serious.

Sarid sneered modishly at the "liberal circles" in the United States whose attitude to the film, he claims, is one of "silence or ... sycophancy." Which liberal circles? As to silence, would it were true. Nobody outside Outer Mongolia has been silent about this movie. I have lost count of the number of articles on it in *Haaretz* alone. Everyone has tried to get into the act. And sycophancy? The columnist Andrew Sullivan has pointed out in the *Sunday*

Times that reaction to the film has divided neatly across known fault lines with conservative pundits praising it and liberals regarding it as a "psychotic piece of sadism." But you can only admire the unprecedented success of the Anti-Defamation League in turning into a blockbuster a movie without a single actor known to the public and without a word of English dialogue.

Like Yossi Sarid, I am in a position to give my forthright opinion on the picture without the inevitable loss of objectivity that I would suffer from seeing it. It may be an accomplished piece of filmmaking, but my nature is far too sensitive to derive pleasure from watching a 20-minute flogging or the sight of one actor relentlessly banging nails into the hand of another.

But aside from its obvious attractions to flagellants and sado-masochists, there is a less obvious aspect to the film that some will find intriguing. Repulsive as it may be, I do confess that my interest has been piqued by its use of Palestinian Aramaic for the lines spoken by Jesus and the other Jewish characters.

Suddenly the eyes of the world are focused on Aramaic. If you know Aramaic, you're in. The *Guardian's* Tim Dowling succeeded in detaching an Aramaist from his ivory tower in the semitic philology department of some ancient university to render into Aramaic such useful phrases as "Yes I'm Jewish, but I wasn't there that day" (*Een, Yuudaayaa naa, ellaa b-haw yawmaa laa hweeth ba-mdeetaa.*) "It sort of reminds me of 'Life of Brian,' but it's nowhere near as funny " (*Ma'hed lee qalleel d-Khayey d-Breeyaan, ellaa dlaa gukhkaa*) and "Please turn off your mobile phone. It is blasphemous" (*Da'ek teleyfoon methta'naanaak, pquud. Guudaapaw!*)

Let me lodge a disclaimer before I am deluged with letters from irate Aramaists; I concede that the quoted samples do not appear to be in the Palestinian Aramaic we know from the biblical books of Daniel and Ezra or the Jerusalem Talmud ... It could be – and I confess I have not looked into it – that the dialect is Syriac, the language of the *Peshitta*, the Christian Aramaic translation of the Bible.

There was a time that Aramaic, a language closely related to Hebrew, was the lingua franca of the whole Middle East. The Jews of two thousand years ago had largely forsaken Hebrew for Aramaic, hence the need for the *targumim*, the translations of the Bible from Hebrew into Aramaic. Yemenite Jews, most of whom now live in Israel, still have a "meturgaman" who recites the Targum in Aramaic after the Hebrew Torah reading. To translate from a language you know well into a language you barely understand is surely the *reductio ad absurdum* of the dead hand of tradition.

Jewish literature has a rich Aramaic content. The language forms an important part of the Jewish liturgy. The most solemn occasion of the Jewish year, the eve of Yom Kippur, opens with the famous Aramaic declaration "Kol Nidrei" and we encounter Aramaic in the Bible; the books of Daniel and Ezra are written largely in Aramaic and Aramaic is the language of both Talmuds and medieval poetry and prose. Much of Aramaic has been absorbed into modern Hebrew; an Israeli child's first words (*abba, imma*) are in Aramaic. So it survives, a linguistic fossil, a faint echo of a once mighty language.

But, unlike Latin, Aramaic is a living language though surely a threatened one. I already had a dim notion that Aramaic is still spoken by Christians in isolated hamlets of Syria, Lebanon and Iraqi Kurdistan. What I did not know, until a couple of years ago, is that it is still spoken by Jews. A cousin of my wife married a delightful young woman whose family belongs to a community that hails from an area of northwestern Iran – by Lake Ormiya near the border with Turkey and Azerbeijan. She told me that her parents spoke Aramaic. I admit I was incredulous. But it is true.

Her small community, which settled in Ormiya at the time of the Babylonian Exile and never left, calls itself "Nash Didan." They speak a dialect of Aramaic they call *lishan didan* – "our language." As I write, I have by me three books, lent to me by our cousin. They are translations from the Bible into lishan didan; the language is recognizably Aramaic. I later learned that Kurdish Jews also speak an Aramaic dialect they call *lishna yehudiyya*.

I find this survival of an ancient Jewish language profoundly moving, an unbroken link with a past that stretches back to the early years of the Babylonian Exile. Sadly, the language will probably disappear within a couple of generations: The young people of the community no longer speak it. Unlike Yiddish or Ladino it has no literature to speak of and we shall not see a chair in lishan didan studies endowed at any university. Truly a great pity.

So one cheer to Mel Gibson for Aramaic. But, as for the movie, if I ever have an overwhelming desire to see a crucifixion I think I'll look again at the DVD of "Life of Brian".

2 April, 2004

*T**arry on, Messiah***

Jews have not had much luck with messiahs. It is not that there has been any lack of candidates. The psychiatric wards are as full of messiahs as of Napoleons; it is the commonest of delusions, and Jewish history is littered with the corpses of failed messiahs. Most messianic aspirants have been innocuous and can safely be relegated to the loony bin of history. But the greatest of the pretenders have caused untold harm to the Jewish people.

Leading the messianic pack by a mile is, of course, Jesus of Nazareth whose followers interpreted his teachings of peace and goodwill as a licence to slaughter those who had the temerity to reject his message. The succeeding century saw Bar Kochba. Acclaimed the Messiah by no less an authority than Rabbi Akiva, his doomed revolt against Rome resulted in the virtual extinction of Jewish life in the Holy Land for centuries.

In the 11th century there came David Alroy. Like Bar Kochba, Alroy, the subject of a highly romanticized novel by Benjamin Disraeli, asserted his messiahship in the form of a military revolt – this time against the Ottoman sultan. The Jews of Baghdad stood on their rooftops waiting for Alroy to arrive from the sky to fly them to the Holy Land.

In the 17th century, Shabbatai Zevi split the Jewish world as no messiah since Jesus had done. Great communities of Europe were split; it is hard to exaggerate the magnetic influence he exercised on Jewry during his years of glory. Until his conversion to Islam, he was endorsed by some of the greatest rabbis of his day and the shock waves from the affair continued to affect Jewry for more than a century afterwards.

And now, once again the hills are alive with the sound of messiahs as we witness the fervour of the protests against Israel's withdrawal from Gaza. It is not that there are no respectable political and strategic arguments to be made against disengagement, but – referendum red herrings aside – it is religion, not politics that dominates the protest rallies. Possessors of the whole truth, the national religious youth who pack the protest rallies are sure that the Redemption is at hand and that the Messiah is on his way.

We recently received an intriguing wedding invitation. The English side of the card, boilerplate in form, invited us to a Jerusalem banquet hall at a named hour. The same hour was designated in the Hebrew text, but at a different venue. The ceremony was to be "(if God wills it") in the courtyard of the Third Temple, but "if the Messiah tarries" – at the hall. If you read both sides of the invitation, you had a dilemma. Do you go to the hall with the Anglophones or to the Temple with the Hebrews?

In the event, there was no problem. For one thing, so far as I knew, the Messiah was still tarrying. Tarrying is something at which he excels. He has been tarrying for 2,000 years and, with a track record like that, you are entitled to assume, in the absence of solid evidence, that he has not ceased his tarrying. Moreover, in spite of whatever informal plans may be afoot on the part of Third Temple enthusiasts to hasten the arrival of the Messiah by removing the existing structures, the current occupants of the site were, when I last checked, still there. In general I detect a distinct lack of enthusiasm for the restoration of the Temple. The business of the Temple is animal sacrifice and 21st century sensibilities are, on the whole, too fastidious to welcome the idea of prayer in an open-access abattoir.

Jewish history has seen would-be messiahs come and go. The difficulty for messiah watchers is that, when a new applicant for the post appears, you cannot tell if he is the genuine article or whether the real messianic McCoy is still tarrying. The job description is pretty demanding: The Messiah has to be a descendant of King David; he must gain sovereignty over the Land of Israel; he will gather the Jews from the four corners of the earth; and – and this is the tricky one – he will bring peace to the world. I know of nothing in the literature that precludes a woman for this post, but the assumption has always been that, like popes and heavyweight boxing champions, the Messiah will be male. I offer a female messiah as a tentative subject for a thesis in one of the mushrooming university departments of feminist studies.

There is one quality the Messiah need not have. Contrary to what you may have heard elsewhere, he need not have been born of a virgin. The whole confusion started with a verse in Isaiah, which Christians interpret as presaging the coming of the Messiah. In English translation, the verse commences: "Behold a virgin shall conceive and bear a son ..." The Hebrew word *alma*, which means a young woman, was translated by the Septuagint from the Hebrew original of Isaiah as *parthenos*, Greek for a virgin. The evangelists Luke and Matthew, who wrote the Gospels that attribute virginity to Mary, knew the Bible only in Greek translation and gallantly, but redundantly, bestowed retroactive maidenhood on the Holy Mother to make her fit the mistranslated prophecy.

Meanwhile the Messiah continues to tarry, a condition that less mystical religious leaders have been content to accept as effectively permanent. Rabbi Yochanan Ben Zakkai, the great first-century hero of Jewish survival, was cool toward the messianism that was prevalent in his time. If someone tells you that the Messiah has arrived while you are holding a sapling, he said, you should first plant the sapling and only then go to greet him. In other words, don't hold your breath.

Jewish doctrine holds firmly that the Messiah will not die until he has completed his redemptive mission. Judaism knows of no Second Coming. This, at any rate, was accepted dogma until 1994, the year that Rabbi Menachem Mendel Schneerson, the Lubavitcher rebbe, died. His death did not, as one might have expected, still the voices in Chabad (the Lubavitch movement) that proclaimed that the rebbe was the Messiah. On the contrary, those voices became shriller. The rebbe was either still alive or would return from the dead to complete the redemption.

The message that the rebbe, the King Messiah, should live forever, stares at you from billboards throughout Israel, and from dozens of messianist Chabad pamphlets. Even in a religion as indifferent to theology as Judaism, there can be little question that this belief, that a dead rabbi can be the Messiah, is rank heresy. Judaism parted brass rags with Christianity over this very question. Jesus could not have been the Messiah, argue traditional Jews because, despite his well-publicized death, the world is still unredeemed; peace on earth remains a chimera.

Chabad apologists maintain that the messianists are a marginal element of their movement. Not so, according to the Orthodox Jewish historian, David Berger, whose book "The Rebbe, the Messiah and the Scandal of Orthodox Indifference" argues that the messianists constitute a majority in Chabad. What troubles Berger is the apathy of the Orthodox Jewish establishment toward what he regards as the most serious departure from Jewish doctrine since Christianity. The rank heresy of the messianic wing of the Chabad movement remains part of the mainstream of Jewish life. Berger, who personally espouses religious pluralism and admires the outreach achievements of Chabad, cannot understand how the religious authorities can countenance messianists occupying the pulpits, or teaching the young, of the Orthodox.

The missionary zeal of the Chabad messianists has penetrated deep into Jewish society. In 1994, while the rebbe lay dying, Chabad Hasidim succeeded in cajoling over sixty members of the Knesset, including Benjamin Netanyahu and Dalia Itzik – who later claimed that they had been hoodwinked – into signing a joint letter to the rebbe declaring him to be the Messiah, the son of David and beseeching him to appear at once, in full health, to redeem the people of Israel.

So messianism, if not the Messiah, is alive and well. You would think that, after all the disasters that messiahs have brought upon us, we would be in no hurry for another one to appear. But, unlike Pavlov's dogs, we do not learn by experience. As I think of the times in which we live and view the passionate intensity of today's messianic enthusiasts, I cannot help thinking of lines from W. B. Yeats' great poem "The Second Coming":

> *Things fall apart; the centre*
> *cannot hold;*
> *Mere anarchy is loosed upon the world …*
> *The best lack all conviction, while the worst*
> *Are full of passionate intensity.*
> *Surely some revelation is at hand;*
> *Surely the Second Coming is at hand.*

As for me, until the son of David arrives bringing universal peace, I shall greet any fresh messianic contender with the words of Brian Cohen's mother in "The Life of Brian": "'E's not the Messiah; e's a very naughty boy".

18 March, 2005

The Power of Prayer

Readers of 19th-century fiction will be familiar with the character of the Gentleman, a species that effectively became extinct with the outbreak of World War I. The concept defies simple definition. Certainly one of the principal qualifications of the Gentleman was that he be in receipt of an unearned income. Freed from the necessity of earning a living, a Gentleman could spend his time in his library in the pursuit of knowledge; he might even have his own laboratory or observatory. Early scientists and men of letters frequently came from this class.

The archetype of the gentleman scientist is Charles Darwin, but his lesser-known cousin, Frances Galton (1822-1911), was in many ways more extraordinary. Galton was one of the great personalities of Victorian science. A man of wide-ranging intellect, he was a pioneer of the modern science of statistics and conducted important research in meteorology, psychology, genetics and anthropology.

Galton is chiefly remembered today as the founder of the controversial theory of eugenics, a word he coined. Galton believed that by selective breeding – encouraging the "fit" and preventing the "unfit" from reproducing – the species could be improved. Until finally discredited by the insane use to which the theory was put by the Nazis, eugenics – though savagely satirized in Aldous Huxley's novel "Brave New World" – had a vogue in the United States in the 1920s, and elsewhere was greatly popular with "progressives" such as H.G. Wells and George Bernard Shaw.

Galton believed that everything was measurable and, being a full-fledged English eccentric, put his theories to the strangest of uses. Using a special counting device that he kept in his pocket, he devised a "beauty map" of the British Isles, classifying girls that he passed in the streets as "attractive, indifferent or repellent." He found "London to rank highest for beauty; Aberdeen lowest." When travelling in Africa – this astonishing man was also an explorer – he used trigonometry to measure the buttocks of native women.

In 1872, Galton published a paper entitled "Statistical Inquiries into the Efficacy of Prayer." He asked whether there are scientific grounds for finding if prayers are answered. How, he wondered, could he go about measuring the effect of prayer? For whom do people pray? He hit upon the members of the royal family and discovered that their life expectancy was poorer than that of people for whom no special prayers were said. Galton then looked at people in what you might call the praying professions. He found that clergymen lived no longer than men of other occupations and that ships carrying missionaries and pilgrims sank as often as other ships. He thus came to the conclusion that prayer brought no measurable benefit.

Is anyone surprised by these findings? That the good often suffer and the wicked flourish is a truism as old as the Book of Job; prayer, if it works, must work in subtler ways. And how can the Almighty deal with prayers that are so frequently mutually incompatible? Each side to a war or, for that matter, to a football game, prays for victory. Even within the same religion God is not always given an easy choice. In the ancient Temple on Yom Kippur, the most sacred day of the Jewish religious year, the high priest prayed for rain, requesting God not to "consider the prayers of the travellers." Travellers would be praying for fine weather, and the high priest was intent on exercising his superior prayer power to thwart them.

One problem I have with prayers is that I find them excessively long. We seem incapable of taking a leaf out of the book of our teacher Moses, whose successful prayer for the recovery from leprosy of his sister Miriam – "Oh God, heal her now" – consisted of six staccato Hebrew syllables: *el na r'fa na la*.

Of course, prayer sometimes appears to work. In the recent US presidential election, the Republicans were unarguably the praying party and their prayers were richly rewarded. Not that American presidents are always lucky with prayer. It is hard to forget the grotesque tableau of the president, Richard Nixon, on the verge of impeachment, persuading Henry Kissinger to kneel with him in prayer. Kissinger should have told him that Jews don't kneel; they have bad knees. At any rate, they could have both stayed standing for all the good the prayer did Nixon.

Yet people who doubt the efficacy of prayer are often inconsistent when it affects them personally. There is some truth in the American adage that there are no atheists in foxholes (the trenches, for Brits.) When confronted by a personal crisis, many rational people resort to prayer or make a "deal" with the Almighty. Just such a deal with God was made by the adulterous wife in Graham Greene's novel "The End of the Affair." Believing her lover to have been killed by a German bomb in the London Blitz, she promises God that she will give him up if he is spared. He is saved – the author leaves you to guess if it was truly a miracle – and she refuses to see him again. Instead she turns to religion. A case of special pleading, yes, but the deal she makes reflects a common experience.

Such solipsism infuriated the late Jewish philosopher and scientist Yeshayahu Leibovitz. Leibovitz, whose practice of his religion was as orthodox as his opinions were heterodox, despised the idea of a personal God who, if cajoled persuasively enough, would answer one's prayers. A highly combative man, he exercised his considerable vituperative powers to ridicule the medieval liturgical poem *Unetaneh Tokef*, which forms a central part of the Ashkenazi ritual for the High Holidays.

Taken literally, the idea of a person's fate being reversible by the power of repentance, prayer and charity, is admittedly simplistic; it may have worked for Nineveh in the days of Jonah, but in the 20th century it did not save Polish Jewry. Yet Leibovitz was surely being unjustly dismissive of the metaphoric power of a prayer that has succeeded in compelling generations of worshippers to take stock of themselves. For Leibovitz, prayer is a duty to be performed toward God, and nothing is to be expected in return. Even to expect spiritual satisfaction is illegitimate. Indeed the literal meaning of a prayer is of peripheral importance to Leibovitz.

Leibovitz's quirky theology has captured many adherents, young practising Jews who can no longer accept the certainties of their religion but remain drawn to its customs and observances. His ideas certainly have a superficial attraction. The fixed prayers of the Jewish liturgy – animal sacrifice; the resurrection of the dead; the suppression of heresy; the return to Zion (which can nowadays be achieved by the purchase of a one-way ticket from El Al, though that news has not seeped through to Boro Park or Stamford Hill) – have little appeal to contemporary sensibilities. But with Leibovitz you can have your cake and eat it, too.

Theology is for me a foreign country, yet I find swallowing Leibovitz's ideas as hard as accepting the dogmas he so contemptuously rejects. But he does provide an answer of sorts to those who are troubled by their lack of spirituality. There are those who are able to achieve a mystical feeling of communication with the divine, what Freud called "the oceanic feeling," and there are others who, in the words of Isaiah Berlin, are "tone-deaf" to religion.

A reductionist but persuasive explanation of spirituality and its absence has been given in a recent book entitled "The God Gene: How Faith is Hardwired into our Genes," by Dean Hamer, a molecular biologist. Hamer claims to have located a gene, VMAT2, that predisposes its bearers to spirituality. In a review of the book, *Time* magazine helpfully includes a quiz entitled "How Spiritual are You?" I regret to record that I emerged from the quiz as "highly sceptical, and resistant to developing spiritual awareness." It helps to explain why, when in synagogue, I so often go into autopilot though surrounded by worshippers clearly pumped up with VMAT2. It's not that I haven't given prayer a chance. I have devoted hundreds of hours to it, but in terms of low return on investment, the only comparable activity is golf lessons.

Why Jews whose faith is shaky continue to pray has more to do with allegiance and belonging than with religion. The close link between cultural identity and religious practice that is peculiar to the Jewish people enables many who no longer accept its doctrines to participate in its rituals without a feeling of inconsistency. Tone-deaf to religion though he claimed to be, Isaiah Berlin found no contradiction in subscribing to some of the practices of his faith.

There is an evening in each year when, all over the planet, Jews stand, as their ancestors did, listening silently to an obsolete legal formula intoned in a barely understood language to a haunting, ancient melody.

Some call it irrational; I call it magnificent.

24 December, 2004

That Titanic Tomb

In terms of the public perception of their value to society, building contractors would languish towards the bottom of any poll, roughly on a par with drug dealers and only a place or two above lawyers. Yet you should spare a thought for the poor builder because in Israel, at any rate, his lot is rarely a happy one. He shares with contractors throughout the world the standard hazards of fire, flood, storm, earthquake and volcanic eruption. He should also beware of Acts of God, but although God is, as it were, playing on his home ground, that particular peril is no more dangerous here than elsewhere. But there is an additional risk that is peculiar to the Israeli contractor; he could hit a grave. Indeed, it is what we specialize in. Saudi Arabia has oil; the Holy Land has tombs. People have been dying around here for millennia and you can hardly plant this year's petunias without stumbling upon the grave of one or other of the hundreds of princelings whose names make the two biblical books of Chronicles about as intriguing as the Manhattan telephone directory.

So when, in 1980, in the course of digging the foundations of a new apartment building in the East Talpiot district of Jerusalem, labourers blasted open a cave that looked like the antechamber to a tomb, it excited no particular interest. The contractor, apparently unable to cover it up in time, reluctantly called in the Israel Antiquities Authority. A team of archaeologists led by Professor Amos Kloner quickly excavated the site. The tomb held ten limestone boxes, known as ossuaries, containing numbers of bones. When he wrote up the find, Professor Kloner reported that the tomb came from the Second Temple period. He can hardly have been accused of sticking his neck out; the period covers a full six centuries - from 538 BCE to 70 CE.

Six of the ossuaries bore inscriptions. What exactly the inscriptions say is still being debated by epigraphers but some have put forward the opinion that the six names were respectively: Yeshua bar Yehosef; Maria; Yose; Yehuda bar Yeshua; Matya; and Mariamne e Mara. This last inscription was written in 'Greek, the others being in Aramaic. If these were indeed the names on the inscriptions, scholars in the field saw nothing unusual in them. The fact that forms of these names crop up in the New Testament meant little. There are at least 21 separate Yeshuas mentioned in the histories of Flavius Josephus and the name has been found in 71 burial caves of the period. Mary, either in its Aramaic form or in its Greek form of Mariamne, was the single most common woman's name of that time. In 1982, the archaeologists, having documented the tomb, duly sealed it.

But the archaeologists had not reckoned with Hollywood. A Canadian documentary film director, fired perhaps by the contemporary success of books and films dealing with early Christianity, scented a scoop. He called in James Cameron, the director of "Titanic," the highest grossing movie of all time, and together they produced a documentary film on the find. While the archaeologists had concluded that, for all they knew, these were the graves of Josh Greenblatt and Miriam Buzaglo, Cameron, who may hold the olympic record in jumping to conclusions, eagerly adopted the nutty theory that one of the ossuaries contained the bones of Jesus of Nazareth and another of the Holy Mother, Mary. Furthermore the theory postulated that the Mariamne of the tomb was Mary Magdalene, who, if these were her bones, had to be Jesus' wife. Finally, to add insult to the injury they were already causing devout Christians, they theorized that Yehuda bar Yeshua was the son of the marriage.

It might surprise those whose knowledge of the Christian Bible is derived from reading the works of Dan Brown, but there is nothing in the whole New Testament even to hint that Jesus was married, let alone to Mary Magdalene. Cameron, while he and Mel Gibson were studying Aramaic, clearly could not find the time to take classes in elementary logic because his argument goes something like this: a) it has to be the grave of Jesus because he is buried with Mary Magdalene; b) it has to be the grave of Mary Magdalene because she is buried with Jesus; c) they had to be married to each other because they are buried together.

To be fair, the Cameron team did not rely on screwy deductive reasoning alone. They added loony statistics. They invited a professor of mathematics from the University of Toronto to assess the statistical probabilities of the cluster of six names being found together. He determined that, common though the names were, the chances were 600,000 to one against that particular combination appearing together. Nothing surprising in that; what they ignored was that most of the names in the tomb could not be comfortably shoehorned into their theory. But the professor permitted the Cameron coterie to give out that there was only one chance in 600,000 that the tomb was not that of Jesus.

Those are handsome odds. Betting men can tell you that if you wanted to back a blind, three-legged horse running in the Derby you would not be likely to get better odds than 100 to one. I am willing to give equally generous odds that the learned professor is talking through his hat. Ever since two distinguished mathematicians came out with the theory that Moses, when writing his five books, slipped in a code which was designed to save Yitzhak Rabin from assassination, I have become increasingly convinced that they slip something into the cappuccinos at faculty meetings of departments of mathematics.

Had Cameron unearthed the *Menorah*, the seven-branched candelabrum from the Temple, you might have been slower to conclude that he was out to lunch. The Menorah, at least, has a provenance and its early peregrinations have been documented. At the time of the destruction of the Second Temple in 70 CE, the Menorah was brought to Rome and its likeness can to this day be seen engraved on Titus' Arch in the Forum. The Vandals brought it to their capital Carthage after they sacked Rome in 455. The Roman Empire, in its Byzantine form, reclaimed the Menorah when the Emperor Justinian's great general, Belisarius, brought it back to Constantinople after conquering Carthage in 533. According to the Byzantine historian Procopius, Justinian, believing that possession of the Menorah brought bad luck, decided to return it to the Jews (let them have the bad luck!) Whether it was actually sent to Jerusalem as Procopius claimed nobody knows, but if those builders in Talpiot had dug up a candelabrum rather than a tomb there would have been less scholarly scepticism.

But James Cameron did not find the Menorah and nor, surprisingly, did his fellow American, Ron Wyatt. With scholarly credentials roughly equivalent to those of Cameron, Wyatt – who had a considerable following among fundamentalist Christians a few years ago – found almost everything else. Near Mount Ararat he discovered Noah's Ark, including its anchors; he identified sulphur balls left over from the burning of Sodom and Gomorrah; dredging the bottom of the Red Sea, he found wheels from the chariots of Pharaoh's army; it goes without saying that he turned up the original stones of the Ten Commandments. And, of course, he located the Ark of the Covenant but then who didn't? As to the location of the Ark of the Covenant, I prefer the Indiana Jones version. As everyone who saw "Raiders of the Lost Ark" knows, it was lost forever when it was boxed up and stored in a vast US Army warehouse.

Believing you have traced the tomb of Jesus while titanically proclaiming, as did Cameron, that "It doesn't get any bigger than this," is evidently some kind of psychosis. I allow that Cameron has not got the IRMs, an epithet - Intense Religious Mania in full - that a now deceased aunt of my wife attached to any of her family or friends who showed signs of excessive spirituality. That is not Cameron's problem; nor does he seem to be suffering from Jerusalem Syndrome. Psychiatrists have given this name to a state of sudden and intense religious delusions brought on while visiting or living in the city of Jerusalem. I do wonder about this diagnosis. As a good part of the population of Jerusalem always seems to me to be gripped by intense religious delusions I wonder how the city's mental health practitioners succeed in distinguishing between sufferers from Jerusalem syndrome and your ordinary Jerusalemite in the street.

But Cameron's delusions can hardly be described as religious. On the contrary, he seems to believe that he has sunk Christianity with the same ease that he scuttled an ocean liner with a studio-produced iceberg. So, if he is suffering from neither the IRMs nor the Jerusalem Syndrome what on earth is his excuse for trumpeting this farrago of nonsense?

13 April, 2007